BEYOND THE FRAGMENTS

BEYOND THE FRAGMENTS

Feminism and the Making of Socialism

Sheila Rowbotham
Lynne Segal
Hilary Wainwright

AAKAR

BEYOND THE FRAGMENTS
Sheila Rowbotham, Lynne Segal and Hilary Wainwright

First Published in India 2016

ISBN 978-93-5002-415-7 (Pb)

Published in agreement with The Merlin Press Ltd., London for publication and sale only in the Indian Subcontinent (India, Pakistan, Bangladesh, Nepal, Maldives, Bhutan & Sri Lanka)

Published by
AAKAR BOOKS
28 E Pocket IV, Mayur Vihar Phase I, Delhi 110 091
Phone : 011 2279 5505 Telefax : 011 2279 5641
aakarbooks@gmail.com; www.aakarbooks.com

Printed at
D.K. Fine Art Press, Delhi 110 052

CONTENTS

CONTENTS

Introduction (2013)
BEYOND THE FRAGMENTS

Sheila Rowbotham

When an American friend recently gave my contribution to *Beyond the Fragments: Feminism and the Making of Socialism* to young women occupying Wall Street , they told her they found it hard to understand. I was puzzled; surely it was clearly written. On reading it through again I decided the reasons it might seem inaccessible were threefold. Many ideas are squashed together because I found them so hard to articulate in the late 1970s; I make frequent references to the history of the left which were then part of a broadly shared radical culture but have now faded from view, and I make several assumptions which were taken for granted at the time but, because of the political shifts which have occurred since, are now unfamiliar and strange.

So, three decades on, some explanatory background may help readers who did not live through those times.

The compression was partly because of my own personal circumstances. In 1978, when I began writing what would become my section of the book, I was the mother of an eighteen-month old son. Though I lived in a communal house and shared childcare equally with my son's father, I still found it hard to think and write. As a consequence I learned to seize time and pack work in. A little hint of my daily life appears in the metaphor about a spirit level. The house had a bulge from war damage and periodically we would measure the wall to see if it had grown bigger. As there was no money to rebuild, the ritual resembled an offering to Fate rather than any practical prospect of house improvement.

The personal roots of the pent-up intensity which drove me to focus so obsessively on how to organise democratically go further back. Ever since I had become involved in the Campaign for Nuclear Disarmament in1962 I had been listening to other people (mainly men) discussing whether the left should work in or out of the Labour Party or form new groupings; whether the Soviet Union constituted a bulwark against international capital or whether it should be opposed by socialists; whether those at the centre of left groups should impose collective decisions on members or whether they should work through federal structures.

Like most other women I remained silent, always thinking I did not know enough to participate. Listening did, however, stimulate me to read widely: Marx, Engels, Trotsky, Lenin, Bakunin, Kropotkin, Emma Goldman, Alexander Berkman, then Gramsci, Sartre, de Beauvoir, Rosa Luxemburg, Alexandra Kollontai – on and on I read. Because I was an historian I plunged into the history of the left and labour movements in Britain and France, then, I began stretching out into women's role in national liberation struggles in Russia, China, Algeria, Cuba. Through this immersion I came across many approaches to organising , though they did not yield much when confronted by the absolute certainties I would hear in socialist meetings. History is not too helpful in enabling you to pronounce succinctly and definitely.

The prevailing organising ideas on the left in the 1960s and '70s were Leninist, both in the Trotskyist groups and in the Communist Party. I was, however, aware through friends of the New Left which had formed after 1956. They had explicitly rejected a politics in which ends justified means and had signalled the need to challenge the values sustaining capitalism. Moreover, during the 1960s, radical community and artistic projects began to appear that adopted anti-authoritarian approaches to knowledge and organising. Direct action, which had appeared in the anti-nuclear movement, was being applied to other causes such as homelessness.

Seeds of doubt had thus been planted which meant I did not accept that the Bolsheviks of 1917 represented the culmination of all earlier forms. Nevertheless I was hesitant about voicing criticisms which dismissed a body of assumptions which were engrained and deeply held by many people on the left. It was to be the women's liberation movement which propelled me to challenge Leninist assumptions. I had watched a movement grow from small clusters of women grumbling amongst ourselves in 1969 to a conference of around five hundred in early 1970 and then to a force which could muster around thirty thousand on demonstrations.

Women's liberation groups mushroomed quickly not only in major cities but in small towns, campaigns were launched for nurseries, equal rights at work, free contraception, abortion rights, family allowances. Centres were set up to protect women from male violence and from rape. We were challenging male domination and sexism in politics, in workplaces, in the trade unions, in academia, in the media, working men's clubs, sport. Gaining courage by speaking and writing in groups we were taking on anyone just about everywhere.

All this had been done through a decentralised movement, consisting of small groups without formal leadership structures. I knew it could be done because I had lived through it with other women. By the end of the decade similar movements had sprung up in many countries, not simply in Europe, Australia and North America, but in South Asia and Latin America too. Hence the existence of women's liberation constituted a tremendous impetus to rethink society, the economy, culture and politics.

In 1978 ,when I began my part of *Beyond the Fragments,* I had so much to say about organising my head was bursting, even so it still felt scary to be taking on Leninism which exerted authority as *the* organising idea of revolutionary movements internationally. It made me feel exposed and on unfamiliar terrain, just as writing about women's liberation itself had felt at the end of 1968. There was nowhere to run for cover and there was no way I would have done it alone.

I was nudged to write because the women's movement fostered supportive values of sisterhood. We practised co-operation in order to overcome our lack of confidence as individuals.

The development of socialist feminist networks and conferences within the women's liberation movement brought together women from differing left traditions. We came to trust one another by doing and thinking across boundaries, united by a desire to connect the emancipation of women to wider aspects of oppression in capitalism.

Over the years we found we had much in common. There were, however, points where we did realise we were at odds. After speaking at a meeting with Bea Campbell, then in the Communist Party, we clashed about Leninism. This led me to do an article in the magazine *Red Rag* which was produced by a collective of Communist Party and left libertarian socialist feminists. I wrote 'Leninism in the Lurch' just before my son was born in 1977 and it resulted in discussion and debate at a conference of the Socialist Unity Symposium in the autumn of 1978.

Then Hilary asked me to speak at the non-aligned Socialist Centre in Newcastle and Lynne at a similar Centre in Islington. These generated yet more discussion. We started to follow up our ideas with friends, men as well as women, and decided we would write down our experiences and thoughts about organising in the women's movement in the hope that people in the many other grass roots movements, campaigns and projects would do the same. We did not pretend to have clear-cut answers but we did have critical understandings based on what we had seen and known. We were convinced that there were complementary recognitions out there on the left.

Initially we intended to do 1,000 copies. But it cost £200 to produce a little book with the help of the Newcastle Socialist Centre and Islington Community Press. Lynne and Hilary who had full time jobs put up the money and I insisted we should do 2,000 so they would get their money back if we charged one pound. It came out in 1979 and sold out. This was the first surprise. When Merlin produced a revised edition in the same year the next surprise was the furore that ensued. One left paper even printed two opposing reviews because the editorial board could not decide how to deal with the book!

We turned into three notorious women who seemed to merge in people's minds like those carvings of female figures on the bows of boats. For many years afterwards people would muddle us up and I became used to being addressed as Lynne or Hilary. This always struck me as curious as we do not look at all alike and our ideas and approaches have always differed.

In my contribution I tussled away with the Bolshevik model of organising which had arisen in the circumstances of underground resistance in Russia. The history of Leninism, combined with my own observation of contemporary examples of it in practice, also had made me aware of a tendency towards centralisation which stifled democracy and the individual's creative inventiveness.

In contrast the American New Left of the 1960s, like some strands of anarchism, had stressed the need for prefigurative forms. I could see the obvious snags of living utopia in the bad old world of capitalism, yet I was sure that the manner in which you organised affected the new society which you could bring about. The interior worlds of both the Communist Party and small left sects were not encouraging and I was convinced the Bolshevik revolution was not an appropriate model for 1970s Britain.

On the other hand I knew that individuals within the Communist Party and the Trotskyist groups were just as keen as I was to develop peoples' abilities and creativity. I also was aware of the fight feminists within all these organisations had had in order to make the case for women's liberation. And I knew these arguments about the position of women were not entirely new in socialist movements. Socialism was not and had never been a homogenous entity. Within each demarcation too there were several currents of ideas.

Moreover, while I believed women's liberation had shown there could be other ways of doing politics which could contribute towards developing a new kind of left, I did not regard our movement as an idealised alternative. To treat it in such a way would be to regard women as somehow apart from politics, an infuriating condescension which left 'politics' with men.

Because for several years I had been involved not simply in innovatory forms of feminist action, but also in exhaustive discussions about the difficulties we encountered, I was well aware that our small consciousness–raising groups and participatory democracy had solved some problems and given rise to others. We were acutely aware of process in the women's liberation movement and we sought to be self-critical. Hence we noted how hidden hierarchies could emerge, we recognised that the suppression of opposing views could be imposed through consensus.

Ironically our anxiety about the process of organising equally and democratically could give rise to a paralysis. Who was to start a meeting when everyone was competing not to be a leader? Sisterhood could be strengthening but it could also smother individuals. When conflicts arose we lacked any formal procedures to decide on our policies. We struggled to keep a space open for debate but by the late 1970s this was contracting and furious arguments about men and about working with mixed groups and campaigns ensued. When differences could not be resolved dissidence could be crushed through guilt and fear.

Despite the bad sides of women's liberation, I still felt the positive aspects outweighed them. We really had devised ways of organising which enabled thousands of women to grow in confidence, express ideas and take courageous action. The key revelation was blindingly simple – every individual involved was capable of making original contributions to a movement which invented itself as it went along. Concepts could be put forward tentatively and built upon by others. We discovered the power of sharing ideas and of mutual help. Meetings were exhilarating learning experiences in which ideas formed collectively.

For several years we were able to allow space for contradictory perceptions and to explore and develop half-formed propositions. We did this face to face and carried it through into international dialogues. Such openness was possible so long as everyone accepted that no individual or group of individuals were absolutely right about everything. Tacitly in the first few years we could agree to disagree. Because this was politics and not an abstract ideal, such compromises were often made by the skin of our teeth. Nevertheless they did happen and were sustained for nearly a decade.

By 1979 when *Beyond the Fragments* appeared, the skin, as Lynne observes, was wearing painfully thin. This was partly because of internal turmoil within the women's movement and partly because of circumstances in society outside. It was evident by the late 1970s that radical social change including feminism was going to be slower than we had envisaged when the first groups formed in 1969. Just how slow we could not have imagined. In retrospect it is clear that we were trying to conceive a larger left movement at a distinctly unpromising time.

In the context of 2012 it may not be evident *why* all three of us should seek to connect our feminism with other movements, campaigns, groups or parties, reformist or revolutionary. It is often the case that what appears mysterious in looking back was so obvious that there seemed no need to explain it. These are the understandings that vanish from view with the passing of time.

In order to make sense of *Beyond the Fragments* it has to be recognised that the women's liberation movement of the 1970s was part of a broader radicalisation. We had lived through a decade of stormy conflicts in workplaces and communities. In Ireland people were engaged in armed struggle. We had marched on massive trade union demonstrations, supported picket lines and learned from men and women on strike and in occupations. Then there were burgeoning movements against racism, around gay liberation. While our main focus in the decade before 1979 had been the women's movement this did not mean we had been enclosed within it.

Though social movements were subsequently to be theorised in academia as expressions of distinct 'identities' and as being in opposition to 'old style' class politics, this was not how most socialist feminists in the 1970s saw the working class. We wanted class to be reconceived through the views and actions of working-class women, but this did not mean we dismissed working-class struggles and organisations. The connections were close. Feminists had worked in trade unions over the previous decade raising equal rights, nurseries, abortion, issues of language and representation. They were also involved in their own unions and active in trade union research groups. Hilary had worked closely with shop stewards organisations, discovering how they shared some of the problems familiar within the women's movement.

Moreover many of us saw the liberation of women as connected to other struggles for liberation and felt our movement had something to contribute. From the early 1970s I had been arguing that realisation of ourselves as women, involved extending outwards from our present circumstances as women. In *Woman's Consciousness, Man's World* (1973) I wrote: 'We have to keep struggling to go beyond our own situation. This means recognizing that the emphases which have come out of women's liberation are important not only to ourselves.'

I went on to discuss the forms of organising, the connecting of work and home, public and personal and argued that the new movement had highlighted areas in which socialists had been weak; authoritarian social relationships, sexuality, daily life in the family and the conditions of reproduction. I could see that it was important not to present the insights of women's liberation as inherent to all women. These were potentials glimpsed through movement, not an ideal to be plonked onto an abstract category of 'womankind'.

In *Beyond the Fragments* I returned to this theme of transcendence, 'If every form of oppression has its own defensive suspicions, all the movements in resistance to humiliation and inequality also discover their own wisdoms.' [pp. 87-88]. I was uneasily aware as I wrote that this phrase was taking me into a subversion which went beyond a critique of Leninism. I certainly thought capitalism could only be changed when it was rejected by a combination of opposing groups and was uncomfortable with the manner in which Marxism tended to impose a hierarchy. Yet I was not sure about entirely dislodging the Marxist view that the working class should be regarded as the key to social transformation – the power to withdraw one's capacity to labour in certain kinds of jobs was clearly a crucial form of power. Nor did I know how a myriad of rebellions might be joined.

I was, and remain, undecided.

Moreover, in the late 1970s, there were already hints that organising around specific oppressions could give rise to a determinism as pernicious as anything in Marxism. The notion of 'identity' focused on individuals in particular types of subordination rather than individuals in broader dynamic relationships. It tended to freeze and isolate specific kinds of oppression, forgetting that personally and collectively people were more than any category of oppression and that each one of us develops our ideas and attitudes in relation to others as well as drawing upon inherited and chosen cultures. Unfortunately, as the possibilities for radical change receded, the assertion of fixed identities would become more pronounced, accentuating fragmentation rather than overcoming it.

All three of us mention, as an aside, the danger of gains being swept away. We had lived through Labour's cuts, and a new kind of Conservatism was sharpening a set of threatening knives around the corner. We could not, however, imagine the extent of the reversals which were to come, nor could we perceive that common sense notions we took for granted were to be so drastically assailed. These are no longer self-evident and so they need to be explicitly stated, for they were the bed rock from which the idea of 'going beyond' sprang.

Throughout the 1960s and 1970s there existed a widespread assumption that society as a whole was connected to and partly responsible for the well-being of individuals. Likewise it was thought that the freedom and well-being of individuals, along with a greater degree of equality, made for a better society. Such thinking was not peculiar to the left, but extended through the Labour and Liberal parties and was accepted by liberal Conservatives. The arguments were around how much equality and social welfare would be desirable and how they were to be achieved. Socialist feminism had grown up and operated within this political and cultural framework. When we wrote *Beyond the Fragments* we had no way of envisaging how it was about to be torn apart and obliterated.

While this context is familiar to my generation it is difficult, I suspect, for younger generations to enter imaginatively, just as it was to prove difficult for us to adjust to changed circumstances. We had dreamed after all not just of society becoming a little better, but of 'liberation'.

We initially saw our readership as relatively small and were overwhelmed by the extent of the impact of our modest proposals. When Merlin Press published *Beyond the Fragments* we were amazed to see how it went off into other countries. As well as being read in English it was translated into Dutch, Japanese and Portuguese, while my section also went into Italian. The response to the book was partly because of the scale of left activism at the time, partly because uncertainty about how to resist was widespread, and partly because unease with left groups and parties was more extensive internationally than we had realised. I suspect it was also because we were clearly feeling our way, drawing on what we acknowledged to be limited experiences and knowledge and distilling thoughts as honestly as we were able, rather than laying down a dogmatic programme. Although we were explicitly so bothered about Leninism we were in fact engaging with wider problems of how to balance the rights of the individual with collectivities and how to overcome inequalities between individuals in groups. These had all predated Lenin and had arisen in libertarian socialist and anarchist traditions as well.

Over the years reactions to the book rolled slowly back. They were not at all what we had foreseen. A group of elegant Italian Marxist feminists arrived to interview me on Leninism. Unfortunately, they arrived when I was looking after a friend's two year old as well as my own. They were exceedingly polite, but I learned later that libertarian left motherhood and the chaos of communal life in inner-city London had confirmed their conviction that the certainties and orderly hierarchies of Leninism were preferable. One angry Canadian man complained to me that we had split his men's group into opposing factions. It appeared we had contributed to fragmentation instead of overcoming it! Then in India at the opposite extreme there was the intense young man who insisted, regardless of my protests, that I must found the 5th International of Fragments. The most startling and humbling discovery came in the late 1990s when I visited Brazil and was told by one of the founders of the Workers' Party how the book had influenced them while in exile.

In Britain, however, instead of people from other movements putting down their experiences and ideas about how to make socialism they were inclined to grouse because we had not written about them or to summons us to come and tell them how everyone should be organising. Perplexed and slightly frustrated we did the conventional thing and called a conference in Leeds in the summer of 1980.

Around 3,000 people turned up. Lenin clearly saw them coming and had a word with the Almighty – it rained all day. Active in the London Nursery Campaign and firmly committed to creative, libertarian education, I had envisaged the crèche as a delight and inspiration. Such utopianism overlooked several contingencies. First there was the weather. This was a strategic disaster because the crèche was some distance from the main conference. Contingencies number two and three proved to be the mothers of Leeds and the vagaries of the libertarian left. Around 140 children appeared, twice the number registered. Perhaps Leninists might have invoked revolutionary discipline and sent them packing; Fragments could not.

I had laryngitis and croaked my way through the day, co-ordinating face-painting and games, helped by a small group of adults and valiant teenagers who rose to the occasion and acted as runners between the crèche and the main conference. The creative, libertarian crèche kept me busy for most of the conference.

In our extensive planning sessions we had agonised about giving everyone a voice and allowing space for diversity. We had, however, relied on spontaneous good will to carry us through the final plenary. This was a mistake. We failed to take into account how small groups, acting in a concerted way, can stymy a large gathering. Anarchists from Class War and a gay Trotskyist stepped into the vacuum. Someone filmed the conference and the grim and relentless video showed the plenary sinking like a pie without an egg cup.

We had hoped that the conference might be the beginning of a new organisational network. Instead, as the cuts and factory closures accelerated under Margaret Thatcher's government, many people on the left including socialist feminists, myself included, took cover in the Labour Party. Issues of gender, along with race *did* enter the Labour Party and the trade unions as a result. But in Britain this occurred when the women's movement had splintered. In contrast in Canada, socialist feminism survived as a campaigning presence through the 1980s and was able to exert a much greater influence within unions and left parties. Getting that crucial combination of agitation without, and pressure within sites of power, is easier said than done.

After 1979, the demise of the women's movement and the strong currents of socialist feminism within it meant that it would become more and more difficult to articulate arguments about how socialism might learn from feminism and to insist that feminism could not be confined only to women's issues.

Within the British media 'feminism' was to be increasingly equated simply with getting women into top jobs or presented as being concerned exclusively with male violence. The innovative and courageous Greenham peace camp would constitute a new kind of feminism which raised the global danger of militarism, though the conclusion which was sometimes drawn, that men were to be equated with war and women with peace, was clearly an oversimplification . We had, after all, Prime Minister Margaret Thatcher at the helm.

Thatcher's skill lay not just in propounding extreme right-wing theories as genteel common sense, she shifted the political compass. Concepts of individual freedom, choice and participation, even the word 'radical' were coopted into the new conservatism. As the centre moved rightwards, socialist feminists along with the rest of the left had to scramble to defend basic trade union rights and welfare provision. Instead of devising a new politics we were fending off a veritable onslaught of Tory measures which left us gasping. A separate women's movement came to look increasingly inadequate in countering these; women's lives were being affected by the changes occurring in society as a whole.

However, when movements dissolve, people who have been active within them are inclined to disperse into other kinds of resistance taking some of the ideas with them.

One unexpected area of activity we never would have foreseen proved to be regional and local government. From the early 1980s both were to become sites for resisting the severe cuts imposed by central government. Moreover, a thorny old question, touched upon and left hanging in *Beyond the Fragments,* would appear and be extended in this surprising context during the 1980s. How were those participatory forms of democracy so important within the women's movement to combine with representative democracy? Lynne describes how feminists had tried to integrate them in practice in the 1970s through working with the Labour Party and the trade unions. I had come to respect the Labour MPs, like Audrey Wise, who resolutely kept the links between Parliament and the womer movement alive. But the wider implications of the relatic between those within the formal structures of politics, and tho: without, continued to dog me.

Both Hilary and I worked in the Greater London Council Economic Policy Unit in the early 1980s. It had an ambitiou brief to establish alternative economic strategies for London industries and services, involving Londoners directly in th process. Hilary headed the Popular Planning Unit which ha the daunting job of involving Londoners in economic an social planning. Hence we were to revisit in practice the haz intimation of the women's movement of how to *combin* representative democracy with direct participation. Wher the obvious strategy of popular assemblies did not work, we developed a whole range of ways of engaging differing groups o Londoners through community and workplace projects.

By activating the GLCs powers to assist the welfare of Londoners, we were able to provide resources to groups struggling to save local hospitals, resisting the building of a new airport, trying to establish community launderettes or workplace nurseries. The GLC could help home workers who were suffering from dangerous materials, immigrant women seeking training, Ford's workers trying to make international links in a period when capital was becoming increasingly global. The key lesson we learned was that to prevent resources being wasted, the initiative had to come from the groups themselves rather than from the Economic Policy Makers or Popular Planners.

By responding to a range of social needs from groups who had not customarily had direct access to the local state, the GLC made it possible, not simply to make links between representative and participatory forms of democracy, but to conceive an alternative to the pro-state and anti-state split which had for so long divided the left. It suggested that forms of grass roots power could, through pressure, ensure that resources went to the most needy and that people themselves could play a much greater part in defining how they were allocated. Moreover it showed that it was possible, at least partially, to also alter relationships *within* the state on more egalitarian, democratic and co-operative lines. We only had a few short years. In 1986 abolition left many questions unresolved. Could this enthusiastic, evangelical approach to social provision have been sustained and how was a large administrative structure, modeled like so many others on the army, to be democratised and remain effective?

I did not know the answer. However, when I was asked to develop a women's programme at the UNU economics institute in Helsinki, WIDER, in 1986, my experience at the GLC was still fresh. With Swasti Mitter I helped to bring together women working around the organisation of women in the informal sector in South Asia and Latin America. We aimed to document the creation of new democratic processes appearing among women in poor countries in their struggles over unequal access to resources.

Our small project was part of something much bigger. Over the course of the 1980s women in poor countries were mobilising around consumption and natural resources as well as production. In Britain women in mining communities took action on a mass scale during the miners' strike, while in the United States, African-American women protested against toxic dumping. Amidst the devastation of globalisation, working-class women were defending their communities, innovating in the process.

By the 1990s I had come to realise that going 'beyond the fragments' was a much slower, more complicated proposition than I had imagined at the end of the 1970s. The passing of time revealed moreover that it is not a linear process either in terms of issues or organising. When the anti-capitalist movement appeared in the mid 1990s I heard young people patiently explaining on the media how saving trees and animals were connected. They were far more aware of the importance of the natural environment than we had been in in the 1970s, though in the dockers' strike they, too, sought links with workers, and someone sent me a moving video of the Seattle demonstration in the late 1990s when these links were to be globalised.

Nevertheless, it did seem that a break had occurred when it came to thinking about how to act. When I asked a young campaigner against GM crops in Totnes where his ideas about anti-authoritarian organising had come from, he blinked and replied 'Buddhism'. 'News from Nowhere' the collective who produced *We are Everywhere: the irresistible rise of global anti capitalism*, published by Verso in 2003, wanted to break down constraining and oppressive fences just as we had, but they cited the Zapatistas in Mexico as their influences. It seemed our efforts to go beyond the fragments had left no direct lineage, even though some of the approaches to organising were being perpetuated.

Hilary, who dwells in the present, was busy connecting with this new activism through *Red Pepper* magazine. But, being an historian, I am always looking for traces and I would spend many years following through the history of some of the themes raised in *Beyond the Fragments.* I have pondered ways in which women of different classes and races have conceptualised emancipation, examined the relations between feminism, socialism and anarchism, dug out dusty visions of co-operative association, at work and among consumers, and marveled at the powerful resolve expressed by so many women to live in freedom as individuals.

I still think that Leninism inclines towards authoritarian forms of organising and see Marxism as a valuable source for ways of seeing which can be mulled over and put into practice rather than as fixed dogma. Yet, because the wheel has now turned so around, and because I am contrary in spirit, I would urge a new generation to read Marx, and yes Lenin and Trotsky as well. I am convinced too that the history of anarchism, along with feminism, gay liberation and movements against colonialism and racism similarly contain understandings which can be valuable for the present. My view now is that the problems of democratic transformation cannot be averted *simply* by adopting new labels. Instead, I believe it is wise to be conscious of the insights and snags in all the radical traditions adopted by people in the past.

Feminism remains an ongoing rebellion. The assertion of women's freedom and equality is as necessary and as subversive of the social order as it was in the 1970s. Indeed I do not think then that we fully understood the extent of the challenge the women's liberation movement was making to hierarchy and domination. For the liberation of women as individuals confounds not just male power but coercive authority. Its free expression requires basic political, legal and cultural rights, an open and just civil society. Conversely these crucial democratic liberties are not practicable for the majority of women without social and economic equality. However this is a *potential* reworking of democracy and society through a gender lens. Historically slips between cup and lip are common indeed and there is overwhelming evidence that the fear of freedom exerts a formidable influence, especially when you and your children are materially dependent on the status quo.

Movements for the emancipation of poor and working-class women thus have been particularly conscious of the need to find ways of mitigating this fear; seeking to support those who were vulnerable by creating co-operative structures to sustain them and by making demands for equality; better pay and conditions of work, more free time, greater access to social resources. However, achieving these reforms has depended on support from a wider labour movement. On a mass scale in capitalist society such agitation has gathered, in the main, under the banner of 'social democracy'.

Though social democratic organisations, revolutionary and reformist, remained male defined, and never fully engaged with the specific rights and needs of women, they did force capitalism to accept checks to the most rampant forms of exploitation and injustice and partially safeguarded the articulation of individual freedoms. Since the 1980s these redistributive gains have been systematically undermined by capital, sneaking in behind the stalking horse of neoliberalism. Decked out in the colours and rosettes of 'democracy', this glossy steed has taken it just about everywhere.

While resistance in the present economic crisis is mounting, each protest and desperate campaign is weakened because it is piecemeal and lacks any broadly acceptable opposing vision of what else might be. This is not simply a problem of structures, programmes or policies but of language, symbols, emblems around which large numbers of contestants could gather. The fragmentation of the present is so extreme it cannot cohere into any single name. Because I have identified so profoundly with 'socialism' that is the word I still carry with me; I am aware however that many younger radicals do not. One of my current uncertainties is whether hanging on to the word itself is of value for the future or whether new terms will re-emerge to fit a new context.

I am though all too aware that any effective opposition would require a mobilisation far beyond the present scope of those who would see themselves as 'socialists' or even as being on the left. How then shall a much broader momentum be nurtured and what can be the connecting ideas which could enable it to grow?

Of course there is the inequality, injustice, prejudice and poverty which has always characterised capitalism. But protesting these alone is not sufficient. Going beyond fragmentation in the early twenty-first century would, I think, involve touching a diffuse but widespread distress which has arisen in response to the recurring short-termism which contemporary capitalism displays towards nature and the environment, human life, work, values, culture and relationships. No political name exists for a movement for a better future in a myriad of everyday manifestations. But it is the basic, underlying yearning which present-day capitalism cannot satisfy; it links people who do not, as yet, assume any alliance. As capitalism gobbles away at the long term, dissenters are left to grumble in isolated clusters.

But the unease is there and it is appearing in many apparently disconnected areas of daily life.

It has been and may still be, that a defence of the long term would result in a reformed capitalism rather than a new kind of egalitarian society. In 2012 I would say even that would be better than this current brand, though this is not the alternative I would wish for. In the 1960s and '70s, inspired by movements against imperialism, people of colour, women and gays imagined a politics of 'liberation' which went beyond rights, or access to resources. 'Liberation' suggested a transformation not simply of the circumstances of daily life but of being and relating. Instead of an individualism of selfishness and greed, there was to be self-definition and expression, instead of competition, association, trust and co-operation. This is the future I still envisage and want to help bring about. But I have to take a deeper breath before admitting to it. When you have experienced many defeats it becomes harder to hang on to hope.

One of my favourite films is *The Never Ending Story* in which a small boy saves Fantasia through grains of sand which contain hope. Hope needs reclaiming .You can't kettle hope. It is one of the most valuable assets of rebellion. Because it is so simple it is easy to take it for granted. I was astounded to hear recently that the British supermarket Budgen's has been charging £1 for a log of wood marked 'hope'. You put it in your trolley and take it to the till but cannot take it away. The money goes to charity. It has proved to be quite popular with shoppers who have been putting down their one pound for hope. Capitalism is truly ingenious and we need to be just as canny. After all, on the left hope comes completely free. True, it is not enough for liberation, but it is an inestimably powerful starting point if we are to go beyond being just anti-capitalism to conceiving what else might be.

REPORTING BACK FROM CONDITIONS NOT OF OUR CHOOSING (2013)

Hilary Wainwright

To look back usefully, with one eye focused firmly on the future, it helps to highlight trends that were then hidden from view but in fact shaped the conditions in which we worked. Thinking back to when we three first met together and began what became 'the Fragments' – in Lynne's communal house, surrounded by copies of *Islington Gutter Press*, people hurrying in and out – my memory fills with people, events, journeys, gatherings, hopes and anxieties. It's only when I stand back and consider those years in relation to the deeper, especially economic tendencies, which began with the Labour government's acceptance of the IMF loan and the cuts on which it was conditional, that the historical significance of those years becomes clear. With an understanding of the growing power of global finance and the multinational corporation and their pressures to restructure the state – and indeed Westminster politics more generally – away from social priorities, we know that what seemed at the time still to be a period of political openings was occurring under conditions that led, at least for a decade, to closure.

The political closure of much of the Thatcher years was not inevitable, was constantly contested and was not of course forever. But when on the last night of the Greater London Council, security men with dogs instructed us out of the wake in the 'members dining room' in London's County Hall and I found myself finally going at midnight to pack up my files at the GLC's Popular Planning Unit, I realised that Thatcher's abolition of the GLC marked the attempt to destroy a lot more than a 'tier of government'. What was taking place then – and in the defeat of the 1984-85 Miners' Strike and the support around it led by the women of the mining communities – was the attempt to crush an emerging radical reinvention of democratic and emancipatory socialist politics with strong roots in a still well-organised working class. This was an unfinished but widely worked-on vision of what, looking back, was a direct alternative to break up of the post-war settlement driven through by Thatcherism, 'Blatcherism' and neoliberalism more generally. It contained many elements which, updated and developed, could be important today, as the economic and political tendencies that were gaining momentum in the late 1970s start to shatter through their own excess.

But historical periods are not neatly divided. Different dimensions of society have different lifespans, which makes for constant unevenness, conflict, ambivalence and surprises with no obvious immediate cause.[1] The sense of possibilities and openings in the 1970s, and with an added feeling of urgency in the years of writing and discussing *Beyond the Fragments*, reflected a political reality, as real (though differently so) as the structural trends to which I have just referred. In ways that I will explore in this essay, they illustrated and laid intellectual foundations for radically democratic political and economic institutions rooted in the capacities, knowledge and self-organisation of so-called 'ordinary' people. These possibilities were premised and prefigured in an understanding of the individual as social and the collective – for example, state, party, trade union – as products of social, and therefore also power relations between individuals, rather than seeing them as reified, supra-human edifices.

Behind the energy and optimism with which we as women experimented with these possibilities were two life-changing political and personal experiences coming in quick succession. Through the events of the late '60s and then the birth and making of the women's liberation movement we'd been through two experiences that changed our lives not only individually, but changed our social relationships to authority – parents, teachers, bosses, states, men – and to each other. Both gave us an important sense of the way institutions and rules are humanly made and can be humanly transformed, or at least changed. We had a strong sense of the flawed and vulnerable nature of supposedly superior authorities previously deferred to as given constraints. At the same time it inspired an awareness of the growing desire and potential capacity for self-government.

Indeed, if I was asked to distil one theme that I carried with me from my experiences in the women's movement for 'the making of socialism' it would be the following. On the one hand I learned never to treat institutions as thing-like, as or irremovably encased, but rather always mentally to get 'inside' an oppressive or conservative institution and identify the relationships by which the powerful depended on the supposedly powerless. This meant looking for where refusal or change could make the powerful vulnerable. It also meant an alertness to hidden forms of power evident in silences and absences. On the other hand, the positive, constructive lesson has been to pay detailed attention, in the process of our own organising for change, to the quality, including equality, of the relationships we create to achieve shared values. It is through those relationships that we develop our shared knowledge and collective power to transform society, and in the process, change ourselves.

In this sense being active in the women's liberation movement made me conscious of both the ways in which we reproduced our subordination through inaction, isolation and/or passivity, but also of how at the same time we could potentially develop the power to transform these circumstances – or at least set in motion a dynamic of transformation. And this applied at many levels in how we saw ourselves: in our relations with men and with each other, in how women were defined culturally, in women's relation to the economy and to state institutions, and in the organisations of the labour movement and the left. This isn't to imply transformation is easy, but rather that it isn't a matter of getting to the promised land, whether a change of government or the revolution, and then making the necessary changes. We found that through refusing to be complicit in relationships as they existed, becoming self-organised around our immediate needs and our anger, developing our self-confidence and our mutual support and also reaching out to make alliances, we could bring about changes in the here and now which opened up further dynamics of struggle and more radical change in the future. For example the organisation of community child care or creation of centres for battered women led on to campaigns for public funds from local councils; dramatic protests against the Miss World Competition shook the culture of women as commodities and spread the confidence to define our own self-images; strike action for equal pay helped to achieve legislation which in turn strengthened a continuing struggle over the gendered division of labour and distribution of wealth.

This emphasis on bringing about change in the present in the direction of the society we aim to create is what I think of as 'prefigurative politics'. Thus this approach to political change is not only about acting consistently with the values of the society you are trying to create. It is that, but in the context of a strategic understanding of social transformation: instead of focusing primarily on the ends, whether they are 'winning government' or 'making a revolution', it emphasises processes of change that draw on the sources of power we have 'from below' positively to transform relationships as we resist and in doing so seek to illustrate and develop feasible alternatives. These developing alternatives, in turn, then guide our continuing struggle.

For this reason, I will start by introducing you to several kinds of organisations that were around at the time of *Beyond the Fragments* and which in the sense just summed up were also prefigurative – around jobs and technology, around housing, local government and cuts in public spending, and around socialists from different traditions and struggles coming together. For all of them a self-consciousness of the relationships they created in the present was essential and evident. So too was the importance of developing feasible alternatives as lode stars of continuing struggle. Certainly, they inspired my sense that the insights we'd arrived at through feminism had a wider political significance for the making of socialism. We thought that if we made these explicit, it could set a process rolling, leading others to reflect on how the kinds of relationships they were creating and ideas they were discovering could also help to renew the left.

Inklings

Three scenes appear as I reflect on *Beyond the Fragments.*

First, a gathering of engineering workers from the Lucas Aerospace Shop Stewards Combine Committee in Wortley Hall, near Sheffield, the stately home turned labour movement meeting place. The 40 or so shop stewards from factories across the UK – Willesden in London to Burnley in Lancashire – were discussing the next steps in the campaign for the plan they'd drawn up for the manufacture of socially useful products: a vehicle for road and rail, medical equipment, energy-saving machinery and more. This was their positive alternative to management plans to close factories and cut jobs. All but two of those present were men.[2] Yet I was struck by similarities with gatherings of the women's movement.

The stewards listened to each other intently. When they spoke, they drew on their experiences, sometimes building up a wider picture of the company's strategies by piecing together information and gossip from different factories and departments. This process of gathering intelligence was vital to how they made their strategy.

The leadership of the combine committee seemed to be shared. There was an awareness of each other's capacities; they turned to each other for answers.

In these and other ways, there was a striking collective self-consciousness of an organisation emerging and a palpable awareness of its success being the responsibility of everyone present and depending on the strength of relations between them. As an 'unofficial' trade union organisation that brought together representatives from at least five different unions, there was no single external structure or authority to which they could pass responsibility. This sense of mutual responsibility made those present especially attentive to new delegates and to sorting out problems and disagreements rather than moving quickly on.

They assumed shared values but not a singular, unified approach to what they meant in practice. People were very open about the stances they started from. In their discussions about the alternative plan, Burnley delegates remembered the disappointments over the nationalisation of the coal industry and how little it increased the influence of miners or their communities; one of the younger stewards proudly proclaimed his membership of CND (Lucas Aerospace made components for missiles, so the alternative plan was an alternative to arms production as well as to the dole); Tony Benn was respected for his encouragement but there was scepticism about the Labour government, whereas Liverpool delegates wanted to steer clear of 'Politics' entirely. There was a shared emphasis on maintaining the combine committee's autonomy from both political institutions and company management.

Sitting in on this meeting, half engaged, half observer, gave me an inkling that the different kind of politics I'd experienced in the women's movement, evident in our autonomous and (more or less) self-aware way of organising, was happening elsewhere. This attentiveness to an organisation's inner relationships – this value given to each other's knowledge and experience, this self-conscious approach to the means of organising being integral to the ends – was not only about gender. In other words, the subordination that we had faced in the traditional organisations of the left and labour movement, which had led us as women to challenge the kind of relationships that were unthinkingly reproduced, not only marginalised and silenced women but also more generally stultified the realisation of people's capacities in the process of organising for radical change.

It was clear that this trade union combine committee too had its own distinctive strengths in the self-conscious ways it paid attention to the process of organising as part of its politics. These came from traditions of organising in the workplace in engineering, arising from a sense of the limits of established and overly conservative trade union structures. The committee had its own constitution, which codified its self-conscious ways of organising; there was a certain formality behind the attentive and reciprocal relationships. One of the main reasons for this was to help ensure their decision-making processes were transparent. This came from its members' constant awareness of their role as delegates, accountable and therefore reporting back to a factory shop stewards committee. They knew they had to convince their fellow workers in the factory to support the decisions of the combine committee at Wortley Hall.

Delegates also described local public meetings about the alternative plan, for example in the North West and the Midlands where unemployment was especially high. They described for example collaboration with local hospitals on ideas for medical equipment and mechanical aids for the disabled. In these ways building the strength of the combine committee and promoting the plan was constantly about creating what now might be called 'horizontal' relationships. With the compass of their alternative plan, they created, as they campaigned, the decentralised connections that illustrated what democratic planning might look like.

Experiments

The second scene I recall was in the cellar of a pizza house in the centre of Newcastle, chewing over plans for the Tyneside Socialist Centre with Kenny Bell, then working as a community organiser with tenants' organisations in the West End of Newcastle (later he became a hugely respected regional trade union leader).[3] The Socialist Centre, including a bookshop and garage converted into a somewhat ramshackle meeting place, was one of many local hubs of left movement activity and culture that were popping up across the country. Often unbeknown to each other, they were all bringing activists together in new, creative ways – like the *Islington Gutter Press* and Socialist Centre that Lynne helped to found in London.

For Kenny, who was organising links between tenants pressing for repairs and building workers resisting the rundown of the council's direct labour force, the importance of the Socialist Centre was that it brought socialists across different campaigns, unions and political parties into contact with each other, on ground that belonged to no single political tendency. This made it easier to build common strategies on particular issues, such as, in Kenny's case, the case for direct labour.

The Labour Party no longer fulfilled this function. Indeed it was because of the cuts imposed by the Labour government that public service activists such as Kenny found themselves making direct, horizontal relationships between users of a service and its providers, local council workers. These relationships had previously been built into the institutions of local government, in forms that were mediated through the hierarchies of representative democracy as it was traditionally organised. So again, in a similar way to the Lucas Aerospace Combine Committee, Kenny and other community organisers were responding to a problem – the cuts – but finding traditional sources of protection, such as the Labour Party, not up to scratch. Consequently they began, again like the Lucas stewards, to improvise and, using whatever organisational resources were available, they built relationships that took them beyond established institutional boundaries. They also became part of a national network of tenants' groups, local council trade unionists and socialist researchers who produced 'the Red Paper on housing', an alternative plan for defending council housing but also making it more democratic and responsive to the variety of needs of tenants.

In practice they were taking on political issues but not doing so primarily through a political party. Instead they were building their own social and industrial power through making new kinds of alliances – in Kenny's case, between tenants' groups city-wide and then between tenants, council workers and the local trades council. These kinds of alliances provided an autonomous base from which political lobbying was one tactic amongst many. The Socialist Centre proved to be a flexible and useful resource for this experimental and direct approach to organising. Its network of relationships proved handy beyond Tyneside too – for example, when Ford workers from Liverpool Halewood were on strike, the Socialist Centre could take them round the factories and shipyards along the Tyne where trade union convenors welcomed them and held mass meetings to hear their case and organise support. This experience, and the new kinds of direct relations built between trade unionists from Liverpool and socialist feminists involved in the Socialist Centre, later fed into the writing and subsequent discussions of *Beyond the Fragments*.[4]

People carrying out experiments need spaces to reflect and think aloud about the implications of what they are discovering and creating. It's helpful too to be able to draw on historical experiences and traditions. The Socialist Centre, as Kenny put it, was also 'helpful as a way of clarifying ideas about strategy', with its debates, courses, bookshop and cultural events.

Working to create the Socialist Centre wasn't easy. Male chauvinism was alive and even proud of itself on Tyneside, with class being used sometimes as a defensive weapon in response to mainly middle-class socialist feminists. But the common commitment to break down constricting divides between workers and intellectuals, communities and trade unions and between culture and politics, and to create an outward-looking, daring organisation, meant that socialists from different backgrounds came to see how dependent they were on each other. Also, many self-aware socialist men were changing through their personal lives and friendships with feminists. There was an intangible and sometimes complicated interplay between these personal changes and the eclectic culture of the Centre. It meant paying attention to the way we organised as part of the process of achieving and elaborating our long term vision. The means and the ends became closely and purposefully connected.

The engineering shop stewards who were among the founders of the Socialist Centre were proud of the traditions of grassroots democracy on which their union, the Amalgamated Union of Engineering Workers, was founded. They pushed us to try to turn our participatory and flexible norms into explicit procedures and some kind of constitution through which the Socialist Centre's supporters could call its co-ordinating committee to account. Questions of process that originated in women's refusal to be treated as secondary fused with principles of democracy long debated in the working-class movement. One spin-off was that many of us, men and women alike, strongly felt the need to rethink radically how the left organises itself.

Collaborations

The idea that 'we make the path by walking' – another feature that these experiences had in common with the women's movement – is fine, but maintaining a sufficiently clear sense of direction isn't easy. It helps to bump into fellow travellers marking the path from other starting points.

My third memory, then, is of the morning after a Socialist Centre meeting organised to spread support for the equal pay strike at Trico, a company making car windscreen-wipers in London. I woke early, on the floor. Sheila, a visiting speaker, was on the mattress. We were off to support a picket of striking bakery workers. It was a good opportunity to discuss the relevance for organising for socialism of what we had learned through the achievements and problems of the women's movement.

The Labour Party in its present state was clearly not going to be an effective opposition to the Tories; it had accepted the IMF's monetarist dictats, and none of the available would-be parties of the radical left seemed viable as mass alternatives or desirable models to follow. Grassroots movements seemed more hopeful but they needed, I felt, to find a means of being more interconnected and politically self-confident – 'hegemonic' one might say – in ways that occasionally I could glimpse in practice but could not put my finger on strategically.

With her knowledge of the efforts of the New Left in the late 1950s and 1960s, her historical perspective as well as her capacity to make connections in the present, Sheila took further these instincts that a new kind of politics was stirring beneath the familiar but increasingly hollow institutions of the conventional left. Further ideas came with a visit to Lynne. A modest plan was born: a booklet sponsored by the two Socialist Centres.

We hoped it would lead others to speak out about their experiences of organising and creating grassroots political power.

We hoped it would spread attempts to generalise from, and see interconnections between, the new ways of organising in all their messy and uneven forms and to learn from the difficulties and obstacles they faced. Hence the stress on encouraging others to write up and reflect on their own experiences: the weaving of such theories involves many different threads. Such a process, however, requires time, which was not to be. Thatcher and Reagan saw to that. Many of the threads remained hanging.

Journeys and encounters

Over the next thirty years, I found myself following a number of those threads – ideas that arose through movement experiences and at the same time were a source of insight for new thinking about a wider social transformation.

International examples – especially in Latin American countries such as Brazil, Bolivia and Uruguay, where a radically democratic kind of socialism was shaped by prolonged resistance to dictatorships – also illustrated how new ways of organising and thinking in the movements were a source of insight for a renewal of socialism. In these countries, grassroots labour movements, urban social movements, organisations of the landless and of indigenous peoples all played important roles, often producing new kinds of political alliances and parties, such as in its first decades the Brazilian Workers Party, the Movement Toward Socialism (MAS) in Bolivia and Frente

Amplio (Uruguay).

On the other hand, an experience which shook rather than reinforced my intuitions about a direct relationship between the growth of transformative social movements and the possibility of a democratic, participatory form of socialism, was encounters with civic activists in Central and Eastern Europe. I found that these new Czech, Hungarian and East German friends were not convinced.

It was necessary to explore directly the possibility and conditions for a non-capitalist or democratically socialised market which would facilitate dispersed and autonomous economic initiatives without leading to the exploitation, inequalities and concentrations of economic power typical of capitalism. This raised the question, one with echoes in our own organising experiences in the women's movement, of how we can achieve interconnection and, where appropriate, co-ordination of dispersed initiatives, but without an overbearing form of unification. Here again, the dilemmas of organising for change in the present had a relevance to how we envisaged the kind of society we desired in the future.

Thatcher's Britain was an inhospitable place to ponder fruitfully on alternatives to capitalism. But through these international discussions it was possible to look again at questions that, for me at any rate, had their origins in the discussions around *Beyond the Fragments*.

Threads

I picked up and followed four threads in particular.

The first concerns how far state institutions can be transformed in response to democratic pressures, rather than being submissive to the financial markets and big business. In this process what might be the relation between direct and participatory forms of democracy and the vote, itself the achievement of earlier social movements? It had become obvious that the formal political equality represented by voting was necessary but not sufficient in societies in which economic and social inequalities were endemic.

A second thread concerned the political significance of how knowledge is understood and organised. We'd found in the women's movement that drawing on and sharing our own experiences (previously dismissed as 'private') and validating the knowledge embedded in emotion (usually marginalised as 'gossip') had been important in developing our collective power and self-confidence. What is the wider significance of these new understandings of the plural sources of knowledge for creating participatory forms of democracy and breaking up concentrations of power?

The third thread, connecting the recognition of the plurality of sources of knowledge with a belief in the possibility of sharing and decentralising public power, concerns the possibility of non-capitalist markets.

And finally, the fourth problem is that of political organisation. Once we recognise the many sources of transformative power and understand state institutions as potential resources – as well as obstacles – for change, what are the implications for how we organise for systemic change?

I will report back on each of the above themes in turn.

What does it mean to democratise states?

In *BTF*, we dwelt directly on a particular aspect of state power. Many of the campaigns and initiatives of the women's movement at the time were concerned with making some part of the welfare state less paternalistic and more responsive to the needs of women. More often than not, women's groups would take action themselves: getting together on a voluntary, rota basis and improvising to raise initial funds for a women's centre or a nursery, then campaigning for the local council to provide funding but under some kind of community control. There was no one model but an approach emerged in practice that not only defended and sought to extend public services but also worked to change the way they were managed.

Out of these experiences came questions of how and through what kinds of democratic relationships, social movements and other kinds of civic initiatives could open up the state and redistribute both power and resources to the many away from the rich and powerful few.

Sheila and I had a glimpse of this possibility through being involved in the 1982-86 Greater London Council, as Sheila describes. This rich experience has been effectively, and I suspect deliberately, deleted from political memory by New Labour, as well as by the right. But it is worth retrieving in order to learn from as an attempt by a group of predominantly left politicians to carry through a radical mandate. Their strategy was innovative. They did not rely on the power of local state institutions, partly because they knew these powers were limited. Their strategy was to work with social and trade union movements who shared the goals of their electoral mandate but were mostly autonomous from the Labour Party and had their own distinct sources (and limits) of democratic power.

One example, the community-led development of Coin Street, on London's South Bank, illustrates how the power and knowledge of organised citizens effectively extended the capacity of the GLC to implement its policies for inner city communities. At the same time this example also illustrates the other side of the relationship: how local state power can be deployed in response to democratic organisations of citizens, rather than, as we have grown all too accustomed to, under the pressure or capture of big business.

In the late 1970s, the streets and community around Coin Street faced destruction through City developers eager to buy the land for speculative office blocks. A strong community campaign developed, which not only protested but drew up a detailed plan of how the local people and their organisations would develop this inner city riverside area: social housing, co-operative and social businesses, cultural and tourist activity and so on. Developing the alternative was part of building wider support. Some of those involved had links with the London Labour Party and along with local activists from other inner city areas they developed a section of the 1982 local election manifesto that gave a high priority to securing and expanding inner city communities against the pressure from property developers to expand office buildings. Several of these campaigners were elected GLC councillors. Indeed the motive behind their decision to be councillors was often to win the political support these campaigns needed to implement their plans.

What finally happened in the case of Coin Street was that the GLC used its powers of compulsory purchase to buy the land and block the property developers. It did so in a collaborative relationship with the community campaign, providing expertise from the GLC's experienced team of architects to complement the knowledge of the community. It convened a regular gathering of community campaigns from inner city areas across London and discussed their needs with the GLC planners. The GLC then supported the creation of the Coin Street Community Trust, on which it was represented until the council's abolition and to which, on agreed conditions, it devolved the development of the land.

Similar kinds of relationships were a hallmark of the GLC's way of implementing radical policies of many kinds, recognising the limits of its own power and knowledge. The pattern was for the GLC to use what distinctive powers it had by virtue of being a particular kind of state body – powers of funding, planning, various kinds of regulation, and so on – to support the capacities of civic democratic organisations to implement shared goals within a negotiated framework.[5]

This pragmatic opening up of the state and effective democratisation of the management of its resources was possible because of the existence of the kinds of organisations, movements and initiatives that inspired us to write *BTF*. Here were organisations, based outside the state and independent of big business, that did not simply make 'demands' on government but sought to bring about, initiate or illustrate transformations in the here and now. On the basis of this autonomy, these organisations had a variety of different kinds of relationships with the state. Generally, however, they sought to maintain their autonomy of both organisation and perspective, at the same time, bargaining, negotiating and collaborating for state support.

These innovations were unfinished and messy. And we do not know what would have happened had the GLC survived. But looking back, especially in the context of both Margaret Thatcher's determination to destroy the GLC and Tony Blair's equally concerted efforts to stop Ken Livingstone becoming mayor of London, this particularly accountable instance of representative politics provided an illustration of an alternative to the market politics of Thatcher and Blair. It was an alternative that opened up this hierarchical and offputting public institution to welcome Londoners to contribute their abundance of under-used capacities to the public good. Moreover it provided funding, legitimacy, confidence and, where appropriate, expertise to do so. Quite a contrast with David Cameron's so-called Big Society today, which bowdlerises our language of empowerment while cutting or privatising the funds, buildings and public spaces on which community organisations depend.

On a very different scale, there are many experiences of a similar kind in Latin America. Participatory budgeting, with all its limits as well as its achievements, is one very specific example. At its best it involves opening up the black box of public finance to transparent and systematic popular participation, with significant consequences for the redistribution of tax revenue towards the poor. The drawing up of a democratic constitution in Bolivia in 2010 provided another illustration of the significant influence on the nature of the state of autonomous forms of more direct kinds of democracy. In Bolivia's case a particularly significant source of non-state public power has been rooted in the struggles of indigenous peoples, leading to the constitutional enshrinement of the principle of a plurinational state. Though the practical dynamic of this sharing of power is now facing serious problems from which it will be important to learn. Finally, judging from recent developments, it may turn out that the participatory models developed through trial and error on the squares of southern Europe could contribute towards the transformations of corrupt and collapsing state institutions.

These, and many other experiences of the possibility of non-state sources of democratic power, mark a significant development beyond a liberal democratic framework of representative democracy. Liberalism has tended to treat citizens as atomised individuals, who are understood as relating to the political process only as voters or as groups lobbying for particular interests. This mentality, built into the institutions of liberal democracy, in turn favours vertical hierarchies in which only the government or the political party have an overview.

The reality of citizens forming horizontal connections across civil society, across politics and economics to build extra-parliamentary sources of public power for democratic social change in turn potentially strengthens the power of the vote, against the extra-parliamentary power of financial markets and the corporate capture of state institutions that has undermined it. The franchise has proven too weak an instrument of popular control on its own to defend itself from those who have sought since the victories of the suffrage movements in the 20th century to subvert its dynamic. But the problem is to reclaim this hard fought for source of political legitimacy and potential power, rather than abandon it.

The politics of knowledge: how to realise the capacities of each for the benefit of all?

A fundamental way in which the movements we described in *BTF*, especially the women's liberation movement, prefigured the society we are trying to create was their self-conscious emphasis on the social production of knowledge from many sources: practical, emotional, historical, theoretical. Many of the initial organisational forms of the women's movement, for instance, were about women sharing and reflecting on each other's experiences to get to the roots of their subordination, including the ways in which they had been complicit.

Much of the personal experiences that women shared at this time would have been dismissed as 'gossip' and never previously been considered a legitimate source of knowledge. Yet they contributed to an explosion of profound and grounded criticism of existing public services and economic policies. This was combined with not only alternative policies on paper but also practical changes in daily life, through campaigns and continuing struggle in new institutions. I witnessed a similar logic at work in the shop stewards committees I mentioned earlier, which I and several other socialist feminists worked with in the engineering industry.[6] What struck me was how they both, quite self-consciously, ensured time and space in their organisation to share and reflect on people's sometimes tacit knowledge and also to draw on academic research. In their practice, they all rejected the sharp dichotomy between theoretical and experiential knowledge that underpinned much public policy.[7]

The question I pursued in the following thirty years or so has been how to organise for radical social change in ways that enabled the capacities of all to be recognised, developed and realised for the benefit of a shared goal.

Recognition of the importance for real democracy of creating the conditions for realising popular capacity is not new. Tom Paine, writing at the end of the 18th century, believed that this was what representative democracy would achieve. It is worth repeating Paine's statement of this aspiration, to contrast it with the elitist rule that representative democracy in reality became. He said in his *Rights of Man:* 'It appears to general observation, that revolutions create genius and talent; but these events do no more than bring them forward. There is existing in man, a mass of sense lying in a dormant state, and which unless something excites it into action, will descend with him, in that condition, to the grave. As it is to the advantage of society that the whole of its faculties should be employed, the construction of government ought to be such as to bring forward by quiet and regular operation, all that capacity which never fails to appear in revolution.'[8]

Since we wrote *BTF* there has been plenty of evidence of his opening observation, if we interpret the reference to revolution broadly as meaning mass democratic movements of various kinds. Such genius and talent was evident among the women of the mining communities in the UK in the 1980s. It flourished for a while in the township 'civics' in South Africa that helped to make the apartheid state ungovernable and created in that period their own forms of self-government in Soweto and Alexandra and the other townships. It was at work in Wenceslas Square in Prague in 1989, and in the dissident movements across Central and Eastern Europe. And it has been to the fore in Tahrir Square and across North Africa, with inspiration spreading across the Mediterranean to Syntagma Square in Athens, Barcelona's Plaça de Catalunya and Madrid's Puerta del Sol, and from there up even more strategically to Wall Street, then across the world to the steps of St Paul's Cathedral, bordering on London's financial centre.

There have also been many attempts to construct lasting forms of political and economic organisation that by 'quiet and regular operation' might continue to bring forward this capacity. Several themes come to the fore.

First, there is the question of time: time to think, learn, plan. While management spends many days planning and thinking strategically, workers have to struggle even to get time off to achieve basic rights, let alone to think and prepare their own positive strategies. We used our resources at the GLC to enable workers to take time off to share information and analysis, to develop their own strategies and bargaining positions for their industry or service – another experiment unfortunately cut short.

A second related theme is education. Education has always been important for the labour movement. But it has not always been associated with a genuinely participatory vision of democracy. In Brazil, however, participatory democracy and popular education have been inseparable. This has its roots in the importance for the struggle against the dictatorship of building organisations of popular participation. The work of

Paulo Freire, the Brazilian popular educationist (and founder member of the PT) was fundamental to this radical view of democracy. This stress on empowerment coming from these traditions of popular education carried over into the way the Workers Party at first approached government power. When it was elected to municipal governments across the country in the 1990s it committed itself to sharing power with popular movements and to try to create lasting institutions of popular power. Pedro Pontual, an ex-Catholic priest and a pioneer of the popular participation in municipal budgets developed in the 1990s, explained to me: 'Freire's philosophy of education is about people becoming aware of their power together to create something new as they overcome what is oppressive. That's the foundation of our participatory politics.'

The third theme which relates to envisaging, in modern times, Paine's idea of a democracy through which human capacity is realised for the benefit of all, is the insistence on transparency. This is becoming an increasingly important dimension of the struggle for 'real democracy' against the opaque means of domination that are characteristic of corporate globalisation: the G8, IMF, World Trade Organisation, credit agencies, and so on. The spread and depth of this resistance owes much to the creative political use of information and communication technology. Important here has been the way that activists have used these tools to create infrastructures of transnational co-ordination in which each collaborating organisation, individual or network is both autonomous and connected.

An important and innovative development here has been the Social Forum process, with its origins at least partly in the experiments in participatory democracy in Brazil, especially the city of Porto Alegre. The legacy of the World Social Forum and the varied kinds of Social Forum organised in continental, national, local and thematic forms is not yet clear. Whether or not they survive as Social Forums, they have helped to create the conditions for a huge variety of political networks to develop the knowledge, expertise and capacity that are essential for democratic collective action on an international as well as local scale. Many of these networks continue or reappear in the movements of today, including Occupy and the *indignados.* So too do the forms of decision-making of the movement the forums were part of, with its emphasis on arriving at a consensus on the basis of shared norms and procedures.

These movements' emphasis on consensus decision-making is perhaps an illustration of Tom Paine's emphasis on the importance of finding ways of realising popular capacities that could otherwise be lost. It was more or less explicitly the methodology of the women's movement and also of the shop stewards movement, in which the consensus to take a vote at certain moments was also important. It is an approach developed through trial and error so that it enables organisations that use it to gain from the diverse capacities of their participants and from turning conflict and argument into a dynamic of innovation and development. How it is being applied and developed by the *indignados*, for example, for decision-making by thousands, many of whom have never occupied anything, let alone been part of deciding how occupations of several months should be governed, has been well documented by Marianne Maeckelbergh, in 'Horizontal Democracy Now: From Alterglobalisation to Occupation'.[9]

The recognition of the necessity of direct, more or less horizontal means of organisation as a basis of sharing the knowledge and mutual support that underpins democratic collective action, long preceded the new technology. But the internet and new developments in information technology have provided tools that have escalated this process exponentially – as well as throwing up new problems. These new tools, now part of everyday life, are also producing a mentality which *assumes* information and knowledge are to be shared. Struggles for knowledge as a common, against attempts to control or privatise knowledge and information are at the centre of today's movements for democracy.[10]

Tom Paine imagined that representative democracy would

'diffuse such a body of knowledge throughout a nation, as to explode ignorance and preclude imposition'. But he underestimated how those whose power was threatened by such a diffusion would work to maintain secrecy and ignorance. If *Beyond the Fragments* has meant anything, it has, I hope, contributed to the processes of direct connection, collaboration and subversion of hierarchy that periodically over the past thirty years has made it impossible for corporate power completely to escape the pressures of what they described in the 1970s as 'excess democracy'.[11]

Beyond the capitalist market

One potentially prefigurative feature of the social and labour movement organising of recent years has been the development of all kinds of networks that are not only critical of the corporate-dominated market but are actively developing alternative trading relationships based on principles of solidarity and democracy. An impressive example of such alternative practice is Twin Trading, which now works with over 50 democratic farmer organisations in 18 countries representing some 400,000 small-holder farmers. It works with them to build capacity, develop infrastructure, get access to markets and promote the products in terms of the social and environmental values guiding their production and their quality.[12] Other organisations have developed links between consumers and workers including farmers, exposing and campaigning against corporate working conditions and damage to the environment. There are trading links between producers and users of goods and services. And there are campaigning links between users, communities (rural and urban), trade unions and co-operatives around the environmental consequences of products and production processes. In different ways all these campaigns and initiatives not only challenge the profit-driven logic of corporations, they also open up the need to envisage non-capitalist markets and explore what state and civic institutions could regulate markets and what kinds of ownership underpin them, so that they become means of exchange and trade within a framework of social and environmental justice.

These initiatives and glimpses of an alternative, socialised market are reinforced by the possibilities opened up by the new technology for distributed production[13] as well as increased decentralised co-ordination between not-for-profits and co-operatives. This in turn strengthens and develops their scope in relation to the corporate dominated economy, creating visible examples of non-capitalist, socialised market forms.

Someone who has done much to build on these developments towards a vision and strategy for non-capitalist markets is the socialist-feminist economist Diane Elson.[14] Moreover, she explicitly addresses the question raised earlier by the failure of the command economies: what are the possibilities and conditions of forms of co-ordination and regulation that do not require a single controlling centre? Practical answers to this question are vital to the development of a feasible alternative to capitalism.

Open access to information is key to Diane's understanding of conscious control of the economy. She rejects as impossible and undesirable a tendency that was common on the left to interpret the aspiration for conscious social control over economics in terms of gathering all relevant information at one decision-making point and taking decisions as if it was possible to have full knowledge of all the interconnections and ramifications. She develops instead the concept of a socialised market in which a key basis for social control is open access to all available information concerning the product and its price, so that any decision-maker has access to the same information as any other.

Her argument treats the activities of shopping, organising a household and the labour of reproduction as part of political economy. This is her original starting point for a persuasive sketch of how a socialised economy might work. It is another example of how the particular experiences of struggling as a woman can feed into the making, or at least envisaging, of new ways of organising the 'social' of socialism.

The relevance here of socialist feminism comes not only from the needs and struggles of women around consumption. This practical idea of socialised markets provides a good example of the prefigurative politics on which socialist feminism has insisted. Here's an approach to a central problem for the future of socialism – the problem of alternatives to the capitalist market – which is grounded in a sensitivity to the practical problems that capitalist relations pose in everyday life and is inspired by existing struggles for change. Building on these, and drawing on a theoretical understanding of markets Diane Elson's ideas have led to a feasible and convincing vision of the future direction of change that makes sense in the present. It provides a strategic compass that could be useful again in a context in which the capitalist corporate-dominated market is deeply discredited – potentially terminally so, if alternatives develop rooted in ways that people are already organising and aspiring.

Can political parties be transformative, or at least supportive of transformation?

Beyond the Fragments marked a particular moment in a redefinition of politics that has been underway for the past 40 years or more. This is a rethinking that has taken place more in practice than in theory and it has been uneven, sometimes like a mountain stream disappearing from view, surfacing unexpectedly and finding new tracks down which to flow. In practice, the many new movements we have seen since its publication have continued in distinctive ways to challenge the boundaries between personal and political, between politics and economics, and between the material and the cultural. They have deepened the rejection of politics as a specialist profession 'above' society. Instead, as in the '70s but more pervasively and in new ways, these movements have emphasised taking action themselves, drawing pragmatically on whatever institutional resources are available, improvising collective and hybrid solutions in their own circumstances and then making wider connections.

Activists for democratic and egalitarian social change do

not invest their hopes and passions in political parties as they used to, even in the 1970s. (When I re-read my contribution, thirty years on, I was a little shocked at the intensity of my own, albeit critical, engagement with the party-focused dilemmas of the British left.) It seems that now most activists put their energies into creating more direct forms of democracy and public power, however partial and unfinished these may be. The scepticism towards political parties as we have known them has shown itself in an exodus from traditional parties and often from participation in elections altogether.

But while the limits of representative democracy as it is presently organised are clear, overcoming injustice and realising conditions of equality and freedom for all requires government/state action even if 80 per cent of the change comes 'from below', from society. Moreover, an electoral mandate for a radical political programme, reinforced by powerful democratic forces in civil society, makes the balance of power more favourable for the use of state powers against capital.

Consequently, there have been numerous attempts to create political parties with the rather vaguely defined purpose of being a 'voice of the movements' in the political system. The balance sheet of these experiences so far has not been positive. The history of the last thirty years is littered with examples of political parties that have either been eaten alive by the dominant political institutions or had their radicalism effectively suffocated. The fate of the Italian Rifondazione Comunista (a party which had particularly strong roots in the alter-globalisation movement in Italy, in its rich variety of forms) since its participation in government in 2006 and the German Greens since going into government and backing the Afghanistan war in 2001 come to mind. On the other hand, we must acknowledge and learn from an understanding of the problems faced by the Zapatistas, the indigenous movement in Chiapas, southern Mexico, and others who decide, often for good reasons, not to participate directly in the electoral system.

Many activists have been attentive to these experiences and

have been learning lessons to guide their own strategies towards the political system. For Europeans, intense collaboration across borders in protests and alternative forums at G8 summits, and at Social Forums more generally, for example, provided ideal opportunities for such mutual learning. Activists involved in forming Syriza in Greece, for instance, cite the importance of the experience at the G8 protests in Genoa and then the European Social Forums in bringing them close to the Italian movements and Rifondazione Comunista. The strong bonds established across the Mediterranean then meant that, when Syriza began to think seriously about government in the face of an avoidable social catastrophe in which all established political parties were complicit, the lessons learned from observing the fate of other radical left parties, especially Rifondazione, were at the back of their mind.

Syriza – a new kind of political organisation in the making?

The result of these international influences, combined with distinctive traditions of Greek political history, is a political organisation, Syriza, from whose impact and challenges we have much to learn.[15] It has been forged in the heat of the most extreme manifestation of neoliberal austerity, which has perhaps speeded up and intensified processes that have equivalents elsewhere. It is only now turning itself from a coalition of twelve organisations into a party. There are many warning signs of problems to come, not least the difficulties that feminists in the coalition have faced in influencing the direction of its leadership, despite the symbolic purple alongside the red and the green on Syriza's flag. However, after spending time in Athens interviewing a wide range of activists and reading the reports of others, it seemed to me that the long and difficult process of inventing a new kind of political organisation, beyond both Leninism and parliamentarism, has begun to produce qualitatively new results.

A foundation of this development is that for Syriza activists, especially the younger generation, it was above all the experience of the movements, especially those that coalesced around the Greek and European Social Forums, that produced their politics, even when they were members of one of the parties that founded the Syriza coalition. An important factor here is that the young activists and intellectuals who helped to found Syriza were part of the first generation that rejected capitalism after the fall of the Soviet Union, and who therefore decided to join the left independently of any 'actually existing' alternative or of debates on its character. Rather, it was the collective processes of knowledge and cultural production in the movements in Greece and internationally in the 1990s that were central to the way that the young leadership of Syriza developed and continue to develop their alternative. These movements were central to their personal political development, rather than being a sphere in which they 'intervened' to promote an alternative that had already been worked out elsewhere.

Syriza's roots in the movements – and Greece, or at least Athens where over 50 per cent of the population live, is a far more politically mobilised society than most – is one of the reasons why so many people decided that Syriza was the instrument they could trust to help them rid Greece of the memorandum. 'Syriza was always with us,' says Tonia Katarina, who helps to organise the Solidarity for All network of kitchens, clinics and other forms of solidarity that have grown up, with help from Syriza amongst others, in response to the devastation caused by the Troika's persistent grinding down of the means of life of the Greek people.[16]

When thousands of people converged on Syntagma Square, to protest against the EU-IMF memorandum of austerity and against the Greek government's acceptance of it, Syriza members were there too. They helped to build the movement, not push a line or take control.

How to take this approach to the institutional level raised new problems. Inside parliament and outside, activists are alert to the dangers of losing their social roots, becoming 'another Pasok', the discredited social democratic party. These dangers are especially acute as the Syriza coalition turns itself into a party. The aim, says Theano Fotiou, one of the new women MPs who make up a third of the parliamentary party, is to create 'a structure for the people to always be connected to the party, even if they are not members of the party, to be criticising the party, bringing new experience to the party.' How to achieve this is one of the questions to which Syriza leaders reply, 'I don't know'.

Interviewing Syriza leaders I found they said 'I don't know' with an ease unusual in political leaders. By this they meant the problem would be discussed in assemblies and other discussions of members and supporters and it was through this process that solutions would be found.

Their approach and culture can be illustrated in relation to two problems: the relation of the parliamentary party to the wider movement, and the pressures of day-to-day politics on the nature of leadership.

One factor that pulled the parliamentary leadership of radical, pro-movement parties in Germany and Italy away from their movement roots was the resources bestowed on them by the state, where the party, and often the movement, lost key cadres to the parliamentary machine. Syriza will receive considerable resources in terms of funds and staff[17] as a result of its electoral success.

The answer of a leading political co-ordinator, Andreas Karitzis, to the question of how these resources will be distributed is interesting. 'The biggest part of the new funds should go to what we can do in the neighbourhoods,' he said when I interviewed him in July 2012. 'For example, to employ people to spread initiatives like social medical centres, to explain what is successful and what is not, or people who would connect people in cities with producers of agricultural stuff. And to improve the ability to build these relationships online. These are the kind of things we are discussing, as well as strengthening the capacity of the party in parliament.' The coalition finally decided to give much to the establishment of 'Solidarity for All' as an autonomous network able to develop without constantly returning for funds. This approach is for Syriza also a symbol of how they would behave in government, redistributing power and resources.

Another pressure drawing the parliamentary party and its leadership away from the needs, initiatives and knowledge of social activists who share its aims and values is what could be called 'the tyranny of the immediate': the way that the day-to-day events of institutional politics and a hostile media require immediate reactions and decisions which can tend to favour an increasing centralisation of power in the hands of the parliamentary leadership.

How to counter this institutional process while being effective at this level of politics is one of the problems Syriza activists are working on as they prepare to move from being a coalition to a new kind of party. Over its complex history Syriza has developed several distinctive capacities which will come in handy for approaching the difficulties it now faces as a result of its success.

First, debate and argument has always been valued as a source of ideas and knowledge. Differences are respected as well as argued over. The value of living with a wide range of views is understood and shared even if it can lead to indecision, a tendency sometimes to the 'tyranny of structurelessness' familiar to the women's movement in the 1970s, and a fuzzy profile that Syriza's ruthless enemies can exploit. There is – as far as I can tell – none of the attempt to close down debate that in the UK has proved so politically and intellectually emasculating for the life of the Labour Party and contributed to the destruction of democracy and the abuse of women in the Socialist Workers Party.[18]

Secondly, there are many levels and focal points of initiative and experiment both in Syriza (partly because of the different political organisations that converged in its creation) and in its surrounding environment. Local branches are enabled and supported by the centre but have considerable autonomy. The intermediate structures have yet to be worked out. The base of

Syriza is, by all accounts, immensely active and self-confident. There is the autonomous research institute the Nicos Poulantzas Institute; *Avgi* the partially independent daily newspaper that recently celebrated its 60th anniversary; the annual three-day 300,000 strong anti-racist festival of which Syriza is one of 250 supporting organisations, and so on.

It is not surprising that Syriza aims to be what it calls a 'mass connective party'. This notion is used to make the contrast with traditional mass parties of the left which have sought to unify all political, social, ideological and cultural anti-capitalist expressions through their embrace and to focus all these activities on the goal of capturing the state. By contrast, what is decisive for Syriza, as Andreas Karitzis insists, 'is what you are doing in the movements and society before seizing power. Eighty per cent of social change comes from society; only twenty per cent through government'. This underpins a politics which stresses the prefigurative: supporting initiatives like, today, the Solidarity for All networks or the resistance to privatisation while organising to transform the clientelist state, and in the process developing people's capacity for democratic self-organisation.

It will be interesting to see how the organisation of Syriza as a party expresses these distinctive and innovative but also often tacit features, at present reflected more in practice than in theory.

Political organisation: neither pyramid nor umbrella but constellation

One line of thinking about transformative political organisation inspired by Syriza is this. First, we must distinguish different purposes, distinct spheres and levels of transformative activity. In part this is related to the different sources of power that different kinds of action and organisation seek to mobilise. Contrast for example the activity of an electoral campaign for Syriza with that of the Solidarity for All Network, or again the building of an alliance to both defend public water and improve it. Second, these activities are inter-related and share the same or overlapping values. Thirdly, we understand that traditional party models and imitations of them, based on pyramid-type hierarchies or umbrella-like forms of unity, are unlikely to have the consequence of enabling the transformative potential of these various activities to be realised.

Instead a more useful metaphor is to understand them as part of a constellation – or more mundanely perhaps, 'network' – of activities, sharing common values, involving all kinds of patterns of mutual influence, each autonomous but interrelated in different ways. Several further implications and questions follow. It becomes obvious that different ways of organising and different forms of democracy suit different purposes. For example, the focused kind of unity required for an election campaign is not what is required for helping to create alliances of community groups and trade unionists around alternatives to privatisation where facilitating the development and sharing of practical knowledge requires a slower pace and more diverse methods.

Moreover, people sharing the values of this multiplicity of organisation and eager to be part of a process of social transformation will have different possibilities and inclinations to participate. A useful concept to capture a necessarily flexible approach to participation is 'an ecology of participation'.[19] It is a concept which takes account of the different means of participation from meetings and face to face deliberation and collaboration to a whole range of new technological tools; and it also acknowledges a variety of skills and life circumstances. Gone is the standardized model of a '*homo politicus*', implicit in so many models of political organisation.

Where this leaves the political party, an organisation with a specific concern with government and the state, I'm not quite sure, and I think will vary from country to country, depending on the nature of state institutions. Certainly though we can say that with the radical widening and deepening of our understanding of the agencies of political change way beyond state power or governmental office, political parties cannot have a monopoly or even leadership of the totality of transformative politics.

Yet as we argued in the original *Beyond the Fragments*, and can reassert now on the basis of practical experience working with the local state – against the national government – the powers of state institutions are often a necessary resource for the success of transformative struggles based in society.

Left political parties or coalitions organised for the purposes of political representation are therefore best understood (and self-understood) as a distinctive part of the constellation of organisations that I referred to earlier. It is then clear that for such political representatives to serve and support transformative movements and initiatives in society, they would need to operate in conditions of transparency and accountability, and take other measures to counter the pressures sucking them into the flytrap of parliamentary politics, away from an enabling role for the wider constellation towards becoming more a part of the political class.

Since political parties have been the traditional form of political unification, I will end this essay by reflecting briefly on what the consequences are today of the changes since the late 1970s for the relations in Britain between autonomous, movement politics and mainstream politics, especially the Labour Party.

Breaking the cycle: the new cultural context of political action

In the UK, the conservative pressures of parliamentary politics have proved almost overwhelming, ensuring that the politics of the Westminster parliament – in partial contrast to the proportionately elected devolved parliaments of Edinburgh and Cardiff – are considerably more conservative than the range and mix of public opinion. The first-past-the-post electoral system draws the main three parties to the centre, leaving radical dissenting views, especially on the left, disenfranchised.

Historically this has led the left in the UK to organise primarily within, or in close alliance with parts of, the Labour Party. This was reinforced by the affiliation of most trade unions to the Labour Party. In the 1960s the actions of Harold Wilson's governments, particularly its attack on trade unions but also its support for the US in Vietnam,[20] led to a mass exodus of members from which it has never really recovered as a party of activists. In the '70s and until the early 1980s this was reinforced by the radical expansion of politics through the activities and culture of social movements, the women's movement especially, beyond the constricted confines of government. But the wider influence of these movements produced such pressures for change inside the party that many activists joined to gain political support for their autonomous campaigns and movements – a process which also grew out of a consciousness of the kinds of resources they needed from the state.

Here is not the place for the full story, but effectively this left turn of the Labour Party in the early 1980s was blamed for Labour's defeat in 1983, setting off a lust to purge the party of all significant signs of socialist life. Many leftists also went out of the party of their own accord. We are now seeing a weak return of this recurring cycle of a (slight) shift to the left and (slight) increase in members. On the other hand, there is also the growth of a new autonomous politics taking forms that have moved on from those that were the subject of *Beyond the Fragments*.

In some cases, most notably UK Uncut and Occupy, they have had an impact on the political mainstream. Particularly significant for our argument, is the fact that they have triggered a shift in the Labour Party towards a (slightly) bolder stance on taxation and financial regulation that would, in present circumstances, have been unthinkable through the traditional tactics of internal party struggle.

One background factor in this is that the new technologies of information and communication have been eroding the traditional monopoly that Westminster politics and the conventional, mainly conservative media had over political culture and the shaping of dominant agendas and opinion. This of course is an international phenomenon.

Consider UK Uncut. This is a group of mainly young people, many of whom had already had the experience of challenging and influencing the dominant political agenda, with considerable success, on climate change, through targeted and media-savvy direct action: the 'Climate Camps' for example at Heathrow airport and other strategic locations. They were frustrated by the absence of any mainstream challenge to the Conservative-Lib Dem coalition's contention that the cuts are 'necessary'. They wanted to organise action that engaged people in a way that the habitual demonstrations of the 'traditional left' failed to do.

They decided to focus on corporate tax avoidance and occupy Vodafone and Topshop, the shopfronts of companies avoiding billions of pounds tax. 'Our aim is to make it clear that the cuts are a political choice, not a necessity,' says Murray Worthy, from UK Uncut, 'that they are avoidable.' UK Uncut activists have a very clear understanding of their role, and its limits. Murray says: 'Our job is to change public opinion, to create a process which will encourage others to speak out, take action. We don't engage directly with the political system, lobby or make policy. There are others who do that.'

The impact of their action and their ability to spread their arguments through social media was dramatic. Two and half years ago, when UK Uncut was formed, there was really no public debate about tax avoidance or progressive, redistributive taxation as an alternative to the cuts. It was the concern simply of a few academics and campaigning groups around international development and the Tobin tax on financial speculation. Two and a half years later it is an issue on which parliamentary inquiries[21] have taken or are taking place into Starbucks, Google and Amazon, all companies targeted by UK Uncut; all three main parties have felt they've got to at least talk about doing something about tax avoidance. Newspapers are now directly talking to the experts on tax avoidance and progressive taxation where before it was UK Uncut using these experts for its campaigning information. The Labour Party in power, with its concern to be 'business-friendly', did very little on the loopholes in tax law. Now Labour MPs and the party's leadership are making strong statements pushing the coalition government, which itself has felt it has to adopt the rhetoric of attacking 'fancy corporate lawyers' and the 'repugnancy of tax avoidance'. Still, however, it is the debate that has been changed, not yet the material policies.

The case of the campaign against the privatisation of water in Italy, like UK Uncut purposefully autonomous of political parties, provides an example of decisive material impact of a new kind of multi-centred, molecular campaign, bringing together all kinds of social actors, mostly based autonomously from national party politics. It managed not only to gain 1.4 million signatures for a referendum petition on whether or not water should be kept as *il bene commune*, a common good, but then to achieve a turn out more than the required 50 per cent of the electorate for the referendum to take effect, with 94 per cent of these voters voting '*si*' to keeping water public. This in a context where Berlusconi directed his media outlets (meaning most mainstream Italian television) not to put out any news about the referendum.

Behind this success is the story of a campaign which co-ordinated horizontally and rotated responsibilities, developing over the years a diffuse leadership through which capacities were spread and developed. It used virtual means of communication as well as extensive popular mobilisation in the streets, market places and cultural centres. These methods overtook and then overwhelmed the mainstream media.[22]

These experiences point to a distinct approach to how we might connect across the fragments, through mutual awareness and shared infrastructures of various kinds rather than being under the same organisational umbrella. And this stress on connection and networks rather than unification through a single centre is spreading in the UK. Several trade unions in the UK, including Unite and the civil service workers' union PCS, have made close and supportive links with UK Uncut. Unite has also created a new kind of community membership, reaching out to people outside the traditional labour market. The TUC has supported a very creative, open and well-used website, False Economy, which provides resources and a platform for all those resisting and campaigning for alternatives to the government's imposition of austerity. These are still, however, signs of potential rather than a dominant trend.

So rather than thinking in terms of unification versus fragmentation, I would emphasise a recognition of the necessity of diverse sources of power, and the need therefore to devise organisational forms for different purposes and contexts. This kind of flexibility and complexity gives importance to the sharing of information, knowledge and connection between each initiative, so we know when to converge, collaborate and develop common decision-making, including in order to intervene in the political system. This in turn points to the importance, as one piece in the organisational jigsaw puzzle, of a purposeful infrastructure to strengthen these flows of communication, cohesion and common political direction, and all the mutual learning that this involves. We all have to be activists and reflective observers at the same time. This is one reason why I became involved with developing *Red Pepper* magazine as one modest step towards such an infrastructure and therefore a practical contribution towards going 'beyond the fragments'.

The organisational models of the past have tended to be based on rallying the masses to a programme worked out by a committed vanguard, to be implemented by a more or less centralised state. *Beyond the Fragments* challenged this model, on the basis of limited though important experiences, especially of the women's movement. And as I have tried to argue here, such a challenge is not only about the means but also nourishes and roots our vision of the society we are trying to create. Now, despite many setbacks and defeats we face a situation where, in practice, alternative approaches are widespread on a global scale. They are based on and realise or express the capacities of the masses rather than presuming their ignorance or 'backwardness'. Moreover, though these alternatives are dispersed, they are frequently interconnected, with considerable mutual awareness and shared values. It is this process which needs to be encouraged so that necessities and opportunities of convergence can be recognised and grasped, rather than any unification sought through a single centre.

I still have to say that I do not know the answer to the question of political organisation, and I guess, never will. There is no holy grail. But I feel confident in saying that we are engaged in a search that is also a continuing struggle and self-conscious process of experiment and argument. And sometimes, this gives good grounds for optimism.

Notes

I want to thank Patrick Kane, campaigner with War on Want and son of Kenny Bell who was involved in organising the conference after the first edition, for his comments on this essay.

1 Like the demonstrations which in 1999 almost stopped a summit of the World Trade Organisation, one of the increasing number of entirely opaque international organisations through which the US and its corporations shaped the economic order to suit their interests.
2 The two women, Jane Barker and Tina Mackay, became leading trade union researchers and organisers, part of a very creative force of socialist feminists who became increasingly influential in the trade unions in the 1980s, contributing no doubt to the fact that in Frances O'Grady we now have the first socialist feminist general secretary of the TUC.
3 He became secretary of the Newcastle council branch of Unison, and the deputy convenor of the Northern Region. Throughout the 1990s and first decade of the 21st century he successfully led a sustained campaign against the outsourcing of council services, always with an alternative strategy of reform – a method inspired partly by the experience of Lucas-style 'alternative plans' developed by engineering shop stewards on Tyneside in the 1970s. See *Public Service Reform.. But Not As We Know It,* Hilary Wainwright and Mathew Little. Brighton: Pic Nic Publishers, 2009. Kenny died in 2011. See Kenny Bell: From Loss to Living Legacy http://www.redpepper.org.uk/kenny-bell

4 John Bohanna, a leading shop steward at Fords Halewood was one of the delegation from Liverpool hosted by the Socialist Centre. Joan Bohanna, leading shop steward at Glaxo, and John became directly involved in organsing the *Beyond the Fragments* conference in Leeds.

5 While we still worked at the GLC, a group of us in its Industry and Employment branch, mainly working in the Popular Planning Unit, wrote up these experiences in *A Taste of Power*, edited by Maureen MacIntosh and Hilary Wainwright. London: Verso, 1986.

6 One of the most notable of these women was Jane Barker, and the respect for her in the trade unions was based in part on this combination of practical and theoretical knowledge, influenced by both her long involvement in the women's movement and her work with the Lucas Aerospace shop stewards. http://www.redpepper.org.uk/jane-barker-one-of-us

7 Helpful intellectual tools for exploring the theoretical implications of these innovations in practice are provided by critical realism, the foundations of which are developed by Roy Bhaskar in *A Realist Theory of Science*, London: Routledge, 2008 and *The Possibility of Naturalism*, London: Routledge, 1998. See also Hilary Wainwright, *Arguments for A New Left, Answering the Free Market Right*, Oxford: Blackwells, 1994, especially pages 1-190.

8 *The Rights of Man* in *The Thomas Paine Reader*, London: Penguin, 1987, p. 277.

9 Marianne Maeckelbergh, 'Horizontal Democracy Now: from alterglobalization to occupation', *Interface*, 4(1), 2012, pp. 207-34.

10 See Manuel Castells, *Networks of Outrage and Hope: Social Movements in the Internet Age*, Cambridge: Polity 2012.

11 The Report of the Trilateral Commission 1975. For a useful discussion of its significance see Boaventura de Sousa Santos' *Democratising Democracy: Beyond the Liberal Democratic Canon*, London: Verso, 2006.

12 Examples here also include Cafedirect, Divine Chocolate and many more.

13 See Michel Bauwens, 'Peer to Peer Production and the Coming of the Commons', *Red Pepper*, July 2012, http://www.redpepper.org.uk/the-coming-of-the-commons

14 Diane Elson, 'Socialised Markets not Market Socialism', *Socialist Register* Vol. 36, London: Merlin, 2000.

15 For an excellent historically informed and inside understanding of Syriza that also draws out its distinctive significance, see Michael Spourdalakis' 'Left strategy in the Greek cauldron: explaining Syriza's success' *in The Question of Strategy: Socialist Register 2013*, London: Merlin, 2012. Also in this volume see Aristides Baltas' 'The Rise of Syriza: an interview' and my own 'Transformative power: political organisation in transition'.

16 See Tonia Katerini, 'Solidarity for All' in *Red Pepper*, December/January 2013.

17 Though the government has cut it to a minimum.

18 See Laurie Penny in the *New Statesman*, http://www.newstatesman.com/laurie-penny/2013/01/what-does-swps-way-dealing-sex-assault-allegations-tell-us-about-left

19 See Mayo Fuster Morell to describe the nature of participation in Wikipedia.

20 Stopping short of military support because of the strength of opposition on the streets, in the unions and amongst a stronger contingent of left MPs than is imaginable today.

21 The Public Accounts Committee chaired by Margaret Hodge MP.

22 See Tommaso Fattori 'Liquid Democracy' in *Transform!*

TODAY, YESTERDAY & TOMORROW: between rebellion and coalition building (2013)

Lynne Segal

Times change, and with them accounts of what is more likely to be seen as politically achievable, or perhaps ridiculous. There is near consensus that Britain at present is facing an ever-deepening recession, with economists such as Will Hutton disclosing that the UK is suffering the worst economic performance since the nineteenth century, while its recovery from the height of the banking crisis has been amongst the slowest in the world. Even the IMF warns that the extent of government's spending cuts and refusal to invest in the public sector is forestalling growth and risking permanent damage to the economy.[1] Moreover, there is widespread awareness of the distressing effects of public sector cuts on the most vulnerable people in the UK, with women hit hardest by job cuts in the welfare system, and half a million people marching against the cuts in March 2011.

Yet in the UK there is nowadays less political cohesion, hope, or anything like an agreed alternative vision between the different forms of resistance to this Tory-led coalition than there was when Margaret Thatcher was elected at the close of the 1970s. With the ethos of market forces so comprehensively triumphant over the last thirty years, fear eats the soul of the British left. Even the once widely approved word, 'socialism', to describe the goal of the radically egalitarian, democratic society many of us hoped to build back in the 1970s, has largely fallen into disuse. Back then, it was the Women's Liberation Movement that exerted the strongest influence on my life, and feminism generally has ever since remained a part of every political move I make. Yet my feminism has never been separate from attempts to make sense of the broader political landscape. Thus, before turning back to that moment of *Beyond the Fragments*, in 1979, I want to survey aspects of the present conjuncture in more detail, to see its possible continuities and discontinuities with that earlier moment. Drawing especially upon the impact of feminism, the problem as we saw it back then was how to facilitate more dialogue and co-operation between the different organized left groups and diverse activist movements to build coalitions solid enough to confront the triumph of the right under Margaret Thatcher. In so many ways we seem back in that moment again, except that the obstacles we face have grown formidably.

'Man does not live by bread alone', the Sydney born anthropologist Michael Taussig reminds his listeners in London, January 2012, speaking of Occupy Wall Street (OWS). Feminists always knew this. '*We want bread, but we want roses, too!*', was one of the classic banners we celebrated, thought to have been carried by the predominantly immigrant women on strike for three months for higher wages and decent working conditions after a threatened pay cut and line speed-up at the Lawrence Textile factory in Massachusetts a hundred years ago. It has been suggested that those banners were apocryphal, having originated in a poem written by James Oppenheim the previous year. Nevertheless they became enduringly associated with the mood of that strike and remained iconic in the reappearance of second-wave feminism, nearly sixty years later. Importantly, the strike, supported by the 'Wobblies' (the IWW or International Workers of the World) had ended with many of the workers' demands being met in March 1912.[2]

Another saying, often joyfully repeated and rephrased by second-wave feminists is wrongly attributed to the anarchist Emma Goldman: '*If I can't dance, I don't want to be part of your revolution*'. Again, the mythical phrase catches Goldman's awareness of the importance of pleasure and beauty in politics, making visible an awareness of what is wanted, alongside anger against the causes of so much suffering. A tireless activist in the early twentieth century, Goldman soon added calls for birth control and women's emancipation to her public speeches in support of workers' and immigrant rights. It is easy to find the source of the historical misremembering of Goldman's words, expressed in her autobiography, *Living My Life* (1931), in which she described her fury when chastised by a comrade who declared her energetic dancing frivolous and harmful to 'the Cause': 'I did not believe that a Cause which stood for a beautiful ideal, for anarchism, for release and freedom from convention and prejudice, should demand the denial of life and joy ... I want freedom, the right to self-expression, everybody's right to beautiful, radiant things ... I would live it in spite of the whole world – prisons, persecution, everything. ... I would live my beautiful ideal'.[3]

The art of protest: direct action today

Living life radiantly is the spirit some tried to capture when reporting from the front lines of the rebellion in Zuccotti Park, which kicked off 'Occupy Wall Street' (OWS) in New York in September 2011: 'To visit the park was like going to a street fair. There were so many smiling people, radiant with happiness, mixed with a few grim, concentrated ones,' Michael Taussig reported in his talk. Living in New York, Taussig was raising spirits in London the following year with accounts of his participation in noisy ebullient days, cold, wet nights, instant democratic networking, during the two months in which thousands of people took part in the occupation in Zuccotti Park. On his favourite terrain, telling stories linking aesthetics and politics, Taussig underlined the necessary ties between revolution, art and corporate capital. The 1 per cent still making obscene profits, that 1 per cent responsible for the entirely predictable economic crash of 2008, are right now busy buying at art fairs around the world. Indeed, as he explains, in financial crises, art is considered one of the safest investments, and top galleries internationally report that their products are selling extraordinarily well: 'As Stocks Fall/Art Surges'.

London art critic Thomas Keane agreed, noting similarly in October 2011: 'While Greece careers towards bankruptcy, the UK is being predicted zero growth for next year, and the phrase "recession" overtakes "postmodernism" as a media buzz word, the artworld can now breathe a microcosmic sigh of relief.'[4] Art work also proliferated in Zuccotti Park, in the sometimes fabulous but fleeting images appearing daily, produced by the small tribe who saw themselves as speaking on behalf of the 99 per cent who, one way and another, were enduring the fall-out of financial crisis. The hundreds of women and men living in the park, black and white, young and old, included some who have lost jobs and homes, those hit hardest by the three decades of deregulated fiscal policies pandering to the always escalating greed of unchecked corporate capital: 'Lost my job but found an occupation', one sign declared. It was out of this art work that Taussig, taking notes, making drawings, constructed his talk, *I'm So Angry, I Made A Sign*: 'This is not only a struggle about income disparity and corporate control of democracy. It is about corporate control of art, too, including the art of being alive.'[5] Reflecting upon the nature and impact of four years of anti-austerity street protests in Greece, the London-based Professor of Law Costas Douzinas similarly points to the cultivation in the squares of a new aesthetic politics, which called upon a lost sense of what should be valued as public expression and cherished as the common good: 'The poems recited, the personal stories and historical references narrated transformed public speaking from instrumental and demagogic act into artistic performance making it deeply political.'[6]

Some have questioned whether feminism is really a dynamic force in recent occupy movements, claiming that it is men's voices that are most often heard in spaces of occupation. Indeed some women reported being harassed, or that microphones were grabbed from their hands.[7] This suggests, of course, the need for constant vigilance in direct action over the stubborn persistence of old hierarchies, and sometimes the emergence of new ones. Nevertheless, the pioneering feminist activist from the late 1960s, Rosalyn Baxandall, who also regularly visited Zuccotti Park, expressed hope that a new movement was being born, one educating itself about the causes of the banking crisis. For while so many North Americans have lost almost everything, she noted – their homes, savings, health insurance and jobs – the salaries of bankers and managerial staff have continued to rise into the millions. Baxandall felt she saw in the park a renewal of her own old ideals: 'The Occupiers have dreams and a vision, too: of a just, peaceful, diverse, democratic world, where democracy serves more than global capitalism and the greedy one percent.'[8] In its opening weeks OWS not only managed to elicit a radical spirit cutting across generational and other divisions but, surprisingly, as British journalist Polly Toynbee celebrated, it quickly gained favourable support from 54 per cent of Americans aware of the protest, with strong endorsement from a quarter of the population, according to a poll in *Time* magazine.[9]

In sudden flurries of activity, there seems little doubt that grass-roots oppositional activity is now back on the political agenda. Rebellion, occupations, civil disobedience, all returned in force some years ago, as ever, in some of the most unexpected places. Some trace the beginning to the riots in the poor suburbs of Paris and other French cities in 2005 and 2007, mainly involving African and Arab youth in violent confrontations with the police. Many would point to the massive demonstration in Athens in 2008, but above all to the Arab Spring beginning December 2010, soon followed by massive gatherings of Portuguese and Spanish Indignados, more Greek street riots, the same year as Occupy movements appeared in New York, London, Sydney, and other cities around the world, late 2011. The most unexpected and immediately inspirational were the Arab insurrections, with the Tunisian uprising at the very close of 2010 followed a few months later by demonstrations of millions of Egyptians in Tahrir Square. The sudden coming together of unemployed graduates, slum-dwellers, union activists, faith groups and feminists, were all at once projecting a host of new dissident voices around the world, many of them, there was no doubt about it this time, talented Arab women's voices, demanding true democracy and a fairer share of their country's resources, beyond any restrictions of gender, religion or class.[10]

Over 800 protesters were killed and tens of thousands injured in Egypt alone. Yet through demonstrations, marches and continuous acts of civil defiance, those first two Arab uprisings rather quickly overthrew their dictatorial, corrupt and self-serving rulers. What has followed in those two countries is more troubling, as economic disorder and political confusion remain, with conservative forces and new elites emerging, supported by the military. Nevertheless, the Egyptian writer Ahdaf Soueif was still writing confidently a year later: 'The Egyptian uprising is like the Nile in flood. It cannot be kept back with barriers and uniforms.'[11] Threatening such optimism is a reality where a revolutionary multitude can for a while make an impact around the world and, at certain moments in history, overthrow a dictator, but they cannot by themselves install a progressive government without the most strenuous of coalition building to create or connect with a political party that might attempt to implement their demands. Such is not yet the case in Tunisia or Egypt although, as we shall see, there are more positive (as well as negative) developments in Greece.

Nevertheless, whatever the ongoing struggles in the Middle East, with complex and far bloodier uprisings in Syria and other regions, they unquestionably served as a further spur for the resurgence of protest movements in western democracies around the globe in the context of the continuing catastrophic effects of the financial crash of 2008. OWS was thus simply one of proliferating occupations of urban spaces in recent years, eager to reclaim the city, with excellent access to global resources for spreading the word that it is possible to imagine and practice ways of living differently: 'This is what democracy looks like', the Marxist geographer, David Harvey, raced into print to declare.[12] No sooner was the occupation in Zuccotti Park violently ejected in October 2011, than people were setting up camp in many other cities around the world. In London, for instance, prevented from settling outside the London Stock Exchange (LSX), tents were pitched nearby, initially outside St Paul's cathedral. They remained for seven months before facing eviction, tents spreading like mushrooms into nearby Finsbury Square, and have been popping up here and there, if more sporadically, ever since.

The goals again were to expose corporate greed and social injustice, the lack of affordable housing in London, the influence of corporate lobbyists on government, as well as environmental pollution globally. Influentially, one of the most eloquent supporters of the occupiers in London was the Canon Chancellor of St Paul's, Giles Fraser, who resigned his post when the Church after some months had the squatters ejected from their forecourt. 'What would Jesus do?', the squatters penned provocatively, raising a tangle of theological issues regarding Christianity's founding Jewish rebel and prophet, who was no friend to money lenders and cared deeply about the poor, the sick, the shamed, discarded and destitute. After the eviction, Fraser became a media figure, writing on the significance of the occupation, sharing much of the occupiers' vision of the destructive values of contemporary global capitalism: 'Occupy's welcome and care for the vulnerable contrasted sharply with the indifference of a City that didn't seem to give two hoots … The demand for social justice was being trumpeted slap bang in the boiler room of global capitalism.'[13]

'You can't kill an idea', was the viral message circulating globally at the height of the occupations, the idea being that there is something rotten in the state of corporate finance and global capitalism: 'We stand in solidarity with the global oppressed and we call for an end to the actions of our government and others in causing this oppression', Occupy London (OLX) declared.[14] 'You can't kill the idea', the activists hope, and their most sympathetic supporters with a voice in the media agree. This is because of the role of the world-wide web, and the instant communications that can keep protest alive. Such is the view of the British economic journalist Paul Mason, who believes the new global revolutions are now unstoppable because 'the near collapse of free-market capitalism combined with the upswing of technological innovation' has resulted in 'a surge in desire for individual freedom and a change in human consciousness about what freedom means'.[15] All that texting, twitter following, instant access for so many to the remarkable resources of internet knowledge and communication, he and others argue, can sustain protest as never before. The paradox Mason notes, like Marx before him, is that the technological advances of capitalism and the free market, which on the one hand has enabled the contracting out of labour in search of ever higher levels of exploitation, has on the other educated ordinary people in much of the world with the 'skill ingenuity and intelligence to swap experiences beyond borders'. Yet he is also aware of the dangerous lack of connection between the protesters and any mainstream politics, noting that most of the people he interviewed were hostile to 'the very idea of a unifying theory', set of demands, or shared pathway.[16] He simply hopes that the movements justified moral outrage at things as they are, with a tiny elite getting ever richer as billions globally get poorer, will somehow combine with their networking skills to help realize their vision of a fairer world, while believing that 'the future hangs in the balance'.[17]

What should we make of this? There is a point to growing old: we have a past. So I can say at once that the imaginative excitement often unleashed in direct action against perceived injustice, actually being on the scene when you hope, rightly or wrongly, that this moment of collective resistance might leave its mark on history, often permanently changes consciousness. Contrary to clichéd opinion, most rebels, young or old, do not significantly shift their political outlook, though they may well become disillusioned. History matters, in discerning the impact of battles of the past; yet, it will also always be contested. Memory matters too, though we recall selectively and must rely upon a shared language of recognition to facilitate our narratives of the past.

The early feminist commitment to sharing and learning from experience was critical for forming a sense of collective agency and purpose, though it would take a battering, some of it useful, when feminist theory began to embrace Continental philosophy.[18] However, early on some feminists realized that the ways in which consensus is formed inevitably sidelines significant controversy in its desire to nurture and protect the ties that bind us.[19] Today there are thriving intellectual debates about the connections and disjuncture between history and memory, and the possibilities and pitfalls of both. Surprisingly perhaps, as some historians have been noting lately, the recent past can be the hardest to know and understand, even when we have participated in some of its most memorable moments. Such indeed were the thoughts clearly articulated by the historian Tony Judt, shortly before he died in 2010: 'The twentieth century is hardly behind us but already its quarrels and its achievements, its ideals and its fears are slipping into the obscurity of mis-memory.'[20] He provides many examples. Nevertheless, for all the growing sophistication of new technology, the instant messaging that does indeed make a difference, one thing ageing activists usually know, when faced with the political dilemma of keeping activism alive after initial exhilaration fades, is how hard that is. Sadly, ideas do fade, or the priority we once gave them, along with the fighting spirit of a movement, especially, perhaps, a movement as volatile, diffuse and vulnerable to attack as the Occupy movement, once the sanctioned forces of law and order move in against it.

Of course it is tiresome to hear, even to say, but to succeed Occupy has to manage to reach out not just in the heat of action, but to build coalitions that survive and manage to have impact upon groups that can affect government policies, once reality bites and fragmentation and exhaustion set in. With or without jobs, a myriad of personal and shared responsibilities take their toll on rebellious spirits and dissident actions. Beyond spontaneous sites of struggle, the question shifts to whether or how 'democracy in action' can be preserved to form a coherent and intelligible opposition. If we actually believe in the possibility of a fairer distribution of the world's resources, and less environmentally polluting uses of them, protest must be preserved and somehow, at least some of the time, made to cohere into something more enduring that can keep pushing for change, attempting to influence those who are in or might form a future government, or who are in some way closer to the levers of power.

Can it be done? The question is all too familiar. As I said, it was exactly the issue that motivated our writing *Beyond the Fragments,* facing the triumph of Thatcher in the UK, Reagan the following year, and wanting to forestall the installation of what would soon become the deregulated economic model known as neoliberalism that has brought us to the mess we are in today. At that time, we were writing from what we thought we had learned from over a decade of activism in different sectors of the then still flourishing radical left, with our own shared feminist, anti-capitalist, socialist perspectives. Today, that economic regime we opposed is itself in continuous crisis, evident in the threatened implosion of the Eurozone and the imposition of harsh anti-austerity measures visibly destroying the lives of many of those in greatest need, while also failing to generate what its own mantra of market expansion and 'growth' requires. This obviously makes it a good time to look back, critically, at the impact, legacy and, let me say right away, as I see it, the failure of so many of the ideas and aspirations that triggered our own largely thwarted attempt to move *Beyond the Fragments.*

Libertarianism writ large

However, I have passed through many lives, and all of them feed into my troubled thoughts of the moment. Before I named myself a socialist, or a feminist, there was a time when a type of anarchism, 'living one's politics', refusing all contact with the political mainstream, was exactly where I positioned myself. Certainly, I and my companions always sided with the poorest and most rebellious, those on the fringes, most in danger of falling through any of the protective welfare nets capitalism might provide, but above all, we tried to live a politics of personal freedom and total disdain for any and all ruling elites. I am transported back to those days in the words and actions of the Occupy movement. As David Graeber, the American anthropologist now working in London points out, the consensus-based, direct democracy favoured by the Occupy movement adheres to anarchist principles, though it may not name them as such. It is not seeking to change the world through gaining state power or working through existing political or juridical institutions, but rather embracing forms of prefigurative politics, setting up its own alternative kitchens, libraries, clinics and networking centres, alongside other forms of mutual aid and self-organisation. From my visits to OLX these were often impressively efficient. This movement, with its self-organization and consensus, is thus busy doing what traditional anarchists have always tried to do, to begin building 'a new society in the shell of the old'.[21]

It was in that anarchist milieu of 'permanent protest', half a century ago, that I first encountered my long-term friend and former comrade, the young Mick Taussig. He was studying medicine at Sydney University, where I was studying psychology, and we both entered adulthood in the 1960s within the then still active, but soon ailing, sparks of Sydney libertarianism. It was a tiny movement that met regularly as the Libertarian Society, with ties to the broader social gathering (meeting in pubs or on the race-course) known as the Sydney Push. As I elaborated in *Making Trouble*, determined to remain on the fringes, never at the centre of institutional politics, we lived our lives visibly at odds with what we could then easily expose as the hypocrisies, corruption and crippling authoritarianism inside all the institutions of state government, law enforcement, trade unions, church, or any other pillar of bourgeois life.

At different times, we would each face arrest or fines for our public stance of principled abstentionism: 'Don't Vote! Whoever you vote for a Politician gets in', we plastered on public hoardings, our message illustrated with three little pigs, poker-faced, bowler-hatted, arms crossed.[22] This was because voting is compulsory in Australia (at least, for those who were allowed to vote, which indigenous Australians in Queensland and Western Australia, for instance, were forbidden to do at the time). The small Libertarian Society sometimes united with the slightly broader Sydney left, briefly joining forces with the Communist Party, the tiny Trotskyist groups, or somewhat larger left Labour supporters and a few militant trade unionists in public protests. At first this involved supporting marches against Apartheid in South Africa or, later, taking to the streets to oppose the war in Vietnam. Later still, libertarians worked with militants in the Builders Workers Union of New South Wales, in support of occupations in old buildings in Kings Cross, Sydney, to prevent their demolition by new property developers determined to replace the beauty of old Sydney with their concrete tower blocks. However, with anarchists as our mentors, the point of our politics was not to capture the state or even to proselytise, but to remain beacons of freedom and alternative ways of living. We believed in 'free love', at a time when any signs of women's sexuality outside marriage was still completely unacceptable, and a 'fallen women' – pregnant outside wedlock – would find it almost impossible to keep the child. We admired the ideas of the American 'Wobblies', founded by radical trade unionists in Chicago in June 1905 (which once had a branch on the docks in Sydney), fighting to end the rule of capitalism and wage labour via direct action and radical workplace democracy.[23]

Thus, strangely, decades before its reappearance recently, Sydney Libertarianism (in line with much of the disenchanted politics of the post-war 'Beat' generation, strongest in the USA), prefigured much of the political disdain and pessimism of today, rejecting any form of party politics. Proud of our lack of illusions and principled pessimism, we thrived then upon just that kind of sceptical pluralism that would be reborn decades later.[24] It is this old permanently distrustful, pessimistic anarchism that I briefly embraced in my bohemian 'sixties that I see back in fashion, both in many involved in Occupy movements and in some fashionable academic circles relating to them. It is promoted, for instance, by the New York based, British philosopher, Simon Critchley, in his book *Infinitely Demanding: Ethics of Commitment, Politics of Resistance.* His ethics of commitment celebrates 'the spectacular tactical politics of contemporary anarchism', one he sees as forging 'a new language of civil disobedience'.[25] This form of ethical commitment is presented as 'an anarchic meta-politics', significant in its 'continual questioning from below of any attempt to impose order from above ... Politics [here] is the manifestation of dissensus, the cultivation of an anarchic multiplicity that calls into question the authority and legitimacy of the state'.[26]

The words are new, but the sentiment is familiar. The modern state, with its inevitable ties to corporate capital, cannot be overthrown. Given the triumph and power of global capitalism, the only role for the dissenter is to withdraw from direct engagement with the state, to create instead new spaces of resistance that remain in its cracks, or interstices, farthest from its control. Voices float back to me from almost fifty years ago (and no doubt from far longer, had I been around when the utopian socialist Robert Owen was founding his co-operative movement).[27] Thus today, at least in much of the direct action in the Anglo-American world, we are back in an anarchist moment, as leaderless protesters take to the streets, many of them understandably convinced that no electable government can be trusted to do more than continue injecting huge amounts of social wealth into rescuing the financial sector, with little concern for the dire economic and social costs resulting from their finance-dominated austerity packages. Meanwhile, anarchy, of a far more destructive kind, also rules in the corporate world, with its equally passionate disdain for government and the state. Even after the global economic meltdown, the pursuit of profit within the corporations still rules supreme, with no fundamental state control over banking and financial markets.[28]

Critchley is surely right to suggest that recent articulations of an anarchist ethics, celebrating open, pluralistic forms of dissent, have been inspiring much of the anti-war and anti-corporate globalization movements today. This draws him into skirmishes today, as it did us yesterday, with those working in social democratic or other political parties seeking government positions, as well as with those, such as his favourite sparring partner, the celebrity philosopher Slavoz Žižek, who believe in the need for a Revolutionary Party fighting for state power. Žižek is contemptuous of those, including Critchley, who accuse him of being stuck within the 'old paradigm', and who imagine that the task today 'is to resist state power by withdrawing from its terrain and creating new spaces outside its control'. In stark contrast, Žižek points with approval to Hugo Chávez, who did the opposite, 'ruthlessly using the Venezuelan state apparatuses to promote his goals', thereby managing to stand up to US-led corporate capital, and empower, even arm, those prepared to take to the streets to defend him, gathered from the grass roots slum committees.[29] This is exactly the sort of confrontation that *Beyond the Fragments* hoped, unsuccessfully at the time, to find a way to surmount. Today, I no longer think there is any way of surmounting the tension between those differing factions of the left, although I still believe, when and as the context allows, we must keep trying to find ways of promoting better dialogue between the two, when and where we see any opportunities for doing so.

Well before any such context appeared, back in Sydney in the early to mid-Sixties, the Libertarians were shrinking fast. The romantic few, mainly men who lived off gambling and casual jobs, refusing all compromise with the mainstream or any centrally organized parties, were being overtaken by the less political, young and hedonistic counter-culture, whose views on world affairs were far more diffuse. Today, some of those surviving Libertarians remain my friends, a few still active as community figures in inner Sydney. Nevertheless, seeking neither to recruit nor convert they have left only a faint trace on history. The Push would be remembered as something like a small exotic tribe, notorious for its promiscuity, gambling and parties. One leading Libertarian, the late George Molnar, would later point out that we were merely creatures of our time. We were so totally opposed to the rigid post-war conservatism, the apparently seamless consensus of 1950s Australia (which continued into the 1960s), and also such a pathetic minority, that we made a virtue of the fact that there seemed no prospect of us ever influencing the course of events: 'We wove a fantasy ... to justify an impotent little group indulging their particular eccentricities ... [talking] about permanent protest, about the impossibility of change.'[30] Ironically, what we didn't realize was that change *was* in the air. We had talked of 'free love', and opposed all forms of censorship, knowing that Australia still enforced one of the most rigid censorship regimes in the Western world. But this was just moments before sexual liberation became the talk of the town, and the draconian censorship that had tried to protect us from any hint or whisper of explicit sexuality was about to be dismantled. As it turned out, the commoditisation of sex was more in keeping with new forms of market consumerism. This should have been my first lesson that change indeed is possible, but when it arrives it is never quite in the form you hoped, and so struggles must begin again. However, it would take some time for me to fully understand this.

The seventies in retrospect

I left Sydney for London in 1970, a single mother, aware that the freewheeling libertarianism I had known (so disdainful of secure jobs and settled life) had nothing helpful to say about motherhood and its dilemmas. In London in the 1970s, the political milieu was rather different, and certainly I needed new ideas to make sense of my position in it. Secretly, those of us most rebellious against institutional certainties, embedded hierarchies and established leaders (which surely must originate in all the unpredictable contingencies of personal history), are often eagerly looking for mentors. It's not easy thinking coherently against the grain, and politically impossible to act collectively for any length of time without guidance, solidarity and rootedness in some sort of comprehensible community, even when the traditions of that community are being reworked or invented day by day.

Fortunately, having just read and admired her writing, it wasn't long before I encountered Sheila Rowbotham who, along with many others, was quickly a key influence on my thoughts. Her writing played a crucial role in the leap in consciousness that helped to consolidate feminist communities in the early years of the women's movement in Britain. Yet Sheila was superficially one of the most unlikely of mentors. Tussling always with her own doubts and dilemmas, her dislike of being centre stage, of telling others what to do, she was always a reluctant organizer. Only in hindsight is it clear that it was precisely her attentiveness to the internal rifts and exclusions in some of the effervescent radicalism that flourished in late 1960s, in particular her dislike of the dogmatic certainties of the small Leninist 'parties' that sprung up in its wake, which inspired her imaginative attention to alternative aspirations. She embraced and circulated the thoughts of radical women that had been marginalized on the left, from Olive Schreiner, Alexandra Kollantai and Rosa Luxemburg, through Simone de Beauvoir to the militant working-class women she interviewed at the close of the 1960s. These voices she combined as best she could with her own reworking of the thoughts of Marx, Fanon, Reich, Sartre and Gramsci, to formulate some basic understandings for a transformative women's liberation movement:

> All revolutionary movements create their own ways of seeing. But this is the result of great labour. People who are without names, who do not know themselves, who have no culture, experience a kind of paralysis of consciousness. The firsts step is to connect and learn to trust one another.[31]

It seemed right to me. Coming from my background in the Libertarian Society, I easily found a political home in Islington, north London, in the 'non-aligned', intensely heterogeneous grass-roots community activism of the early 1970s, which had sprung up in most large cities in the wake of the political militancy of the late 1960s. At that time, this community politics was definitively part of the left, explicitly aligned with socialism and quickly a crucible for the diverse movement politics, especially women's liberation. It consisted of loose alliances between a myriad of local community resource centres, campaigning groups and radical trade unionists, all intermingled with the burgeoning women's, gay, Black and ethnic minority movements. However, political life now made sense, above all, because of the essential ingredient of women's liberation, a movement uniting me, this time, not just with a small tribe of determinedly rebellious outcasts, who were happy to remain that way (though we still had plenty of them in our midst in the Seventies), but also with women and men equally determined to see themselves as part of a mass movement, one capable of effecting change in state policies. In absolute numbers at that time, the non-aligned radical activists would almost certainly have outnumbered those in the biggest far left groups, although none of us were busy counting our 'recruits'. In this milieu, there was still for the most part a shared emphasis on autonomy, spontaneity, living in alternative ways in the present, now called 'prefigurative' politics, and above all exemplifying ways of working that were ideally open and devoid of formal leadership structures. However, at least locally, we were always looking for alliances to foster any campaign of the moment. Sites of activity were often unpredictable, although back then, seemingly ubiquitous, as my own essay for *Beyond the Fragments* outlined.

Overall, for those around me, the Seventies was a time of constant excitement, rising hope and confidence. I spent much of my time engaged in or reporting on a diversity of struggles and campaigns, or (mostly) enjoying the festivals and alternative cultural life of the left. Feminism, in particular, had unleashed enormous creativity in women, poured into the formation of bands, such as Jam Today, theatre groups, including Cunning Stunts, the Monstrous Regiment, Gay Sweatshop, art-works of every stripe, including film, poetry, magazines, dance, and more. Yet, what is so surprising for me to register today is that most retrospective discussion of the Seventies presents it as a bleak and depressing decade, a time of growing tedium after the exhilaration of the Sixties. A description of decline, producing fears of crisis and decay, especially in the late Seventies is certainly the mood that the astute commentator Andy Beckett reports in his assessment, *When the Lights Went Out* (2009), which illustrates once more how differently we perceive and recall the very same eras in recent history.[32]

It was hardly any sense of decline, but rather of a wave of huge optimism that was the most notable feature of the landscape I inhabited then, especially that energizing feminists throughout most of the 1970s. Indeed, feminism managed to reach out to embrace hundreds of thousands of other women, near and far. Moreover, many feminist struggles, especially those around recognition of the extent of violence against women, discrimination in the workplace, women's right to reproductive control, the need for nurseries, met with considerable success. Much of that success has lasted, despite having to fight over and over again to ensure its preservation – never more so than at this present moment of austerity cuts, known to be hitting women hardest, and threats to abortion clinics imported from the American right. Feminists throughout the decade also remained amongst the most committed political activists, often to our own surprise becoming increasingly competent and confident players in the public domain that would take us into the new and soon very different political landscape of the 1980s. From the margins, where some remained, to the centre, where more professional women ended up, feminist thought had begun shifting ways of seeing, influencing state policies, union practices and opening doors hitherto closed to women, while transforming cultural spaces generally.

Again as I described in *Making Trouble*, by the close of the 1970s, ideas had begun flowing across from the new social movements to more traditional forms of community politics, including local government, not infrequently resulting in meetings to promote more participatory democratic practices. Although often mutually mistrustful, this interaction left its mark on mainstream politics, broadening political agendas to include problems hitherto barely discernible, let alone thought addressable. It would also pave the way for many more militants, myself included, to make their way into the Labour Party, in what would be for us its glory days of radicalism in the early 1980s (for others, its wilder years of unelectability). In fact, we did get a few militant MPs elected, including Jeremy Corbyn in my borough of North Islington, who to this day remains one of the most left-wing and rebellious of Labour figures. He fiercely opposed the Iraq war and is still busily campaigning: whether nationally against the austerity and privatization practices of the Tory coalition; or internationally, against military aggression, or Israel's continued occupation of the West Bank and blockade of Gaza. It was the success rather than the failure of struggles at municipal levels across Britain, that led to Thatcher's targeted offensive against possible funding for more participatory democratic structures at local levels. New Labour did little to reverse this when in government.

Retrospectively, however, it has been clear for some time that part of the success of feminism related to broader economic change. With government and market priorities allowing the decline of Britain's industrial base in favour of the expansion of the financial and service sector, women's position in society was shifting. However, feminists were not mere pawns of market forces, mostly remaining in critical dialogue with the broader left movement fighting for a more egalitarian and peaceful world. Even in the USA, where more conventionally liberal movements were far stronger than in Britain, one prominent wing of the movement was militantly leftist and radical. Meanwhile, given its influence and success, neither the mainstream nor the left could afford to ignore feminism.

Testifying to its deep and lasting impact globally, it was from 1977 that the UN General Assembly formally marked International Women's Day to support women's rights around the world, as Jocelyn Olcott highlights in an article on women's representation internationally.[33] Women's victories in the 1970s were also aided by the broader political moment, with Labour in government and in charge of many local councils. This facilitated our belief that self-organization and collective action could indeed begin to transform everything, from personal lives to workplace conditions, social policy and the law, while impacting on culture generally. It is of course this confidence that enabled us – three women – to think we might make an impact on the left's ways of organizing, promoting both alliance and autonomy, in forums that could encourage the creativity of all who became involved.

Yet, for all its successes, the close of the 1970s was already a confusing time for many feminists in Britain and elsewhere. Indeed, it was the very success of the movement that intensified the divisions within. It was this same success that led to us writing *Beyond the Fragments* during the run-up to the general election that would usher in the momentous upheavals of Margaret Thatcher's decade in power. We hoped that feminist ways of working, at their best, might help broaden and regenerate the left. This broad left would be stronger, we argued, if it were genuinely supportive of the multiplicity of grass-roots struggles, instead of either disdaining or attempting to direct them. Conversely, those grass-roots struggles would be stronger if they obtained genuine support from a broader left. For much the same reason, I had joined the small left group Big Flame, the previous year, since it was a national organization that stressed the need for some sort of central organization, while also supporting the autonomy of oppressed groups and espousing a politics that emphasized the interconnections between community and workplace struggles, seeing both as essentially anti-capitalist in their rejection of existing conditions in and outside the workplace. So, despite the sense of doom that many shared, 1979 was an exciting yet turbulent year for me and my political allies.

The interest triggered by the initial slim pamphlet *Beyond the Fragments* generated a noisy conference of almost three thousand people in Leeds the following year. As Sheila and Hilary say, over the years *Beyond the Fragments* has continued to influence feminist groups and trade union activists in India, Turkey and even the Brazilian Workers Party, to name a few. Indeed, even today, I found on the web a recent article by Pam Currie, a leading member of the Scottish Socialist Party, citing *Beyond the Fragments* for its emphasis on tackling sexism in political parties.[34] Looking back, I think we were right to suggest that many feminist priorities, such as stressing ties between the frustrations of personal life and the need for political change, or focusing on working locally, while supporting women's struggles globally, did play a significant role in the political achievements of the 1970s. As it turned out, however, with certain very significant exceptions, especially in the early 1980s, we were over-optimistic in imagining that people with similar but far from identical political goals and ways of organizing could work together and agree on common action.[35] The recurrent antagonism disrupting the final session of the conference underscored this. Some feminist groups and other individuals voiced their forceful opposition to our calls for greater ties with the organized left; members of left groups rejected the importance we gave to direct action and autonomous ways of working over democratic centralism and 'party' building.

Defeats and retrievals

What happened next? Or as many from left and right both like to ask, 'who was to blame' for the defeat of progressive forces by the close of the 1980s? No story is linear. With the right in power, not just in Britain, but in a Britain insistently welcoming the increasingly belligerent hegemony of the right in the USA, it was never going to be easy for the left to manage to shift the overall political direction and increasingly harder to agree on the best strategies for doing so.

Nevertheless, significant struggles were still being waged in the early 1980s, evident in the widespread support across the left for the twelve months miner's strike against threatened pit closures, begun in March 1984. It was a battle determinedly instigated by Margaret Thatcher, with quite extraordinary levels of police mobilization and the orchestration of all possible media demonization of the miner's leader, Arthur Scargill. The final defeat of the strike in March 1985 significantly weakened the British trade union movement, in which a once united NUM (National Union of Mineworkers) had operated as one of its strongest members.[36] Meanwhile, as Sheila and Hilary both illustrate, the years of Ken Livingstone's GLC (Greater London Council) provided another broad-based, creative surge of resistance to Thatcher, often drawing directly on the ideas of *Beyond the Fragments.* Nevertheless, there is more to say than we expressed in that text about the difficulties of using feminist insights in the recurring challenge of uniting the radical left by building coalitions that genuinely make space for spontaneity and autonomy.

First of all, it now seems clear that the very real strengths of the outlook, ways of working and achievements of the women's movement in the 1970s were tied in with inevitable limitations. The shared energy and close friendships built up in the small groups most feminists preferred, with their principled rejection of any structures of leadership, worked well for bringing more people into politics. The informality fostered individual creativity and encouraged those shifts in identity and sense of agency that bring confidence to hitherto marginalized groups, enabling alliances (or confrontations) with others in the political arena. Yet, this same strong, ideally relaxed sense of collectivity and bonding could also leave some women feeling distanced from the effects of its more hidden premises, leaving them suspicious of the imagined joys of 'sisterhood'. Relatedly, the lack of prescribed structures of leadership in no way precludes certain controlling individuals, or simply the most charismatic, sharp, or ebullient of people, from becoming dominant figures, whether they wish to or not. Early on, this is exactly what Jo Freeman argued in her widely read, much anthologized essay, coining the now familiar phrase 'the tyranny of structurelessness' to describe her experience of the unwitting bullying and hidden mechanisms of control in the women's movement in the USA.[37]

The dedication to ideals of equality, where everyone was encouraged to develop all possible skills, could obviously prove inefficient, while also evoking resentment against those seen as too authoritative, ambitious or successful. Again from the USA, the feminist psychoanalyst Muriel Dimen has suggested that the disavowal of envy and competitiveness between women made its inevitable concealed expression all the more embittered, seen in some forms of 'feminist rectitude'.[38] The resulting prescriptiveness created problems within movements apparently relying upon consensus, which usually entailed dismissing any views seen as inconsistent with the dominant one as inherently 'anti-feminist'. This is what triggered the fiercest conflicts over feminist sexual politics, pornography and images of power in erotic fantasy, especially as strands of radical feminism insisted that men's sexual violence against women (seen as instilled by pornography), should become the overriding concern of feminists everywhere from the close of the Seventies.[39] In the UK, the conflict came to a head in the very last annual women's liberation conference in Birmingham in 1978. It descended into chaos when women attempted to debate the motion of a small but determined group of revolutionary feminists aiming to name men's sexual violence against women as *the* fundamental cause of women's oppression. The acrimony this generated brought to an end any further attempts to hold national conferences of the whole of the women's movement.[40] From the USA, Joan Nestle, among others, would describe similar debates over sexuality tearing feminism apart in her feminist milieu from the close of the 1970s.[41]

Bringing all the divisions between women around sexuality,

race, class, heterosexism, into the open thus destroyed any notion of women's cosy unity. Race would soon prove an even more explosive issue than class and sexual orientation, whether in the USA or UK, for although both in theory and in practice poverty and racism were constant preoccupations of women's liberation, feminist groups remained overwhelmingly white and predominantly middle class. Thus, by the close of the Seventies division was more apparent than unity in many feminist gatherings, as newly empowered groups of women expressed their sense of marginalization within the movement itself. In Britain, the first Black women's conference was held in 1979, and here, as in the USA, the most painful clashes over race would occur in the second decade of resurgent feminism, with Black women challenging the priorities of white feminist analysis over the previous decade for privileging sexism over racism, and ignoring the particularities of ethnic difference. Thus, Valerie Amos and Pratibha Parmar argued in the early 1980s that 'the gains made by white women have been and still are at the expense of Black women'.[42]

Nevertheless, whatever our distinct identities, what few of us could predict then was the extent of the subsequent selective incorporation or mainstreaming of key feminist demands by the state and corporate capital. Attending to some of women's struggles for equality while ignoring others, would launch one tier of professional women, including Amos herself, into positions of considerable power, authority and financial reward. (Valerie, now Baroness Amos, was the first Black woman to hold cabinet office. She is currently UN Under-Secretary-General for Humanitarian Affairs and Emergency Relief Coordinator and a Labour Party life peer in the House of Lords). However, other women, especially ethnic minorities and poorer women everywhere, are still grappling with most of the old problems that women have always faced – juggling paid and unpaid labour in a landscape where violence against women, sexist and racist behaviour, though now officially condemned, remain deeply entrenched. Thus one partial success of feminism, allowing more women into ruling elites, could be aligned with the intensification of divisions between women in ways that were barely conceivable in the egalitarian politics we once fought for.

However, in my view it was not primarily conflictual internal dynamics that destroyed the early energies of grass-root movements, feminist or otherwise. Those who felt sidelined in the heyday of movement politics regrouped into new clusters in which they could work. It was rather the ruthless and unyielding forces soon confronting activists of any progressive stripe in Thatcher's Britain. The internal divisions within feminism were real enough at the close of the 1970s, accompanying the inevitability of hidden, and not so hidden, hierarchies and self-policing. But even as new groups kept appearing within feminist spaces, what was disappearing was any forward motion towards the more egalitarian or caring world we all apparently desired. The world was moving in the opposite direction.

As economic survival became more precarious for many, the social networks sustaining progressive thought and practice withered. The public mood shifted, gradually becoming more aligned with Thatcher's (and then her successor's) increasingly hegemonic anti-welfare, market-driven culture. The levels of political activity that grass roots struggle demands is harder to sustain in unfavourable conditions, and certainly the confidence needed for initiatives at left unity, such as that promoted by *Beyond the Fragments*, was difficult to achieve. There would nevertheless be many other attempts in the decades that followed to try again, never free from the difficulties faced by that first conference in Leeds. Indeed, it is the same strategy that emerged at a global level at the close of the 1990s with the sudden upsurge of interest in the World Social Forums. Those working hard to create unity and pursue change through flexible consensus and networking, however, are still beset on all sides by voices from distinct far left groupings, re-emerging in their tiny splinters to dominate them. It leaves the rest of us ensnared, as ever, between fuzzy fragments and invasive vanguards.

In between, the politics of direct action continued in new

sites, the most significant was at the women's peace camp at Greenham Common. This began in 1981 after a group, *Women for Life on Earth*, marched from Wales to the military airfield in Berkshire in protest at the decision of the British government to allow American cruise missiles to be based there. Lasting more than a decade, the camp attracted huge media attention, especially in its early years when tens of thousands of women took part in various days of action to blockade the base, holding hands around its fourteen-mile perimeter fence. During that time hundreds of women set up camp at different gates around the common, later speaking of their experience of the unique ties of affection and solidarity it created between the most heterogeneous of women.[43] The predominant, though far from exclusive, outlook of the women's peace movement saw women as more naturally peacemakers, men as the initiators of violence, whether at home or in military encounters. However, the fact that it was a female prime minister, and an exceptionally belligerent one, triumphantly waging war on the Falklands in 1982, provided an anomaly that was downplayed in this perspective.

Many others, including the significant minority in Big Flame that I supported, assessing our own weakness as an oppositional force capable of driving out the Thatcher government, joined the Labour Party in the early 1980s. This was a time when it seemed important to us tactically to consolidate a radical left within the Labour Party, reinforcing the mainstream opposition to Thatcher and her, almost literal, worship of the market, accompanying her soon successful attempts to defeat and dismantle all the forums of resistance in which we had hitherto found spaces to work or build progressive alliances. The hegemony of the right seemed unstoppable, as Thatcher had systematically weakened the unions, local government, and any other regional bodies of resistance, most strikingly in her annihilation of the GLC in 1986. For a few years, my own branch in north London included an eclectic bunch of many of my old collaborators, who pursued much the same politics inside the Labour Party as we had outside it, busily putting forward motions for conferences that were usually defeated, but nevertheless often discussed. I don't regret those years in the Party, which I saw as equivalent to being a member of my trade union, though I drifted out by the close of the 1980s, along with many others who had joined, when our membership no longer seemed politically significant in making further changes in the Labour Party, which itself proved unable to defeat Thatcher.

The 1990s was thus largely a decade of gloom and mourning across a fragmented left and dwindling labour movement. There was, however, a sparkling resurgence of gay and lesbian activism in that decade, with the formation of Outrage in the UK in 1990, campaigning primarily on behalf of gay men and others who were, for a while, demonized in the press, and often neglected by the social services, as the first group facing the catastrophe of the spread of the HIV-AIDS virus within their ranks. Also around this time, another broad-based, multi-ethnic, but predominantly Black and Asian group, *Women Against Fundamentalism*, was formed to fight the resurgence of fundamentalism in their communities, after the fatwa against Salman Rushdie for insulting the prophet, Muhammad, in 1989, supported by the Iranian government and certain other Muslim groups around the world. Many former feminists also remained active in anti-war and justice movements, such as the Women in Black, formed in Israel in 1988 following the first Palestinian intifada, and soon spreading to become a world-wide network of women committed to peace with justice, while actively opposed to war, militarism and all other forms of violence. In a sense, however, it was *back to the fragments* for most activists who remained politically engaged from the late-1980s, including myself. Tragically, however, it would be following the election of New Labour in 1997, and Tony Blair's soon evident respect for the rhetoric and policies of the Tory government, accompanying his affinity with the disastrous George W. Bush and eager subservience to US military aggression abroad, that finally sealed the disenchantment of much of what remained of the left and, for a while at least, any hope of forming coalitions that could make an impact on government policies.

Cherishing autonomy; building alliance

So what has brought us to this new moment of significant resistance in the second decade of the 21st century? For any with eyes not glued shut, it is the obvious failure of the dream of the right. Through its own greed and mismanagement, the seemingly invincible grip of the various institutions of corporate capitalism on governments around the world instigated the biggest financial collapse since the 1930s, necessitating huge bailouts from those very governments who had in recent decades granted them so much freedom. Yet, following such spectacular refinancing of the banks, creating massive government debts and the implementation of severe cuts in welfare to lower them, there has been no fresh thinking at government level to counter the hegemony of free market ideology. The neoliberal faith in markets should have been completely discredited, but no attempt to reverse the abyss of social inequality they have produced has been implemented. Quite the reverse: financial institutions and heads of private companies continue to award themselves huge bonuses; the poorest and most needy are in danger of losing the scant social supports they could hitherto rely upon, with cuts directly targeting low income families, those on disability benefits, or receiving housing aid. The scandal of this situation is hard to hide when we read that in 2011, just as all these cuts had begun, the pay of directors at the FTSE 100 campanies has risen by 49 per cent (to an average of £2.7 million) in a single year, while the average employee's pay rose by a mere 2.7 per cent, and workers in the bottom tenth of the pay scale received virtually no rise at all or were thrown out of work.[44]

For decades we had been hearing that the distinctions between left and right are obsolete, whether coming from academics such as Ulrich Beck and Anthony Giddens, or from leading politicians, such as Tony Blair and Barack Obama. Of course, those two political leaders were swept into office on huge surges of hope and massive organizational work coming from, precisely, large segments of the left. It was a left so very determined to jettison what they correctly saw as the near seamless hegemony of the right, consolidated in Britain and the USA since that start of the 1980s. Never could this have been clearer than in the extraordinary mobilization supporting Obama in 2008, although there was briefly a similar mood of elation with the election of Tony Blair in 1997. The make-up and in particular the methods of the left may indeed have always been contested, however all its traditions and lineage point in one direction only, that of working for social change for greater equality, not just of opportunity but of actual outcome. The right, in contrast, has always accepted social hierarchy as inevitable, standing for strong national defence, traditional moral values and the protection of individual rights and property, especially via support for free markets and limited government regulation of the pursuit of profit. The left will doubtless always be divided, unsure how best to confront the monoliths of power it opposes and, for any number of reasons, will encompass competing interest groups within it. Nevertheless, whatever the inevitable divisions and blindness within the left itself, the notion that the two poles are not analytically separable is absurd. This is why people have taken to the streets, the squares, or in other ways begun to call once more for a new vision for the left.

Nowadays, when I turn back to that paradoxical moment, 1979, when we worked together on the pamphlet, *Beyond the Fragments*, I know I am returning to another world. It is strange to revisit those times, when we were able to take so much for granted about commitments to equality, direct democracy and the need to develop and share the skills and imagination of everyone. At the community press that first printed *Beyond the Fragments*, people had begun working for nothing. Certainly, we expected no financial compensation for the labour we put into the alternative paper we produced, not even personal kudos, for names were rarely attached to articles. The bottom line was the prefigurative politics that expressed our belief in mutual aid and the sharing of talent and resources. This was the sort of society we wanted to create. Of course we joked about it. 'After the revolution' we can spend all our time in meetings, working for nothing, printing, collating, distributing materials, receiving naught but the political satisfaction of serving the community. I think our old goals are still worth fighting for, fighting over, though I have one or two final thoughts on how to do this.

Foremost, now as then we need to cherish any progressive oppositional spirit that is critical of the values and assumptions of unregulated market capitalism, undemocratic regimes and entrenched oppression. Today, for instance, it is the jailing of Pussy Riot in Russia and the brutality of rape cultures around the world that have been responsible for some of the most passionate gestures of protest and solidarity. Moreover, it is as evident now as it was forty years ago that people are drawn into collective resistance in a multitude of different, unpredictable ways. It is rarely established political parties, mainstream or radical, confident in their certainties of the best way forward, which bring new groups into politics. It is rather any number of shared personal issues and collective identifications in specific cultural contexts. I see this wherever I look. It was sharply evident lately, for instance, with the two election victories of the maverick (recently again somewhat discredited) politician George Galloway, after he was expelled from the Labour Party in October 2003 for his fierce opposition to the Iraq war. He went on to found the left-wing, anti-racist Respect Party in times of heightened racism, directed especially against those seen as Muslims. Twice, Islamic communities rallied successfully to support him and overturn hitherto 'safe' Labour Party seats, first in Bethnal Green and Bow in 2005, then even more startlingly in Bradford West in 2012, with a 36 per cent swing from Labour, the third-largest in modern British political history.[45]

I also know personally the significance of individual identifications quite outside party politics: as a young woman drawn to libertarianism when faced with the stifling conservatism and sexual hypocrisy of life in Australia in the early 1960s; as a single mother seduced by women's liberation in the 1970s; much later, as a person of Jewish descent, influenced by what soon became a movement of Jewish people opposed to the policies of the Israeli state, with its ruthless occupation of and expansion into the Palestinian West Bank and brutal blockade of Gaza. It is personal issues that bring people into politics, and it is a multitude of contingencies that then determine when, where and how people might go further, perhaps forming coalitions and alliances in pursuit of their goals.

Context is critical. At present, for instance, it is clear that in Greece it was four years of radical street protests, in the circumstance of extreme economic melt-down, that created the sudden impressive strength of Syriza – an acronym for the broad-based Coalition of the Radical left, led by Alexis Tsipras (originally from the youth wing of the Greek Communist Party). Syriza did extraordinarily well in the Greek elections of June 2012, receiving almost 27 per cent of the vote, less than 3 per cent behind the winning New Democracy party. As Costas Douzinas pointed out just before the election: 'The squares and mass disobedience were crucial in preparing the vote for the radical left. The unemployed and unemployable, men and women, Greeks and migrants, young and old, coming from different political ideologies and historical trajectories rose and learnt the importance of disobedience and insubordination.' As he sees it, there were three steps needed for these protests to become a serious political force. First, there was direct action, in particular the significance of aesthetic politics (taking us back to my opening section), second, the development of direct democracy (taking us back to those movement priorities of the 1970s), and finally, and crucial for the formation and strength of Syriza, the building of a hegemonic left block capable of seeking state power: 'It found its parliamentary representation in the elections which rewarded those parties and groups and ideas which participated in the occupations from the start without attempting to dominate the multitude. The radical left won all the big cities where the occupations took place. ... Direct democracy acquired its parliamentary companion.'[46]

Hilary also elaborates on the impressive success of Syriza in her essay here. However, there is the danger that these new hegemonies or large-scale left alliances that many of us on the left have always hoped to see are only occurring in exceptional circumstances. Greece at present is in just such a situation, facing catastrophic bankruptcy or brutal penalties imposed by the very institutions that were happy to make loans and encourage the expansion of debt only yesterday, before requesting its pound of flesh today. Nevertheless, it is an exception that may well become something of a rule, certainly at present in Southern Europe, as other nation states find themselves in similar situations. There is another danger here as well. Terrifyingly, the far right fascist party, Golden Dawn, also did unexpectedly well in the last Greek elections, produced by the very same set of circumstances mobilizing their supporters via traditionally nationalistic, patriarchal, racist and homophobic values. They too have continued to grow, despite and because of daily evidence of their violence against immigrants, ethnic minorities, women, gays and leftists.

More alarmingly, as the moving reports from Maria Margaronis illustrate, this openly fascist group is working with support from legitimate authorities, including the police and their own elected MPs: 'Golden Dawn is opening branches in towns all over Greece and regularly coming third in national opinion polls. Its black-shirted vigilantes have been beating up immigrants for more than three years, unmolested by the police; lately they've taken to attacking Greeks they suspect of being gay or on the left. Their elected MPs participate proudly in the violence.[47] It was just such situations of dire economic crisis that mobilized support for Hitler and other fascist leaders in the 1930s. On the one hand, the threat of fascism produced the sudden rise and significance of communist parties and other left formations and peace groups around the world. On the other hand, this did not prevent the devastating success of Hitler, Franco or Mussolini. Once we add in what we now know of the effects of climate change, and imminent water and food deprivation in swathes of the world, it is hard to know whether fear of our possible futures will strengthen or weaken the seeds of hope the left requires to nurture belief in its goals.

Perhaps surprisingly, given the changes I have witnessed, my thoughts today are not so far removed from my position over thirty years ago. If we hope to see a new and more vibrant left again, we need to support and try to connect both the multiplicity of expressions of direct action as well as any emerging, genuinely democratic and inclusive coalitions of resistance against contemporary corporate capital, and the environmental pollution that comes in its wake. We need today, as yesterday, direct action, movement politics and any coalition of resistance to seek diverse ways of influencing national government. The old familiar anti-statism of some of the left is far too closely attuned to the dominant refrains of neoliberalism, promising to 'get government off our backs'. In the UK, with our still unchanged electoral system, this means once more helping to strengthen left Labour (whether from inside or outside of the party). Or perhaps, as some of my erstwhile feminist and other left allies are doing, joining and trying to strengthen the left forces within the Green Party, working for a safer environment as well as a more egalitarian and peaceful world. Different strategies are possible and the most effective hard to gauge. Intellectual pessimism is surely inevitable, knowing the brutal forces protecting every pot of gold. However, even if we fail to win, we can perhaps agree with John Berger when he says: 'One protests because not to protest would be too humiliating, too diminishing, too deadly. One protests … in order to *save the present moment*, whatever the future holds.'[48]

Contrary to market idiocy that can only encourage us to consume more (preferably with tags on), being human depends on our acceptance by and concern with other people, not primarily the individual consumption or pursuit of profit that neoliberalism has made its mantra. Being human is also about savouring the time and place in which people leave their mark on us. For this reason I want to conclude with some recent thoughts of Stuart Hall, which I notice I echo, expressed in a talk at the celebration of his eightieth birthday. He was speaking of the continuities that have sustained him through time, and the political aspirations that have guided his life, which, even in these bleak times, suggest that change is always possible:

> For someone who is committed to political and social change, I am astonished, looking back, to find how consistent I remain. I still believe that the poor should inherit the earth, that capitalism is a barbarous way of organizing social life, that despite all its political complexities social, sexual and racial justice is possible and worth fighting for. I think that while sometimes the situation looks extremely bleak – as it does at the moment – there are always what Raymond Williams calls 'emergent forces and ideas', which cannot be contained within the existing structure of settlements and compromises which constitute the dominant social order. Other wishes, desires, ideas and interests cannot be indefinitely contained. They will always break through in ways you cannot anticipate or predict.[49]

His words speak directly to and for me, explaining why some of the dreams of old, looked at again, critically, just might be put to use to help us imagine futures better than the present.

Ageing, it is hard to retain the confidence of earlier youthful dreams of radical transformation. Apart from all the obstacles we have encountered, we usually become more aware of, and prepared to admit, just how much we fail to understand about the complexities of power bearing down on any who challenge its manifest operations, not to mention its largely hidden ones. Entering the libertarian left in the 1960s and becoming a feminist in the 1970s, the better part of my life's ambition was trying to work for greater equality overall and increased democratic accountability, seeing feminism as a key player in the process. Today, I can see the significant changes that feminism helped to create, in making the world a less harsh, less confusing, more fulfilling place for many women, raising people's awareness of sexual oppression, domestic violence and the exclusion of women as significant players in cultural, political and economic life.

I also see what has worsened. At the bulky base of those old class, ethnic, and geographical hierarchies, both women and men have crashed down into a deepening chasm separating the rich from the poor. I can register as well the connection between what we have won, and what we have lost (as certain women and some ethnic minority members straddle the heights of power). This paradox only provides more reasons to think things anew, remaining in some sense true to those trampled hopes of yesterday, whatever the terrain. Returning more cautiously to where I began leaves me still welcoming the direct action of today, while also hoping as strongly as ever to see more consolidation of the diverse forms of resistance into some challenging left coalition – so long as that coalition, whatever its inevitable failings, tries to remain as open and democratic as possible.

Notes

1 Will Hutton, 'The worst post-war chancellor?' *The Guardian*, 25 July, 2012, p. 32; see also, Larry Elliott and Dan Atkinson, 'Little Britain: why the UK is no longer a superpower', 8 June 2012.
2 See Gerald Side and Gavin Smith, *Between History and Histories: The Making of Silences and Commemorations*, Toronto, Toronto University Press, 1997.
3 Emma Goldman, *Living my Life*, vol. 1 [1931], New York, Cosimo Classics, 2011, p.56.
4 Thomas Keane, 'Frieze Art Fair All's Well That Ends Well', *Artlist*, 27 OCT 2011, http://www.artlyst.com/articles/frieze-art-fair-alls-well-that-ends-well
5 Michael Taussig, 'I'm So Angry, I Made A Sign', Goldsmith College, text of talk, delivered at Goldsmith College, 16/01/2012, sent as personal correspondence by the author.
6 Costas Douzinas, 'What did the squares vote *for*', *Greek Left Review*, May 15, 2012, accessed May 26, 2012, http://greekleftreview.

wordpress.com/2012/05/15/what-did-the-squares-vote-for/

7 Feminist Peace Network, 'Empowering the Feminist Voice at Occupy – Confronting the Silencing of Mic Check and Other Misogynies', Nov 16, 2011, http://www.feministpeacenetwork.org/2011/11/16/empowering-the-feminist-voice-at-occupy-confronting-the-silencing-of-mic-check-and-other-misogynies-in-the-occupy-movement/

8 Rosalind Fraad Baxandall, 'The Populist Movement Reborn, At Last, In Occupy Wall Street', October 14, 2011, in *The Issue Magazine*, http://www.ontheissuesmagazine.com/cafe2/article/175

9 Polly Toynbee, 'Here in the City protest has occupied the mainstream', *The Guardian*, 18 October, 2011, p.33.

10 Laura Gibbon, 'Translating Egypt's revolution: Images from Tahrir, *Open Democracy*, 9 March 2012, http://www.opendemocracy.net/laura-gribbon/translating-egypts-revolution-images-from-tahrir, accessed 1 August, 2012.

11 Ahdaf Soueif, 'Egypt's revolution has carved its path to parliament', *The Guardian*, Comment is Free, January 2012, http://www.guardian.co.uk/world/2012/jan/24/egypts-revolution-parliament-ahdaf-soueif

12 David Harvey, *Rebel Cities: From the Right to the City to the Urban Revolution*, London, Verso, 2012.

13 Giles Fraser, 'Occupy LSX may be gone, but the movement won't be forgotten', 28 Feb 2012, http://www.guardian.co.uk/uk/2012/feb/28/occupy-london-gone-not-forgotten

14 Statement issued from the assembly on the steps of St Paul's Cathedral in October 2011, reported in two of the leading UK Newspapers, *The Guardian* and *The Telegraph*, see, for example, Murray Wardrop, '"Occupy" protests: activists deliver charter of grievances', London: *The Telegraph*. 17 October 2011, http://www.telegraph.co.uk/news/uknews/8831851/Occupy-protests-activists-deliver-charter-of-grievances.html). Retrieved 17 May, 2012.

15 Paul Mason, *Why It's Kicking Off Everywhere*, London and New York, Verso, p.3.

16 ibid. p. 3.

17 ibid. p. 152.

18 Joan Scott, 'Experience', in *Feminists Theorize the Political* eds. Judith Butler and Joan Scott, New York and London: Routledge, 1992.

19 See Sheila Rowbotham, *Dreams and* Dilemmas, London, Virago, 1983, p.59; Lynne Segal, *Why Feminism: Gender, Psychology,*

Politics, Cambridge, Polity, 1999, pp.14-22.

20 Tony Judt, 'What Have We Learned, If Anything?', *The New York Review of Books*, www.nybooks.com/search/?q=tony+judt.

21 David Graeber, 'Occupy Wall Street's anarchist roots', 30 Nov., 2011, *aljazeera*, http://www.aljazeera.com/indepth/opinion/2011/11/2011112872835904508.html.

22 Lynne Segal, 'My Sydney Sixties', in *Making Trouble: Life and Politics*, London, Serpents Tail, 2007.

23 Mark McGuire, 'The I.W.W. in Australia' in *Red and Black, an anarchist journal*, No 8 1978/79.

24 See, Gerd-Rainer Horn, G-D. 'Outcasts, Rebels and Provocateurs: Nonconformists Prepare the Terrain', in Horn, *The Spirit of '68: Rebellion in Western Europe and North America, 1956-1976.* Oxford: Oxford University Press, 2007.

25 Simon Critchley, *Infinitely Demanding: Ethics of Commitment, politics of Resistance*, London and New York, *Verso* 2007, p. 12; 13.

26 Ibid.

27 See Barbara Taylor, *Eve and the New Jerusalem: Socialism and Feminism in the 19th Century*, London, Virago, 1983.

28 Trevor Evans, 'The 2002-2007 US Economic Expansion and the Limits of Finance-led Capitalism', *Studies in Political Economy*, vol. 83, Spring 2009; Bethany McLean and Joseph Nocera, *All the Devils Are Here: The Hidden History of the Financial Crisis*, New York, Portfolio/Penguin, 2010;John Lancaster, *Whoops!: Why Everyone Owes Everyone and No One Can Pay*, Allen Lane, 2010.

29 Slavoj Žižek, 'Resistance Is Surrender', *London Review of Books*, vol.29 no.15, 15 November, 2007, p.7.

30 See, Susan Varga 'Twice the man: The Two George Molnars', *The Sydney Morning Herald*, August 9, 2003 (accessed on the web)

31 Sheila Rowbotham, *Woman's Consciousness, Man's World*, Harmondworth, Pelican Books, 1973, p.27.

32 Andy Beckett, *When the Lights Went* Out, London, Faber and Faber, 2009.

33 Jocelyn Olcott, 'Globalizing Sisterhood: International Women's Year and the Limits of Identity Politics', in Niall Ferguson, Charles S. Maier, Erez Manela and Daniel J. Sargent eds., *The Shock of the Global: The 1970s in Perspective* Cambridge, Mass.: The Belknap Press of Harvard University Press, 2010.

34 Pam Currie, 'Reaching Beyond the Fragments', *International Viewpoint Online magazine*, IV440, September (2011)://www.internationalviewpoint.org/spip.php?article820

35 For a critique of the libertarian politics of the 1970s informing *Beyond the Fragments* see, Elizabeth Wilson, 'Beyond the ghetto: thoughts on Beyond the Fragments: feminism and the Making of Socialism by Hilary Wainwright, Sheila Rowbotham and Lynne Segal, *Feminist Review,* 4 (1980), 28-44; Max Farrar, 'The Libertarian Movement of the 1970s: What can we learn?', *Edinburgh Review,* 82, Winter (1989), 58-74.

36 Seamus Milne, *The Enemy Within – Thatcher's Secret War Against the Miners.* London: Verso, 1994.

37 Jo Freeman, 'The Tyranny of Structurelessness', *The Second Wave,* 2, 1, 1972.

38 Muriel Dimen, 'In the Zone of Amivalence: A Journal of Competition' in Susan Weisser and Jennifer Fleishner, eds., *Feminist Nightmares: Women at Odds,* New York: New York University Press, 1994, p.362.

39 See Catharine MacKinnon, Feminism Unmodified: Discourses on Life and Law, Mass., Harvard University Press, 1987.

40 Jeska Rees, 'A look back at anger: the Women's Liberation Movement in 1978', *Women's History Review,* 2010, 19(3), pp. 337-356

41 Joan Nestle, 'A Fems Feminist History' in DuPlessis and Snitow, (eds.) *Feminist Memoir Project,* p.345.

42 Valerie Amos, Pratibha Parmar, 'Challenging Imperial Feminism, from *Feminist Review: Many Voices One Chant,* 17, Autumn, 1984, p.5.

43 Sasha Roseneil, *Common Women, Uncommon Practices: The Queer Feminisms of Greenham,* London, Continuum, 2000.

44 Ian Jack, 'What a carve up!, *The Guardian Review,* 26.05.12, p.9.

45 Gilligan, Andrew (30 March 2012). 'A runaway victory for George Galloway – and all praise to Allah', *The Telegraph,* 30 March, 2012, http://www.telegraph.co.uk/news/politics/9176195/A-runaway-victory-for-George-Galloway-and-all-praise-to-Allah.html Retrieved 1 August, 2012.

46 Douzinas, 'What did the squares vote *for*', cited above.

47 Maria Margaronis, 'Fear and loathing in Athens: the rise of Golden Dawn and the far right', *The Guardian,* 26 Oct 2012: http://www.guardian.co.uk/profile/maria-margaronis. Downloaded, 10.1.2013.

48 John Berger, *Bento's Sketchbook,* London, Verso, 2011, p.80; p.79, italic in original text.

49 Notes taken from the talk of Stuart Hall, on the celebration of his eightieth birthday, Rivington Place, London EC2, 1 April, 2012, Later checked by him.

BEYOND THE FRAGMENTS

1979 edition

FOREWORD (1979)

Since it first appeared as a pamphlet, published by the Tyneside Socialist Centre and the Islington Community Press, Beyond the Fragments has sparked a wide ranging discussion of issues that have been lurking sometimes on but generally beneath the surface on the left: the relationship of the women's movement to the male-dominated left; the ways in which we organize for socialism and what we mean by socialism; how we encompass and make sense of the breadth of experience and struggles that have been part of the anti-capitalist movement in the last ten years; the contemporary validity of Leninist politics, etc.

This resonance itself has shown how fragmented the various movements have been and how important the issues at stake are in the making of socialism, particularly at a time when so many of the small gains that have been made are now under attack from all quarters.

This new edition is, partly due to that wide-ranging discussion and interest, an almost quite different book. While Sheila Rowbotham has only made minor changes to her piece, both Hilary Wainwright and Lynne Segal have considerably rewritten and reworked their contributions. Hilary outlines some of the wider problems that face all sections of the left. Drawing on the experience of militants from all parts of Britain she points out how the demands and insights of the women's movement are vital to any present or future socialist movement. As well, she argues that the loosely organized, but strongly supportive structures of the women's movement will be important in creating the kind of mass socialist consciousness that is an essential part of any socialist movement. Lynne, on the other hand, has expanded her piece in a way that has enabled her to draw out in more detail some of the ideas and feelings that emerged from her experience as a feminist active in a local area over the last eight years or so.

Taken together, the three parts of this book are now much more than one long article, an introduction and an 'appendix'. They are now three distinct, but complementary parts, reflecting slightly different concerns and preoccupations. As Hilary wrote in her introduction to the original pamphlet:

> We have all travelled differing political journeys and it will be clear we do not come at the question of how we can think about organizing from the same place... We have worked together on this because we feel the need to air actual political experiences, reassessing our politics by sharing these, not because we think we have the 'answer'. We feel that any genuine, new form of socialist organisation will have to grow from such a collective process.

ACKNOWLEDGEMENTS (1979)

The contents of this book were written individually but became very much a collective project not in the sense of a shared complete agreement about all the ideas but in suggestions for clarification and development We have also all needed one another's reassurance amidst doubts, exhaustion and despair. We are indebted to Jean McCrindle for being continuously part of this process.

Thanks also to Sally Alexander, Paul Atkinson, Kenny Bell, Huw Beynon, Bea Campbell, Luise Eichenbaum, Ralph Edney, Julian Harber, Jane Hawksley, Marsha Rowe, Vic Seidler, Sue Sharpe, Barbara Taylor, Chris Whitbread, Stephen Yeo, Roy Bhaskar and Karen Margolis for comments, criticism, ideas and sustenance. For help with particular points thanks to Juliet Ash, Bob Cant, Chris Goodey, Jeff Weeks.

Sheila's section originated in a talk for the Socialist Unity Symposium in Autumn 1978, which was later repeated at the Newcastle Socialist Centre and, with Lynne's account of her experience locally, at the Islington Socialist Centre.

INTRODUCTION (1979)

Hilary Wainwright

After a decade of intense socialist agitation, more working-class people than ever in post-war years voted Tory at the last election. At the same time, fewer people than at any election since 1931 voted for the Labour Party. It seems then that as far as the mass influence of socialist politics is concerned, not only have we a long way to go, but in one respect at least we have not been moving forwards.

Of course, the way people vote does not sum up their consciousness. Many of those who did not vote Labour will undoubtedly have been active in militant strikes and demonstrations over the last few months. And a low vote for the Callaghan government was more indicative of the crisis facing the Labour Party than the failure of socialist agitation. But when the reactionary rhetoric of Tory 'freedom' can evoke such a groundswell of working-class support, socialists need to ask a few questions about our inability to translate the awareness of a vanguard of socialist activists into any lasting change in mass consciousness. The inability applies both to socialists organized through the Labour Party and, in a different way, to socialists organized in Leninist parties.

The flaw which they have in common is that they both are organized in ways more appropriate to seizing power – governmental power and state power respectively – than to the necessary preliminaries of raising and extending socialist consciousness and grass-roots organization among the majority of working people. In the former case the priorities of the electoral machine, the overriding imperative of retaining or gaining parliamentary/council power tends to suppress political debate and inhibit political involvement in industrial and social struggles. In the latter case, the pretensions and disciplines of democratic centralism tend to produce an arrogance and sectarianism which make the Leninist groups unable to contribute to and encourage the many sources of socialist initiative and activity. The Communist Party too has its own version of organizing for power before organizing to change consciousness, in its desire for trade union positions often at the cost of challenging the apathy and conservatism still prevalent on the shop floor.

We feel that the women's movement has, at the very least, raised the consciousness, and encouraged the self-organization of thousands of women. In doing so it has also begun to challenge relations of power. If the left is to achieve the change in consciousness and the growth in self-organization which is a condition for resolving the problem of power, then there is much that socialists can learn from the women's movement's values and ways of organizing. For we cannot just put the problems down to 'objective conditions' like socialists tended to during the boom years of the fifties and sixties. In many ways objective conditions have never made socialism seem so necessary and so achievable. Capitalism's self-justification as the natural means of meeting human needs and expanding human possibilities seems more obviously groundless than ever, with every structure of the economy out of joint with human needs (not just the 'declining' sections of industry as in the thirties). Health services are short of money while private corporations keep millions in 'deferred' – unpaid – tax; thousands are homeless with building workers on the dole; millions are spent on the technology of defence while cheap heating, nurseries, aids to the handicapped, preventive medicine, public transport systems, etc., still remain primitive; and so the list goes on, touching on everyone's day-to-day experience. In such conditions the possibility of producing for need rather than profit, of planning production by working people rather than by the civil service or the corporations should seem more relevant than ever. Moreover, the means – or at least the groundwork – for achieving such a society, the organizations created by working people themselves, have grown in numbers and, with occasional setbacks, in strength, as the crisis has deepened. It's not like the thirties when a socialist vision was there – whatever criticisms we may now make of it – but the strength was lacking. Not only have the traditional workers' organizations, so far, retained their grass-roots strength but also oppressed groups which were previously passive or angry in isolation, women, gays, blacks and youth, have become militant and organized.

Why Go Beyond The Fragments?

Our concern in writing this book is with the forms of organization necessary to develop socialist consciousness out of this grass-roots industrial and social strength. Perhaps this concern in itself needs some justification. 'Why go beyond the fragments?' radical feminists, syndicalists and others might ask. After all, they might say, socialist organizations have not been spectacularly successful in fighting against inequality, arbitrary power, exploitation, racial, sexual and other forms of oppression. A wider political organization, they might add, blunts the power of the autonomous movements. Their conclusion is that the best chance of success for each movement is through the direct exertion of their own power.

There might be some logic in this if all the inequalities and sources of exploitation and oppression which the women's movement, the trade union movement, the black movement, etc., are up against were separate, unconnected to each other. If workers were simply up against bosses, women up against the sexual division of labour and sexist culture, blacks against racial repression and discrimination, with no significant connection between these forms of oppression, no state power linking and overseeing the institutions concerned, then strong independent movements would be enough. But it is precisely the connections between these sources of oppression, both through the state and through the organization of production and culture, which makes such a piecemeal solution impossible.

For example, consider all the connections which lie behind the demands of the women's movement. To win these demands there would have to be a massive shift from corporate profits to socially useful facilities (nurseries, abortion, day-care facilities, and so on) and from defence expenditure to expenditure on health and education; there would have to be a radical reorganization of work and control over work, to provide men and women with full opportunities for childcare and leisure, without jeopardizing job prospects; there would have to be a democratization of health and education and of the media, among other things, if women's needs were to be met. The list of all the wider ramifications of women's liberation could be extended, but from this list alone it is clear that our demands challenge all the priorities of the present – and previous – governments. Moreover they challenge the vested interests of the armed forces, the big corporations and hierarchy of the civil service. Changes of this sort affect and concern all the other movements of oppressed people, workers, blacks, youth, and so on. Unless women's demands are integrated with the needs of these other groups then it is unlikely that women's demands will ever get the support necessary to take on the powerful vested interests they are up against. For example, without incessant argument for an alternative which meets the needs of all oppressed and exploited groups, trade unionists in the private sector will see our demands for more social expenditure as a threat to their jobs; council house tenants will see our demands as competition for scarce resources, and so on.

So one problem is that of drawing up a common programme of political and social change, meeting the needs of all oppressed groups, and arguing for it among each group. The other problem is that of gathering together all the different sources of strength, uniting the social power of the community with the industrial power of those in production, and pitching this popular power against the existing state. This requires a strategy, based on the ideas and experiences of each movement, and drawing from the lessons of past struggles and from international experiences. The solution to these problems needs more than just ad hoc contact between the different movements. Neither is the merging of the movements any solution; there are good reasons for each movement preserving its autonomy, controlling its own organization. For women, blacks, trade unionists, gays, youth, and national minorities have specific interests which may sometimes be antagonistic to each other both now and probably in a socialist society. The solution lies in bringing together all those involved in the different movements and campaigns who agree on a wider programme of socialist change, based on the demands of the different movements in the context of organizing for social ownership and popular political power.

New Ways of Organizing

In organizational terms this could imply some sort of federal structure which provides a framework for united actions following from the fundamental principles on which revolutionaries could agree, for collective discussion of our differing experiences and traditions, and autonomy to take initiatives where tactical disagreements keep us apart. But this book is not about organizational prescriptions, it is rather intended to begin a discussion of the limits of traditional principles of revolutionary and social democratic organizations, in the light of the advances and insights made by recent movements, starting with the women's liberation movement

The method by which Sheila Rowbotham theorizes the problems of socialist organization is very different from that which has dominated discussions within and between left groups; though it is not hostile to these discussions. Her argument draws on a variety of past experiences of creating socialist organizations – including but not restricted to the Leninist tradition. It draws critically from the classic theorists of socialist organizations. But her central contribution is to theorize and give political credence to many of the organizational principles and insights of what most political organizations would treat as a 'sectoral' movement, of significance only within that 'sector'.

Of course the struggles of the women's movement are focused on a specific oppression: the oppression of women as a sex. But the women's movement, like all other movements arising to resist a particular oppression, also has a wider significance for the way we organize as socialists. For every form of subordination suppresses vital understandings which can only be fully achieved and communicated through the liberation of the oppressed group itself. No 'vanguard' organization can truly anticipate these understandings. For example, no such organization had any real understanding of the subjectivity of oppression, of the connections between personal relations and public political organization, or of the emotional components of consciousness, until the women's movement had brought these issues to the surface and made them part of political thought and action.

If a revolutionary movement is to be truly able to encourage, develop and guide the self-activity and the organized power of the oppressed then it must be able to learn from and contribute to these understandings. It must be organized in a way which can bring them together into a vision of socialist transformation. To a very large extent socialist politics should derive, and at times has derived, its main content from these understandings. But one reason why socialism has become so sterile and dead to most working class people in the post-war years is because it has not, until recently, become open to the understandings arrived at through the movements of oppressed groups and classes. The debates of political parties have, until the late sixties, tended to be seen as 'above' the concerns of specific movements, except insofar as an item might be added to a programme. In relation to this, Sheila quotes Fernando Claudin, who, in his book on Eurocommunism, pointed to this tendency in the Communist Party and other left parties:

> to regard political action as a private reserve and to try and restrict other organizations – the trade unions, organs of

grassroots democracy, the women's movement, etc. – each to their own 'specific problems', preventing them from taking initiatives in relation to general questions.

In the past five years or so some process of learning and dialogue has gone on within the political organizations. But in general it has been limited to the specific 'sectoral' concerns of each movement. Fernando Claudin's description still applies. For example, revolutionary organizations will readily admit that they've learnt about sexism through the women's movement, racism through black organizations, etc. But when it comes to developing the principles of revolutionary politics, the principles or organizing which seek to overthrow capitalism as a whole, this has traditionally been the internal concern and monopoly of formally political organizations. Such a view had some justification at the time of mass socialist or communist parties as in Europe in the 1900s and the 1920s, when the vast majority of socialist activists in the various social and industrial movements, for example the shop stewards' movements of that time, were also members of mass political parties. In these conditions the developments within the movements would have a direct political expression, and an influence on the shape of the political organization. New political initiatives and sometimes new political organizations would arise from debates and sometimes splits would be stimulated by the movements, but occurring from within these parties.

By contrast, one reason why socialists now have to make a much more conscious effort to theorize the understandings of these movements is because we do not have such a close relation to a mass socialist party. On the contrary, we are now faced with creating a socialist organization not primarily through debates, struggles and splits within existing parties (although that will be an important part of the process especially in relation to the Labour Party), but through the coming together of socialists based in the various 'sectoral' movements, the majority of whom are not members of any political party. For the radicalization which took place in the late sixties occurred against the background of a virtual political vacuum and a real discontinuity in the influence of the traditional workers' parties, the Labour Party especially. The conditions of the boom were one factor: militant industrial organizations had grown accustomed to gaining partial victories without any active involvement in the Labour Party. And when the Labour Party returned to office it became so quickly integrated into the capitalist state, and the Labour left showed so little sign of activity that industrial militants, plus the new movements of students, women, and black organizations, were quickly thrown onto their own resources.

In this situation the women's movement, solidarity movements with international struggles, many shop stewards' combines or local action committees, the anti-fascist movement, theatre groups, alternative newspapers, militant tenants, squatters and community groups have themselves become a political focus. That is to say, the vast majority of people who became socialists – through many different routes – after the boom, tended to concentrate their energies on activities and organizations directly concerned with their own lives, experiences and skills. Many briefly passed through, worked with, or eclectically drew on the activities and ideas of the revolutionary groups (the IS and IMG especially). And these groups have at different times been very important catalysts and educators. But only a small minority of socialists have found either these groups, or for different reasons the Communist Party or Labour Party, to be an adequate political framework. The rest have applied and developed their socialism in more specific areas of struggle, building up ideas on broader ways of organizing from these limited and often localized experiences.

By pointing to the present strength of these fragmented working-class activities we do not want to imply that these are timelessly superior to a co-ordinated national organization. As Lynne describes later in this book, there are serious limits to, for example, isolated local organizations. She explores the question of organizing from her experience of the efforts of libertarian

Marxists and anarchists to form non-hierarchical networks in the early 1970s. She shows the similarities and interconnections between libertarianism and some aspects of the women's movement in this period. Both movements shared a basic openness to tackling dilemmas which faced people in their everyday life. She traces the development of these politics in the area of London in which she lives, through women's centres and the *Islington Gutter Press*, which has shown itself to be among the most resilient and popular of the local papers which sprang up in the late 1960s and early 1970s. Such accounts of local radical activity are vital. Unrecorded they disappear even from the recent political memory.

Nonetheless, after spending eight years within the local movement of Islington radicalism she has become very aware of the real vulnerability and limitations inherent both in women's community activity and indeed of an isolated localism which lacks political links to activity elsewhere. This slow but growing realization was behind her decision to join a small nationally-based group, Big Flame, last year.

At a more general level it is also obvious that the National Front could never have been so effectively challenged if it had not been for the national focus and leadership the Socialist Workers Party, as well as members of other organizations, in the Anti-Nazi League. Most industrial struggles, whether against government wage restraint or closures in a multi-plant company, require national – if not international – co-ordination. The women's movement derives strength and support from being international as well. A mass socialist newspaper – which perhaps *Socialist Worker* or *Women 's Voice* could become if they were more open to rank and file organizations and less party recruitment papers – and a paper for the left, like *Socialist Challenge*, clearly require national co-ordination. And looking into the longer term, a revolutionary movement will only succeed through the overthrow of the national state machinery and its international supports. What I would suggest though is that in creating the wide network of links which make up a political rather than single issue movement, the local impetus will at this stage be crucial. When a new movement is not emerging only as a split from an existing, cohesive political party, people will tend to build these wider links with people they know and trust; and they will do so in ways that are close to their own experience. This will tend to mean that the possibilities in the localities, of going beyond the fragments, of creating the foundations of a revolutionary movement, will for a time be far greater than on a national level.

We have had occasional glimpses of what such alliances could be: a means of exchanging the understandings arrived at by different movements – industrial militants, for example, contributing their sharp sense of the material sources of working-class power, that flows from a detailed knowledge of how production is organized, or feminists challenging the competitive ego-tripping and ego-trampling arrogance which still erodes the collective strength and democracy of many trade union and socialist organizations (it afflicts feminist organizations too sometimes but at least we're very conscious of the problem); a forum for political debate and discussion through which the truths and weaknesses of different traditions can be sifted and tested in relation to the contemporary problems; a focus for socialist culture and ideas, and a resource centre for organizing campaigns and struggles. It was partly from a desire to build on and improve on these beginnings that we decided to write this book.

The Insights of Feminism

In the three contributions which make up this book we discuss some of the difficulties which need to be overcome to create such a democratic, and united – albeit loosely – socialist organization out of those involved in all the fragmented movements, campaigns and political groups in which socialists are involved. We have written it because we feel the experiences of the women's liberation movement have much to contribute to overcome the problems which hold back the growth of such an organization.

The women's movement, arising as it does to resist an oppression which comes from inequalities of power and confidence in interpersonal relations, and from a hierarchical division of labour, has been intensely sensitive and self-conscious about inequality and hierarchy in the creating of its organizational forms. In this process the women's movement has made important insights which are directly relevant to how we organize as socialists. Moreover, again because of the form of oppression which it confronts, the women's movement has radically extended the scope of politics and, with this, has changed who is involved in politics and how. Much of the oppression of women takes place 'in private', in areas of life considered 'personal'. The causes of that oppression are social and economic, but these causes could only be revealed and confronted when women challenged the assumptions of their personal life, of who does the housework, of the way children are brought up, the quality of our friendships, even the way we make love and with whom. These were not normally the subject of politics. Yet these are the problems of everyday life, the problems about which women talk most to other women (and about which many men would talk more if they could). When the women's movement made these issues part of socialist politics, it began to break down the barriers which have kept so many people, especially women, out of politics. Before the women's movement, socialist politics like all other sorts of politics, seemed something separate from everyday life, something unconnected with looking after children, worrying about the meals and the housework, finding ways of enjoying yourself with your friends, and so on. It was something professional, for men and among men, for the shop steward or the party activist. The activities of the women's movement have begun to change that as far as women are concerned. But it's meant a different way of organizing, a way of organizing which does not restrict political activity to 'the professional'.

The insights of the women's movement then do not simply concern the issue of 'sexism' in a socialist organization. They could contribute in general ways to creating a more democratic, more truly popular and more effective socialist movement than was possible before.

Answering the Criticisms

Since we produced the first edition of this book the issues raised have been debated at many meetings and taken up in reviews. We have received a large number of letters, more requests to speak than we can possibly manage and been involved in lengthy discussions.

In response to the first edition of *Beyond the Fragments* a lot of people would say, 'It's all very nice your talk of the need for a socialist organization that can both allow for the open expression of conflict between different groups and develop the particular understandings which these differences bring to socialism, but you don't really say anything practical about getting there!' That's a true comment but there are good reasons. First, our limited experiences do not give us the grounds for confidence to arrive at such general practical conclusions. Secondly, we question the idea that you can really only step into the debate about political organization when you have a general solution, a clear way forward. There would never have been a women's movement at all if we had accepted this approach. Often the inadequacies of traditional ways of organizing initially become apparent through very specific experiences, it is important that these are expressed and reflected on, partial though they be. If change and innovation to cope with new conditions, new problems had to wait for a new masterplan (or mistressplan for that matter!) the old ways would become ossified and there would be little chance of change. So we have written from our common experiences in the women's movement and from the interaction of these experiences with our other particular involvements in revolutionary groups, in local socialist newspapers and socialist centres and in work with other working-class organizations. We have written in the hope that others would complete, develop or modify the picture from their different experiences; and that maybe out of that process would come a clearer way forward.

The discussions we have had since the first edition have not changed our view of these necessary limits of what we are doing. But they have made us see the need, first, to be more explicit about the general political assumptions behind our discussion of the insights of the women's movement; secondly, to draw out more practically the general political directions in which our conclusions tend. Thirdly, we have become aware of the need to move outside arguments which are only about the revolutionary left, the women's movement or local community politics and tackle the wider context of, labour politics. So in 'Moving Beyond the Fragments' I try to draw together some of the developments on the extra-parliamentary left and consider their relationship to the Labour Party and the contribution feminism has made and would make to them.

There has also been criticism that in *Beyond the Fragments* we did not discuss the nature of the state. We do not make it clear whether we think socialists should be aiming to control it, change it, overthrow it and what will be our alternative. A full discussion of this requires several volumes! All we can do is make clear our basic assumptions.

The Women's Movement and the State

The women's movement has come repeatedly into conflict with the state. The force of the police has been used against for instance the 'Miss World' demonstrators in the early seventies; against women picketing during strikes, Irish women, Astrid Prou, 'Reclaim the Night' marchers. But on the whole, the areas of struggle have been around male-dominated definitions of the law, e.g., in relation to lesbian mothers and rape, and around the everyday and apparently benign aspects of state power, some of which Lynne and Sheila describe – for example, conflicts over social security, child benefit, for nursery provisions, against the attitudes in medical institutions towards women's bodies and minds. In contesting the law women have been challenging important areas of power behind the 'common sense' of male-dominated capitalism. In demanding control over welfare, which because of women's position in the family is such an immediate concern, the women's movement has focused on an old problem for socialists. Socialists have tended to either emphasize the need to strike at the directly coercive force of the state or, obversely, to make demands as if the state were a neutral force. The women's movements has been part of a new recognition which the welfare state has made possible. First, that we need the gains made by the working class and the feminist movements of the past. Secondly, that the existence of these gains makes possible new forms of resistance in which we can fight for control over welfare. Thirdly, that no improvement is ever finally 'achieved'. For within a capitalist society, the original radical intention can be channelled or transposed into quite different purposes. For example, welfare networks can accumulate a considerable amount of information which is sometimes used against people. When the economic tide turns no legal or social gains are secure.

The practice of the women's movement points towards the need for an understanding of how we are faced not simply with a coercive state with a military machine which we must destroy, but also with the complex ramifications of the law and welfare, and intervention in industry and the economy, in which movements of opposition to capitalism have established a certain – albeit limited – presence. This continuing process of everyday contestation is a crucial factor in weighting the balance of forces within capitalist society. To say this is not to argue that the making of socialism will not come up against coercion, but that struggle in areas in which the state power appears to many people to be legitimate is equally important. The women's movement has contributed towards challenging how this legitimacy is defined – for example, in questioning the dominant notion of the family in social policy. It has also begun to search for forms of resistance which acknowledge that the social resources which modern capitalism has been forced to concede are needed by people, while insisting that these must be in the control of those who use them. This requires a strategy which does not simply oscillate between rhetorical repetition of the need to smash the bourgeois state and a policy of piecemeal demands for bits of social welfare, the proverbial crumbs from the rich man's table, easily given or taken away at his discretion. We need instead to see our everyday struggle for control as part of the creation of a new form of political power based on local, regional and national assemblies of working people controlling all areas of social life, social services, production and distribution, internal order, external defence, and foreign trade.

Such a political system could only be achieved against such sources of extra-parliamentary power as the big corporations, the financial institutions, the institutions of international banking and trade, the leadership of the army and NATO and sections of the civil service. It could not be achieved in Britain alone or through parliament alone. As the experience of Labour governments demonstrate, the extra-parliamentary institutions we have just mentioned have a power which far outweighs the power of a majority government. This is especially true of countries like Britain, so dependent on international trade and investment and therefore on the 'goodwill' of international financial, trading and state institutions.

For socialists to win a parliamentary majority will be important, but only on the basis of, and accountable to, a strong extra-parliamentary movement able to confront the existing state apparatus and the financial interests it protects. For it is this movement which, having destroyed the coercive powers of the present state, will provide the basis of the new democratic form of political power. The exact form of the political organizations that will be capable of giving this movement a lead, fighting for its interests within the existing political system and organizing its defence against repression and violence, cannot yet be seen. It cannot be determined until the working class and other oppressed groups have developed a level of consciousness, sense of purpose and degree of self-confidence to re-make society. The purpose of socialist organization now should be to develop that consciousness together with a vision of an alternative society.

For this we need a very flexible and yet co-ordinated form

of organization. It needs to be able to build on and make links between all the initiatives towards popular democracy and control which working people are already making, however limited and fragmented these initiatives may be. Such initiatives have a long history; no socialist organization can wipe the board clean and create only the initiatives that fit in with its own scheme. At this stage, for example, it might include strengthening initiatives which are taking place in political frameworks that are not in themselves revolutionary. For example, the socialists fighting within the Labour Party for the accountability of MPs to the extra-parliamentary labour movement have at one level a common cause with socialists who are seeking to strengthen the power, and develop the consciousness of industrial organizations, women's groups, black movements, and so on. The principle of parliamentary accountability is an important principle in strengthening the extra-parliamentary power of working people and their local organizations. It will be a necessary part of the organization which eventually emerges as the socialist alternative to social democracy.

So we do not see the ideas in *Beyond the Fragments* as a one-way communication about or within the women's movement. We hope they will be discussed among groups of socialists involved in a whole range of activities and we hope that other people will be encouraged to speak their minds and communicate their own understandings by our effort.

The three of us have travelled differing political journeys and it will be clear we do not come at the question of how we can think about organizing from the same place. Whereas Lynne has just joined a left group, Sheila had a brief connection to another, the Socialist Workers Party, and I had a longer involvement with the International Marxist Group. But we have all three been involved in the women's movement. Through this we have come to agree on the questions that need to be asked, though we still argue about the answers.

We have worked together on this because we feel the need to air actual political experiences, reassessing our politics by sharing these, not because we think we have the 'answer'. We feel that any genuine, new form of socialist organization will have to grow from such a collective process.

THE WOMEN'S MOVEMENT AND ORGANIZING FOR SOCIALISM (1979)

Sheila Rowbotham

PART ONE

I think it helps to say how you've entered a particular train of thought. Behind what I'm saying are four main political influences, the New Left of the late 1950s to early 1960s, International Socialism (now the Socialist Workers Party) from the mid-1960s to the mid-1970s, libertarian Marxism in the early 1970s, and the Women's Liberation Movement since its beginnings in the late 1960s. Like all influences, the impact of these has not been linear or even. They have jostled together inside my head, pushing and tugging at one another for space. The nature of my involvement with them has not been at all the same.

When I began thinking of myself as a 'socialist' in 1962 the great upheaval in the Communist Party which had occurred in 1956 was still a persistent reference point. An event of six years before was for me at nineteen a distant happening. But the assumptions of what politics were about were still being set by CND and the New Left. 1956 appeared to me as the beginning of modern times. It was a break, just as 1968 was to be a break to a later political generation.

The recoil from the Communist Party was part of my political inheritance but it was not part of my own political experience. This meant I rejected the possibility of a socialist renewal from within the CP intellectually, but I had no understanding of the inner life of communism before the impact of 1956. This was further complicated by meeting throughout the sixties Young Communist League members, older Communist trade unionists and intellectuals who were shaken by the consequences of Hungary and later by Czechoslovakia, and increasingly open to discussion with socialists outside the CP. They were less dogmatic than the Trotskyists because they had no longer illusions about being omniscient. I always winced at the self-satisfied tone with which members of Trotskyist groups called all Communist Party members 'Stalinists', for I knew it didn't fit. I felt Cold War anti-communism became mixed up in the stridency of anti-Stalinism. Somehow by over-shooting the mark Trotskyism blocked many aspects of the New Left resistance to Stalinism proper, which was not only a political system but a particular stance towards being a socialist.

There were other ambiguities which can be partly explained by being politically formed by the New Left of the late fifties without being actually part of it. The possibility of making an alternative left movement to the Labour Party and to Stalinism did not have any reality for me. The New Left as a practical movement of left clubs and centres like the Partisan coffee bar in Soho was waning by 1962. By the time I arrived on the left the Campaign for Nuclear Disarmament was the 'movement' and its atmosphere was radical rather than socialist. Committee of 100 and a new left students' journal were the first kinds of activity I encountered. Committee of 100 was far more exciting – this was the period in which Regional Seats of Government were being discovered and exposed. There was a feeling around that 'direct action' was the thing, not discussion of ideas. But CND itself was in the process of disintegration and when I left University in 1964 it seemed as if pressure on the left of the Labour Party was more realistic than the creation of an independent left movement.

Nonetheless the timing and shaping was rather important. For if I had become a socialist too late to be part of the first wave of the New Left, I was still deeply affected by an approach to politics which had not only broken with Stalinism but was quite alien to the assumptions of the then tiny Trotskyist sects. Indeed until I met Trotskyists in the Hackney Labour Party in 1964 they seemed simply odd with an inward, self-confirming intensity like evangelical religious groups. Even as I encountered Trotskyism and neo-Trotskyism (international Socialism) I was never quite of them. I could never be quite so sure somehow. They had all those certainties as if everything was known, the whole world and its history was sewn up and neatly categorized. How could anyone know so much? But what it was that I was or why I couldn't be sure was quite unclear. In face of the clear-cut polarities which various Trotskyist groups shuffled between one another like counters I had only puzzlement. 'Middle class', they said. Forced to peel through class prejudice by their challenge I could acknowledge that it was partly this.

But class was only part of it because some of them were middle class too. It was also the legacy of New Left politics. The emotion of my socialism was too rooted in an interconnecting quest between circumstance and consciousness – consciousness and circumstance. Trotskyism's emphasis on the 'analysis' of an unfolding objective crisis suggested the professional revolutionary going in, extracting the salient bits of reality and fashioning a programme accordingly. The New Left (the movement rather than the journal which kept the name) never seemed to have such detachment. We were all immersed in the real world. Our understandings flowed out of the actual movement of existence and dissolved back within it. Against the preparation for an externally developing 'moment' into which the professional revolutionary organization was to insert/inject itself was the conviction in the New Left that human beings could and would resist an unjust and inhuman society because it denied the possibility of creativity and love. We were all responsible agents of our destinies and must act in our lives. I could consequently never accept the notion of 'training' which was present in the Leninist tradition and important in Trotskyism.

In varying degrees the Trotskyist groups believed that personal feelings should be curbed and in some cases sacrificed – whereas the New Left in resisting Stalinism wanted to allow space for personal feeling as a source of humanity. It was assumed that personal relationships and values were to be respected and that Stalinism had denied and destroyed them. They were to be recognized as important in their own right even if they denied the immediate possibility of commitment to any organized resistance. In 1960 in 'Outside the Whale', Edward Thompson explored the sources of apathy and the personal anti-political rebellion among the young. He argued the radical potential of the response expressed in Shelagh Delaney's *A Taste of Honey*. If love had become falsified perhaps it appeared better to shed illusions and seek honesty instead. But in the search for honesty we could rediscover the source of love in opposition to its caricature.

> The anti-political find themselves once again in the arena of political choice. Because 'love' must be thrust into the context of power, the moralist finds that he must become revolutionary.[1]

The New Left stressed the possibilities of personal choice within particular contexts. It was not an abstract freedom, but it was an historical freedom. They did not assume that everyone had to make socialism by the same route. They did not insist on there being the one way to truth which seems to me to be essential in the make-up of the Trotskyist groups in the 1970s. I think this arminianism was shared by most IS members in the 1960s and was one bond with the New Left. No single left group could claim with conviction any way to having absolute truth. They were after all so tiny. The pretensions of the Socialist Labour League (now the Workers Revolutionary Party) seemed simply grotesque to most socialists in the early 1960s. Unselfconsciously we read Kropotkin and Bakunin as well as Marx, Gandhi and GDH Cole, Camus, Sartre and Emma

Goldman. We bought *Anarchy* as well as *Peace News, Sanity, Tribune* and *Labour Worker.*

By 1964 when I left University it seemed as if people in the New Left were becoming less preoccupied with finding new forms for class struggle which the ex-CP members had sought, and were more involved in cultural analyses of popular working-class attitudes and customs. I did not understand then why it was important to study the relationships between the stereotypes of the media and consciousness. It just seemed rather owlish. I was too closely involved emotionally in the music of popular culture to want to study it. I knew nothing of the differences on the journal. While I was friendly with some of the group round the *New Left Review* after 1963, I could not understand how they could be socialists and not bother about being personally remote from working-class people. This made them very different from the initiators of the New Left.

So I joined the Young Socialists in Hackney Labour Party where I met Trotskyists who were in Militant and International Socialism. I could not see Trotskyism from outside anymore. I learned about Trotskyism from young working-class people, many of whom came from left Labour families and remembered the anti-fascist struggles of the East End or quite violent confrontations with the law and state going back over several generations of trade unionism in class-conscious families. The precarious tradition of Trotskyism was strengthened because it combined with personal experience of class. I learned from them about theory (J.P. Cannon) and proletarian art (*The Ragged Trousered Philanthropists*). I was told you could never trust the middle class (me among others). I learned how to dissect Labour Party policy statements and argue (just about) with right-wing MPs about incomes policy. We had no illusions that the Labour Party leadership was going to bring us socialism. But we tended to underestimate the capacity of Labourism to exhaust left opposition.

Within the Labour Party Young Socialists I was drawn towards the International Socialism Group (now Socialist

Workers Party) around 1966 and I joined briefly in the late 1960s. Its attraction to me and to other socialists influenced by the New Left was that it appeared to combine theoretical openness and flexibility with an orientation towards a grass-roots working-class politics. In the sixties IS seemed to be able to assimilate and learn from new movements while retaining an understanding of exploitation. This was important both in the student movements and locally for me in the Vietnam Solidarity Committee in Hackney. But before these, IS had supported various kinds of community action, a campaign about racialism in Islington and the organization of private tenants in Hackney which contributed to their involvement in the council tenants' movement in the late sixties.

I joined for about eighteen months, following a drive to recruit people who agreed very generally with their aims after Powell's racist speech in 1968. A debate about organization was just coming to an end. I puzzled over various position papers in bewilderment. In a sense I'm still puzzling, for ideas take years to sink in and grow out of me. Anyway in retrospect this argument seems to me to have been crucial. It involved discussion about the degree of autonomy local branches should have. The case for a centralized structure was eventually accepted. This debate came to be referred to as a closed issue – as if it had been settled. But its implications were critical for the course which IS was to take as an organization. Closing up on these issues was a mistake. It was implied there was no time for further discussion.

Martin Shaw, in his account of the history of IS, 'The Making of a Party?', comments that the political basis of the new 'democratic centralism' which was then accepted, '... was not fully understood either by many of the pre-1968 members ... or by the new recruits'.[2]

This was certainly true in my case. In retrospect again this episode which remained mysterious to me for years was in fact an elaborate conjuring trick. Tony Cliff held the rabbit of Rosa Luxemburg's criticism of the undemocratic features of Leninism and the dangers of the Party substituting itself for the working class in one hand. Then, in the twinkling of an eye, it had gone into the hat and out came a knotted scarf 'democratic centralism' and a long Leninist tradition – more and more and more of it.

Martin Shaw points out that Cliff's turnaround was a reaction to the failure of May 1968. He says it was a response which eclipsed any other 'lessons'. This incident could be dismissed as simply an example of an 'opportunism' peculiar to IS or to Cliff as an individual. But I think it has more general implications. For the assumption that the end justifies the means we use in organizing need not only apply to recruiting on a fuzzy basis. It could be combined with a formally democratic internal regime but involve the tactic of entrism, a fundamentally deceitful operation which has contributed to great distrust of both the Communist Party and Trotskyist groups. Or it might mean the covert control of front organizations or the use of smear tactics to defeat any opposition from non-aligned socialists.

Somehow there has passed into Trotskyism (and into the neo-Trotskyism of IS) the assumption that the manipulation of people is justified by the supposedly superior knowledge which leaders of revolutionary groups presume to possess of the end they believe they are pursuing. It is certainly possible to find justification for such a view in Lenin's dictums on morality. But there was enough historical evidence for questioning these. The disastrous extension and intensification of such an approach to politics had been a crucial feature of the Stalinism which Trotskyism professed to oppose. Trotskyists have levelled precisely these kinds of criticism at the CP's period of popular frontism for example. Yet Trotskyists can also still lack scruples about stacking the cards against a real process of discussion and learning for everyone before decisions were taken. Why should it be justifiable for Trotskyists and not for Stalinists?

It was not only a question of accepting a formal democratic process. It was a corrosion of the inner responses about how a socialist should behave. Awareness of this was present actually within Trotskyism. The dissidents grouped around ' Facing

Reality' argued in 1958 that contemporary Marxism was inhibited and cramped 'by a habit of mind and a way of life' which included 'a psychology of leadership'. They maintained that,

> The vanguard organisation substituted political theory and an internal political life for the human responses and sensitivities of its members to ordinary people. It has now become very difficult for them to go back into the stream of the community.[3]

I think this comment was to be curiously prophetic of the relationship which the Trotskyist leaderships were to have with the younger generation of socialists after 1968.

The energy which erupted in May 1968 was overwhelming. You could catch a glimpse of that extraordinary concentrated force of people's power to dissolve constraining structures which must be the subjective experience of a revolutionary process. I resisted identifying too hopefully at first. I couldn't bear the disappointment of defeat. But events pushed this reluctance away. The upsurge and its creativity were undeniable.

In a way there was too much to absorb. You couldn't believe your own ears sometimes. Nothing seemed impossible. The experiences of 1968 opened your political eyes and ears. It revealed vulnerabilities within capitalist society which were making it possible for people to imagine socialism in different ways.

Capitalism was seen as claiming your whole being. We were all colonized and had to become total resisters. The focus was not only on production or even on a wider concept of class struggle but on oppression in everyday life particularly the family and consumption. 'The revolution' must liberate the imagination. The opposition to capitalism was not only a power contest against an external system but against its inner hold. Not only the rational but the irrational was the sphere of this rebellion. There was a stress on subjective feeling and a suspicion of structures of any kind, including demands. 'Don't Demand – Occupy!' declared *Black Dwarf.* The stress was on learning through doing and on the need for experience to be the source of theory. It was assumed that your politics were communicated not only through what you said but in what you did and how you did it. This led to the assertion that the attack against capitalist society should carry the future within the present. Thus there should be no hierarchy, no elites, no chair, no committees, no speakers and even no meetings in some cases. Or the meeting merged into and became life. Life thus became meetings!

It is easy to cast a cynical eye backwards onto such utopianism. 1968 'failed' so it can be dismissed. I don't believe it can. For unless we understand how such a politics came about, how it influenced the emergence of the women's movement and crystallized within libertarian Marxism in the early seventies, we have no context in which to place the alternative assumptions about organizing which have been central in these movements. Aspects of these have persisted in innumerable community and cultural projects, communes, ecology, alternative technology, therapy and the growth movement.

In retrospect I think the late sixties were an enormously creative period which have been too easily dismissed in the quite different situation of the late seventies. The ideas which sprang up around the May Events deserve much more serious conscious consideration.

Nonetheless with the passing of time the weaknesses of many of the assumptions about organizing which have been bequeathed half consciously are apparent. The idea of oppression is both vague and rather static. It fixes people in their role as victim rather than pointing to the contradictory aspects of relationships which force the emergence of new forms of consciousness. The stress on the way capitalism devours our whole beings could lead to a fatalism once the initial voluntarist enthusiasm was exhausted. Similarly there is a problem inherent in the slogan 'the personal is political' for it tends to imply that all individual problems can find a short-term political solution.

Thus a politics which asserted subjectivity could ironically become a means of reducing human beings to the functions they perform for capital. Notions of individual potential could thus be obscured and denied. The stress on total solutions and the fears of co-option could give way to despair and disillusion when the world went on in its bad old course. The conviction that organization should carry the future, breaking down all hierarchy and denying all skills, could become an inturned and moralistic network which excluded people. The alternatives could seem like the lifestyle of a sub-culture, almost a fashion coming out of an anti-fashionable stance. Perhaps it was some such combination of factors which contributed to that paralysis of libertarian Marxism as a challenge to the hegemony of the Trotskyist groups in the British left which is apparent from the mid-seventies.

This paralysis, combined with the defensiveness against theory has left the situation open for both 'workerism' which disregards new movements at one extreme and the abstruse high theory which has become a form of practice among academic Marxists.

I think it would be illuminating to disentangle the continuities and differences between the New Left of the fifties and this second wave, the New Left of the late sixties/ early seventies.[4] I suspect that in fact the New Left response to 1956 did not simply 'end' when the *New Left Review* changed hands, or 'fail' as Trotskyists imply. Instead the people involved went into quite diverse forms of activity in the course of which their cohesive similarities were fragmented and transformed but never completely dissolved. This process has never been examined in any detail. Jan O'Malley, though, traces one strand of New Left development in Notting Hill. In her book *The Politics of Community Action* she describes the contribution made by people from the London left clubs in tenants' and anti-racist groups before 1966. She also mentions their involvement with the London Free School, the Nutting Hill Community Workshop in 1966, and their support for the May Day Manifesto's statement in May 1967. This said that socialists needed to make a political movement which would make 'democratic practice effective throughout the society, by activity and locality rather than in some closed, centralized, ritualized place'.[5]

The use of the term 'workshop' echoed the community organizing of the American New Left. The Free School also prefigured the politics of the libertarians of the early 1970s. Libertarian Marxism in this period also stressed the grass-roots community organizing which had been developing in Notting Hill since the late sixties. Perhaps some of the differences between this community politics of the mid-sixties and libertarianism in the early seventies is the much greater influence of the ideas of the French Situationists and the Italian far left upon the latter.

Strands of the New Left in other areas could be traced within the Labour Party, Anarchist groups, in Solidarity, international Socialist groups, and trade unions in the mid-sixties. From the late sixties they could be seen helping to create 'History Workshops', becoming involved in the women's movement, in left cultural movements and in radical intellectual work.

I could not attempt to unravel these strands myself for I feel personally that I am too stuck in a particular crevice somewhere between the two new lefts. I am close to both but belong to neither. I was too late for the fifties but too formed by the late sixties to be completely swept up in the student movement of the late sixties or the voluntarism of libertarian Marxism in the early seventies. So I was drawn emotionally towards libertarianism but remained intellectually full of doubt. Though I identified with the struggle to solve the actual problems presented by capitalism, without forcing everything back into the terms in which Lenin, or whoever, had said things should be happening, I felt they were continually cutting corners and over-simplifying Leninism.

It's frightening to set off on new journeys without any maps. Perhaps the hardest bit is deciding what to hang on to and what to shed. There seemed to be an atmosphere which would annihilate history as if the past was too compromised to be acknowledged. This has had a destructive effect in the American New Left and appeared in the left libertarian politics of the early 1970s. I suspect it has contributed to contemporary left attitudes towards history in opposition to 'theory'. I felt distrustful of this, for while acknowledging many of their criticisms of the Old Left, I was wary of what seemed like an extreme subjectivity, it was true that immediate feelings of the moment were ignored in the rituals of both the Communist Party and the Trotskyist groups. But, on the other hand, what of the strategic consequences of actions? Libertarianism seemed to dismiss these. The past is always part of the moment of the present whether we consider it or not.

So I had become an 'old leftist' by the early seventies. This meant I remained psychologically close to IS as a kind of reference point even after I left early in 1970. I think this was a situation shared by many socialists who were to varying degrees affected by the 'old New Left'. The subsequent hardening of IS from around 1972 which intensified in the mid-seventies propelled me (and some of them) into personal dissent. It has finally forced me to start confronting the differences between the impulse of the New Left and that tradition of revolutionary organizing of which IS was an idiosyncratic part–Leninism and Trotskyism.

My real involvement was with the emerging Women's Liberation Movement but this closeness to IS meant I was forced to try and understand the leadership's resistance in the early 1970s to discussing aspects of oppression which were not directly related to class exploitation. I went to the first IS women's conference as an observer and identified strongly with the women arguing for women's liberation. It was a particularly confusing situation because many of the first women's groups outside London were started by women in or close to IS.

At first it seemed enough to put resistance to women's liberation down to the bias of a male-dominated leadership – though the picture was never that simple as some women in IS opposed women's liberation and some men supported it from the beginning. The effort to change the class base of IS and orientate towards working-class economic struggles also certainly contributed towards a dismissal of women's liberation as middle class – the pot being disposed to call the kettle black. But by the mid-seventies neither of these seemed adequate explanations for the greater overt sectarianism shown by IS than by the Communist Party or the international Marxist Group to the women's movement. Why should a group which had historically broken with both Stalinism and orthodox Trotskyism on the issue of socialist democracy and worker's control be more incapable of digesting not only feminism but issues like gay liberation, radical psychology, struggles around cultural and community life and personal discussion of what it meant to be a socialist? Why should a group which had rejected dogma hold its ideas as moralistic defences? Ostensibly committed to learning from workers' struggles, the initiator of rank and file groups, opposed to bureaucracy in the labour movement, IS baulked at extending these ideas into the wider issues of everyday life or at applying them within their own organization. Even the commitment to workers' rank and file struggles and experience came to be narrowly defined in terms of recruitment. Looking at the tussles from outside it looked as if the various groupings in the leadership adopted a rhetoric about who could put in the best claim to be the interpreter of workers' experience.

It is a mistake of course to expect a political process to be a smooth unfolding. People in the very act of breaking out of some forms of politics, protect their behinds tightly with the corners of the old covers.

Perhaps the consequence of breaking from the tradition of the Communist Party and Trotskyism made it more imperative to hold on to a limited economic concept of class struggle. For strait is the way between the perils and blandishments of centrism, reformism, etc. Especially if you are petit bourgeois to boot!

But with this dismissal of new movements and democracy

many aspects of the politics from which they had partially detached themselves grew up within yet another walled garden.

Critics within IS explained the strange twists of fortune and recessions of democracy as a series of coincidences which could be put right. But how many coin cadences could you explain away? The same dilemmas seemed to be coming up about the relationship of a political organization to rank and file groups which had been held up by IS as awful warnings of the CP's Stalinist sectarianism in the late twenties and early thirties. The experience of the women's movement also indicated that the question of the connection of a political group to movements and campaigns could not be solved by the kind of political break IS had made with Stalinism and orthodox Trotskyism. This went deeper than the actions of IS. It involved the whole approach to being socialists.

In its early days IS really did try and break with sectarian traditions and with the windbag rhetorical rituals on the left. But this hardened into a refusal to talk about the politics of what they were doing within the left. Martin Shaw has described how IS members came to feel they were above sectarianism. But the refusal to deal with dogma meant that in trying to go outwards they dismissed other socialists. In rejecting some of the obvious pretentions of orthodox Trotskyism, righteousness grew within. It was as if they had a special calling which was never stated and was somehow invisible. Their politics became those of a chosen elect. They could never do everything themselves but felt no one else could be relied upon to do anything worthwhile. Under this strain their ideas were held in abeyance. There was no time to learn from new developments. Increasingly their theories did not fit new realities outside IS so they stiffened into dogma and became defensive. Ideas and open debate became almost suspect as inherently middle class. They seemed to be regarded as a waste of time with 'the Crisis' upon us. The instinct towards criticism was to attack the opponents for their class or lack of activity. Paranoia mounted as secret internal documents inevitably leaked. If the circumstances of the mid-seventies could produce this change, the mind boggles at what a civil war and famine would have done – Uncle Joe apart.

By the mid-seventies I was being nudged into trying to understand why it should be that the politics of IS should end up this way. I know this need to understand is shared by those socialists who have been close to IS and who became critical of its development in the early 1970s. This experience cannot simply be shaken off. Our past is not an indulgence. A lot of people's lives have been affected by their membership of IS/SWP – political faiths have been scarred much more deeply than the socialism of someone like me who was not a member for very long. Such negligence is never without its nemesis of cynicism and paralysis. The expelled members or people who left were erased from the memory of what is significant. Their opposing politics were constantly confused with moral failing. This has sinister echoes and has resulted in bitterness and waste. But the implications go even beyond this. I think that unless we try and understand what were the sticking points which limited IS's move away from Stalinism and from orthodox Trotskyism we will not see what allowed this process to occur. This means we are back to square one with no guarantee we won't repeat the same circle.

So I think the process of opening up what happened in IS and exploring its consequences for how we organize in the future is as important as a reassessment of the impact of the 1956 New Left and libertarian Marxism.[6] I am aware that my preoccupation with IS/SWP may have a hermetic quality to people who have not lived any aspect of such an encounter. It may seem a strange, intense passion splashing around in the proverbial parochial duck pond. But I believe it has a significance beyond the political involvement of ex-members or members. For roughly a decade from the mid-1960s IS represented in Britain the main organizational hope that the Leninist and Trotskyist traditions could be renewed by a generation which had not been scarred by the horrors of Stalinism and the extreme isolation of the minority Trotskyist opposition. The renewal promised was to carry the revolutionary tradition of 1917 and yet face outwards to the problems of modern capitalism. I think this promise has proved to be illusory. However the existence of such a hope meant that many implications of the New Left challenge to Stalinism were evaded. Also, as Martin Shaw argues, the IS leaders did not really understand 'the structural changes... which the student movement highlighted'.[7] More than this though, they did not acknowledge the significance of the changes in consciousness which these developments involved. The insights of both movements could thus be absorbed, channelled and finally abandoned by the sectarian husk which had consumed them.

This has had a most confusing effect on the contemporary left in which the SWP can raise great dust storms while digging itself further into the sand. It means that the substantial problems raised by the New Left after 1956 and by the May Events in 1968, about how we should make socialism, have been almost completely obscured.

I suppose this effort to understand IS/SWP could be described as a continuing niggling external puzzle for me. An internal pull towards thinking about organization has been experiencing a completely different politics within the women's movement since 1969. The differences between this kind of practice and socialist politics have seemed so great that it has been hard to compare them. I've increasingly felt this as a paralysing split. There is a danger that we might acquiesce to such a division, accepting one way of organizing for socialism and another for feminism. Given the existing balance of power between the sexes in society as a whole this would undoubtedly mean that our organizing as feminists became increasingly ghettoized.

In the women's movement for nearly ten years there have been organizing assumptions growing, mainly communicated by word of mouth. The difficulty of translating these assumptions into a language which can touch current definitions of organization on the left have been enormous. This is partly because these have emerged from the practice of a movement in a piecemeal way. They challenge the left groups implicitly rather than explicitly. But also they cannot be contained within the accepted circumference of debate established by the male-dominated left. Coming partly from the experience of feminist women's lives they reach continually outwards towards new forms of expressing defiance and resistance. This is a creativity which has not been shared by the left groups within the Leninist and Trotskyist traditions.

We have stressed for instance the closeness and protection of a small group and the feeling of sisterhood. Within the small group it has been important that every woman has space and air for her feelings and ideas to grow. The assumption is that there is not a single correctness which can be learned off by heart and passed on by poking people with it. It is rather that we know our feelings and ideas move and transform themselves in relation to other women. We all need to express and contribute. Our views are valid because they come from within us and not because we hold a received correctness. The words we use seek an openness and an honesty about our own interest in what we say. This is the opposite to most left language which is constantly distinguishing itself as correct and then covering itself with a determined objectivity. (This is not only true of Leninism but sometimes also of the opponents of Leninism. Here the name becomes inadequate to express the problem. It becomes a problem within the use of the concept of science in Marxism itself.) it is very important to be able to say 'I don't know' and 'Nobody knows, we need to find out' without being dismissed as stupid.

Our politics have tried to allow for the expression of vulnerability and openness to every woman's feelings which consciousness raising at its best implies. We have rejected central organization, hierarchical structures and a leadership. This has not meant that we have no organization, for example, regional networks, women's centres, conferences, publishing groups, theatre groups, folk and rock bands, film collectives, trade union caucuses, food co-ops are aspects of the women's movement.

The structures which have arisen have been seen as serving particular needs. The making and communication of ideas have been an extraordinary collective process in which thousands of women have contributed. The organizational initiatives which have been spread through the movement have been extremely diverse, involving women in quite different ways. The women's movement has touched many areas of politics socialists have neglected and its hold goes deeper. It absorbs more of your being.

We've been close to our own weaknesses and pain in all this. It is hard to disentangle ourselves enough to make more distanced theoretical criticism while holding on to the realization of how creative our organizing has been. Though setting ourselves more exacting practical and personal standards in politics than the contemporary left, we nonetheless have found that criticism and differences bear too closely upon us for comfort. The distancing which is present in male-dominated groups is alienating. Yet it allows for the release of differences. The agony of division can be turned outwards rather than imploding the soul. Sisterhood can become a coercive consensus which makes it emotionally difficult for individual women to say what they feel rather than a source of strength. Consciousness raising can put too great a pressure on women to change by an effort of will alone. Feminist politics can become preoccupied with living a liberated life rather than becoming a movement for the liberation of women. Our lack of structure can make it difficult for women outside particular social networks to join. It can lead to cliquishness and thus be undemocratic. The stress on personal experience makes it hard to communicate ideas which have been gained either from the women's movement in the past or from other forms of radical politics.

Awareness of these weaknesses has made some women join left organizations. Their problem is then that many of the understandings of the women's movement are still unrecognized. Some women have opted instead for a pure theory which dismisses the vital importance of a politics in which subjective experience is always present. I can see how this response arises but I think it's a denial of a crucial source of our creativity as a movement. The recent growth of socialist feminist groups carries the hope of an integration of ideas, personal feeling and activity. It has come from several sources. Within the women's movement there have always been socialists and women who have become socialists so there is continuity with these earlier groupings of socialist feminists. But many women have also joined socialist feminist groups as exiles from Trotskyist and other left groups. For others the socialist feminist group is both their first women's and socialist group. This means there is no longer an automatically shared background of movement politics.

The women's movement has had a great reticence about blowing trumpets. For a woman like me familiar with the left this was one of the strangest things I had to learn. There was no bluffing but a careful, scrupulous examination of the minutiae of behaviour, with much more exacting inner standards. On the left everything is a hurry and there is a pressure for results. Exemplary myths can substitute in the short term. I think the realism has been a long-term strength of the women's movement. On the other hand, it sometimes becomes a self-denigration, a dismissal of what we have achieved. This is true of our attitude to activity and ideas but most particularly to organization. I think it's important now to begin to assert explicitly understandings which have been passed on by word of mouth or even been implicit in how we've done things. For understandings which are not formulated explicitly have a way of vanishing like dust under a carpet of 'correct' ideas.

Our discussions of organization have dwelt on immediate problems, for example, the lack of structure, embarrassed silences in meetings, the relationship of co-ordinating centres like the London workshop to local groups. There is a shared understanding of the need for an independent movement, though some women interpret this as remaining completely separate from men and other movements while others see it as keeping our organizational autonomy but working with other groupings against a common opponent. Beyond these assumptions and understandings we have tried to solve organizational problems as they come up with the general aim of making situations in which all women can participate fully. Despite feminist interest in women's history, we have not referred what we are doing much to past traditions of revolutionary organization, Leninist or otherwise. In this way the women's movement has shared with libertarian Marxism a sense of beginning anew. This has meant we have avoided the dogmatism with which these traditions have become encrusted. But it has put us on the defensive in relation to people on the left who appear to have very clear versions of revolutionary tradition and 'an analysis' off pat. It has also deprived us of the valuable confidence which a sense of belonging to a complex culture of resistance brings to the labour movement. The growing numbers of women exiled from left groups could bring the positive aspects of these traditions into the women's movement.

Our debates have been grounded in real conflicts but it has been difficult to generalize beyond the particular. We have no means of placing them in any context. Experience which is not theorized has a way of dissolving and slipping out of view, even when it belongs to the relatively recent collective memory of a living movement. We can retain attitudes and responses towards forms of organizing which we prefer but it is hard to pass them on or give them a more general validity.

I think the need to theorize our organizational experience using past traditions creatively is becoming more urgent, for as time passes it becomes impossible to communicate what happened or why decisions were taken by word of mouth. You can't keep telling it like a story. 'Well you see at the Skegness Women's Liberation Conference we got everyone down off the platform. And then we had to do the same a few years later at the Mile End Women And Socialism Conference.' It's too long-winded and it means everyone is just going backwards and forwards, up and down the same hill. It evokes a vision of a small body of intransigent feminist old age pensioners still hauling Trotskyist women off platforms armed with a memory which is incomprehensible to most people. Without a theory you get stuck defending entrenched feelings. Making a theory gives you enough bounce to leap up in the air, meet critics head on and land on your feet with an alternative without getting too puffed. It gives you the advantage.

There has become more of a need for such leaps since we have been trying to work out how we approach issues like anti-fascism, Ireland, mass working-class confrontations like Grunwick, legal repression, or imperialism. Violent demonstrations, mass pickets, torture and the consolidation of the power of the state to suppress radical resistance internationally have stretched the response of feminist organizational structures which were devised for quite different kinds of politics.[8] There is strong pressure to simply dismiss the significance of the more intimate and personal areas of struggle. Instead I think we need to clarify the different kinds of resistance we are engaged in as feminists and develop a more strategic sense of opposition and alliance and new combinations of personal and public forms depending on the nature of the political issue.

One aspect of such a strategy would be a more worked-out understanding of what the feminist experience has taught us about how to organize and what aspects we feel are relevant for making socialism.

I think it would be to go down a blind alley if we simply presented this in terms of a defensive idealization of the women's movement as 'the alternative' and a caricature of the 'authoritarian male' left. This puts an impossible weight on women's liberation and lets men off the hook as they can leave it to women while presenting a more-feminist-than-thou facade. The women's movement can't carry some finished alternative, though the experience of an alternative practice and the search for different relationships within the political process can contribute a great deal. But despite its creativity, feminism, by definition, expresses the experience of one sex. It is necessarily partial. Moreover there are actual class and race biases as well. Women's liberation has mobilized mainly women from a particular strata, teachers, social workers, librarians, journalists or clerical workers, as well as women working in the family. They are largely people involved in the communication of values and the administration and servicing of capitalist society. These are crucial places to contest. They give important insights into raw sensitivities apparent in relations of control between the sexes in these areas of capitalism. But many women are not included in this particular social relationship. While some manual working-class women have been involved and many others influenced by the women's movement their experience has not been central to the emergence of the new feminism. There is a similar racial limitation. Feminists are predominantly white. Asian and West Indian women are in a minority. This has restricted the full understanding of lived similarities and differences in the predicament of women of various classes and races.

I don't think the women's movement or small groups of men and women can provide some neat alternative model out of a hat. The great historic force of Leninism is precisely that it has been created and used in revolutionary situations. It has worked up to a point and adapted to more complex situations than either anarchism or syndicalism,. Nor is there any denying that Trotskyism's origins in resistance to Stalinism when such opposition was tortuous and lonely make it a crucial source of revolutionary experience.

But there is no need to stop there. It must also be admitted that the Bolsheviks, even before Stalin, have a lot to account for, and that Leninism destroyed vital aspects of socialism even in creating a new kind of left politics. It was not only that revolutions have faced the most dire external circumstances. Leninist assumptions are actually weighted against the integration of many of the understandings present within pre-Leninist forms of socialism.[9] The persistent traditions of anti-Leninism have not been mere intransigence. But they have been limited to tiny sectarian groupings or abstract theory by the historical impact of Stalinism and this has affected how opposition has been expressed.

It feels now as if new light is being cast on these old disputes. I have taken heart from the debates which have been going on internationally in the Communist Parties, from the discussions in Britain around Socialist Unity, Big Flame and the International Socialism Conference and articles in *The Leveller* and *Socialist Register*. I feel personally closest to the growth of the network of socialist feminist groups and the things written about the left in *Red Rag*, *Gay Left*, *Lesbian Left* and *Achilles Heel* as these are not the papers of any political organization and are concerned with the connection between socialism and sexual politics.

In a recent interview in *The Leveller*, 'Recovering the Libertarian Tradition', E.P. Thompson criticized 'the unreconstructed Leninist and vanguardist strategies, which once again situate a sectarian leadership proclaiming themselves to be the embodiment of the proper revolutionary consciousness of the working people: and not inquiring very closely into what the actual demands and needs of the people are'.

He added that this was not 'a blanket criticism of Leninism as such – Leninism was a specific product of very special historical circumstances' which seemed to him 'to be irrelevant to this country and this time, and which could often entail anti-democratic and anti-libertarian premises'.

He asserted the need for an 'affirmative politics' which could avoid the passions, hatreds and paranoia which flourished within the contemporary left and could include 'an immense number of active supporters of the existing labour movements and Labour Party'.[10]

I see the growth of new forms of organizing within the women's movement as part of such a larger recovery of a libertarian socialist tradition. I think that this requires a sustained re-evaluation of the tradition of Leninism, and in Britain, because of its particular influence, of Trotskyism.[11] I will confess to being a reluctant contributor to this process, for such a realization is still in its early days with confusion and doubt on one side and a more tenacious clutch of doctrinal purity on the other. While there is a growing muttering and mumbling among the dissatisfied it is still being met by a pother of rhetoric from the Trotskyist and neo-Trotskyist leaderships.

Not only fear at stirring the pother has restrained me but respect. Organizing ideas, male dominated and handed down from above or not, are laborious creations and root themselves through usage. There certainly are skills which need to be passed on. There are things you need to learn from people who know more. Everything does not pop up in our heads. I know I have learned from both Lenin and Trotsky. It would be prodigal to dismiss the depth of understanding which the Russian revolutionary tradition and the enormous upheaval of 1917 made possible. Leninist ideas have obviously been well tried and practiced sanctions. Whatever criticisms I'd make of Leninism there was always some friend in the Communist Party or one of the left groups to explain Lenin hadn't meant it like that or he'd said something different. Sometimes I feel even naming the problem as Leninism is wrong. For I know that in all left organizations there are always people with complex understandings which are lived in many dimensions. So I've thought for years perhaps it was best to leave well alone whatever uneasiness I felt. Why tussle and worry when you have no worked-out alternative?

Now though, it seems to me to have become inescapably important to bring the real disagreements about how to make socialism which exist in the left and the labour movement out into the open in order to develop new understandings. We can best begin by examining our own political experience and see what might be generalized from that. We need to uncover what we have been actually doing without claiming an ascendent correctness or disguising weaknesses.

All this is just the story behind the main plot which in summary is: how I think some of the approaches to organizing which go under the headings of Leninism and Trotskyism are flawed; how I think the assumptions of what it means to be a socialist carried within Leninism and Trotskyism and which prevail on the left now block our energy and self-activity and make it harder for socialism to communicate to most people; why I think the women's movement suggests certain ways of reopening the possibility of a strong and popular socialist movement.

I am not dealing systematically with the 'works' of Lenin or the works of Trotsky, or the history of the Communist Parties, or Maoism's specific application of Leninism. Nor am I tracing the origin and growth of the Fourth International or the disputes within Trotskyism which led dissidents like C.LR. James, Raya Dunayevskaya, Michel Pablo and Tony Cliff himself to revise aspects of Trotsky's thought. Absent are great chunks of debates which Leninists and Trotskyists have been chewing away at for years, for instance the question of state power, imperialism, the law of uneven development, the theory of permanent revolution, and many more.

I am approaching Leninism mainly as it has appeared through the resurgent flourish of Trotskyist groups on the British left since the late sixties. I am focusing on the points of conflict which have developed between these Trotskyist forms of Leninism and the women's movement. This is not because I don't think there is much more to be said – but because I know I am not the one to say it. Hopefully other people will explore the ways in which these confrontations have occurred in other contexts and extend the implications of feminism into those areas of left debate in which we are still absent.

The general terms of these criticisms could not have been formulated without the experience of being in the women's movement. But the specifics of what follows is me writing as an individual. I hope this might contribute to a more thorough discussion.

PART TWO

Introduction

I want to begin to explore the challenge I think the women's movement is making to the prevailing assumptions of how revolutionary socialists should organize. These involve how theory is conceived, how the political organization sees its relationship to other movements, how consciousness is assumed to change, how the scope of politics is defined, how individual socialists see themselves and their relationship to other people, now and in the past.

I don't see this as a matter of biological people, women, scoring off biological people, men. Feminism for me is a movement to assert the interests of women as a sex. But more than this it is a means of releasing and communicating the understandings which that subordination holds in check. The movement for women's liberation is part of the creation of a society in which there are no forms of domination. This society cannot be separated from the process of its making.

Relationships between men and women have undoubtedly changed historically along with the great upheavals in which the production and reproduction of all the means of social life and material existence have been transformed by people in the past. This does not mean that sex-gender relations can be either dissolved into economic changes in how things are produced or seen as a function of biological difference. We know very little of the forms these relations have taken for most people in the past. But socialist feminists have begun to assert the need to look at the sexual division of labour and the power relations within kinship networks as they have appeared historically. We are not arguing then either for a biologically universal kind of relationship or for one which is totally contingent on change in the mode of production.

Rosalind Petchesky in 'Dissolving the Hyphen' stresses the need 'to study concrete revolutionary situations in order to determine whether women, because of their particular material conditions, develop particular ways of fighting and organizing.

If we understand that patriarchal kinship relations are not static but, like class relations are characterized by antagonism and struggle, then we begin to speculate that women's consciousness and their periodic attempts to resist or change the dominant kinship structures will themselves affect class relations.'[12]

Felicity Edholm, Olivia Harris and Kate Young point out that we cannot simply assume that antagonism and struggle are constant. They ask, in 'Conceptualising Woman': 'Under what conditions is it likely that women will not accept their situation as natural and "god ordained"?'

They suggest a hypothesis which it would be most useful to explore both historically and through anthropological studies of particular societies, '... that this occurs when changes in the productive process bring the sex/gender system into contradiction with the sexual division of labour, when there is no longer congruence between the two, this incompatibility provides the potential for struggle and questioning, for sexual hostility and antagonism. The direction that such struggle takes, however cannot be "read off" in advance.'[13]

Potentially Marxism is a valuable means of understanding how historical transformations affect our lives and how we are both limited by these processes and help to make them. The existing shape of Marxism has itself been made by the forces and dilemmas uppermost for socialists in the past. The emergence of the women's movement has shown the underdevelopment of Marxism on relations between sexes and the connection between this and women's subordination within the left. It has meant that socialist women, both inside and outside left groups, have challenged the power of men to determine Marxism in their own image. The imperatives of feminism require that we make many aspects of Marxism anew.

The experience of feminism has been that the specific gender oppression of women requires an independent movement in order for us to develop and assert a new collective consciousness of being female, whether this is seen as separatist or autonomous. Bea Campbell has described in *Red Rag* how this autonomy was defined in practice from the start as autonomy from men. Implicit in this though was the assertion of sex-gender relationships as an area of social conflict neglected by socialism. This went beyond any definition of femaleness. In delineating what was specific to us as a sex we were necessarily transforming the boundaries of identity.

> ... feminism necessarily identifies both the subjective and objective condition of existence as problems of politics. In other words, the person became a political problem. This challenged a way of practising politics that treats revolutionary personnel as agents rather than subjects.
>
> Feminism proposes that the lived relations of subordination, the way of being subordinated, must be a central problem for revolutionary strategy. (It is not alone in doing that, but it is the most coherent and persistent of the 'new' politics.) This prompts a form that is about mass engagement, that is about a process of preparedness.[14]

A. How We Relate to Ideas

One aspect of the lived relation of subordination has been the exclusion of women from all generalizing concepts and from the dominant definition of culture. This is partly a shared subordination. Other forms of hierarchical relationship, around class and race for example, are also excluded. But women's subordination is particularly internalized, it even appears in the words which express the hope of a new collective identity. It is not just a matter of 'mankind', but of 'Liberty, Equality, Fraternity'. It is not only 'chairman', but 'brotherhood' and 'yours fraternally' as well. This language of the socialist and labour movement expresses the way men have defined what is important within the radical tradition as well as in capitalist society as a whole. When women on the left began to criticize this language we were told we were just being petty. But the ideas and politics of women's liberation emerged out of precisely these small everyday moments of dismissive encounter.

The women's movement in challenging every aspect of men's hold over culture, ideas and power has begun to illuminate the bias in the language which expresses the power to define how the world is understood and acted upon.

But the mere existence of a movement, though vital, does not end this cultural subordination because the values we are contesting are rooted in actual power relationships. It does, however, mean that the contours of oppression come into sharper relief and can thus be confronted.

A problem we share with other groups of people who are not powerful, the ignoble, unknown people, is how to explore and reveal our experience in the moment of transforming our culture. If we simply dwell upon our suffering and the ways we have shifted for ourselves, we can produce an idealized icon of the earth-mother, whore-with-a-heart-of-gold or the madonna. We will not dissolve the existing assumptions about womanhood. On the other hand, if we do not recognize and grow within the specific lived experiences of women we can just create another ideal, this time a feminist stereotype, which does not relate to real life and will not touch the heart.

In order to explore, we need good maps. (I nearly wrote workmanlike!) We need to be able to take stock of the situation and communicate any general principles to other wanderers. We have to establish certain staging posts to refuel and assess the journey. This means we have to sit back momentarily from our immediate response to the route and try to sum up the relationship of what we have travelled to the whole journey. Some of this will be from our experience, with information from other travellers' tales and from any existing maps. Some will be speculation about the way things will be likely to go.

Our summation of the whole may be incomplete and imperfect, but we still need it in order to get our bearings. Even if we abandon this assessment subsequently, the attempt can still be decisive and the effort to be as accurate as we can is still vital if we are not to trundle down every dead end or take enormous detours.

It is this kind of activity I mean when I use the word 'theory'. 'Abstraction' should help us to move when we wish and to settle in the best camping places. It should help us to communicate and spread experience, feelings, understandings and ideas and thus facilitate action. It should not be a series of coded sign-posts that only a small elite can de-code and which lead us round and round in circles.

I realize that 'theory' has a rather more weighty meaning on the contemporary left. It has a grand resonance which comes from the towers of academia and the fossilized authority of sectarianism. Both these approach 'theory' as something unattainable except by the few. It becomes fixed, hanging above us in a kind of ahistorical space. But ideas come from our experience of our lives, from the past wisdom of others and from the movement for change. Our efforts to abstract upon our practice and history through theories of how to make socialism for example are not good for all time, to be handed on like dusty catechisms, repeated by rote as 'correct thought'. They have no universal validity. If they serve more than their time, well and good. But this does not make them sacred texts; it makes them more fitting to be used and enjoyed and developed. I think that each effort of abstraction must be constantly re-examined, criticized, dipped back into experience, merge and be born again.

Because the process of abstraction requires a conception of yourself which can be generalized, there are enormous and serious difficulties in the relationship between groups of people who have been subordinated and theory. A movement helps you to overcome some of the oppressive distancing of theory and this has been a considerable and continuing creative endeavour of women's liberation. But some paths are not mapped and our footholds vanish. The theorizing about organization remains in the quick sands. It is unclaimed territory still. I see what I'm writing as part of a wider claiming which is beginning. I am part of the difficulty myself. The difficulty is not out there. I feel the effort physically still in the act of writing this. I am stumbling in the dark. There is the floundering feeling I got in writing about women's liberation before there was a movement to be part of in 1968. But this time I feel weights against thought. They press on my shoulders and on my breasts. I find myself catching my breath. A kind of helmet grows on my head. The words slither around and seem to slip onto the surface of my consciousness unless I make an enormous effort to remain within them. The difference is that I know such huffing and puffing is not a personal eccentricity but a social experience and this knowledge is something felt, not just something I understand intellectually.

When the women's movement began it seemed that socialist ideas were external because mainly men made and defined them. It seemed that the fear came because we were women. This is broadly true within a culture in which men are still dominant but it needs qualifying. The existence of the women's movement affects men as well as women. It is not just a matter of the ideas but the relationship to them. If men try and hold ideas differently they encounter a similar paralysis and panic which women know. We need to help one another through this – we are at separate ends of the same quicksands. Similarly if women are willing to accept a formal recognition, if we do not seek to overturn the whole relationship to theory we will be accepted grudgingly by the leadership of the male left just as we can be accommodated within a masculine bourgeois culture.

Yeats commenting on Maud Gonne's involvement in the Irish movement provides an external unsympathetic description of the price women have paid even in relation to male-dominated popular movements.

> Women, because the main event of their lives has been a giving of themselves, give themselves to an opinion as if (it) were some terrible stone doll ... the opinion becomes so much a part of them that it is as though a part of their flesh becomes, as it were, stone, and much of their being passes out of life.[15]

It is a terrible cruel price and feminism has clawed a way through to ideas which do not involve this handing over of our beings because we are within them.

But a violent and painful struggle leaves scars which harden. We need to create as well as oppose. The implicit understanding of this has been one of the strengths of feminism. Creativity involves transformation by going beyond yourself. It is nurtured by the collective experience and knowledge of people now and in the past. One aspect of domination is the denial of such nurture. We cannot afford to be negligent of the understandings carried in past socialist ideas of how to organize because those ideas have been defined by men and tend to be held by small leaderships who train others in their image. Nor do we want to hand ourselves over to ways of thinking which turn parts of us to stone. We need to bring the strengths of the feminist movement to bear on this wrenching agony. We have the experience of a living movement in which thousands and thousands of women have made and shared ideas with love. This is the source of a most extraordinary power.

B. And To The Past

Feminism requires an enormous interrogation of the past, just as other movements of people who are held down have sought a past which does not maintain their subordination, by exclusion or distortion. One aspect of this critical encounter must be with the history of the socialist and labour movements.

It is not only that we are persistently on the lookout for women. Socialist feminists have asked many questions which have come up because of the political practice and understandings which we have reached through feminism. We want to know, for example, what has been the relationship between socialist and feminist movements. We have asked how the way work is divided at different periods of capitalism has affected men's and women's involvement in radical organization. We are concerned with the interconnections of sex/gender relationships and production at various times and how this has affected people's consciousness. We want to find out what kinds of socialist and labour movements have attracted large numbers of women or excluded them and why these have happened. We have asked have socialists imagined how women and men, men and men, women and women, children and adults might live together differently? How have socialists seen personal relationships in society as a whole, in their own lives and in their organizations? Did socialists believe that women's liberation meant women should become like men; did they argue that women had specific qualities as a sex which men might acquire or develop; or did they imagine men and women contributing towards making a culture in which notions of 'masculinity' and 'feminity' would dissolve? How did relationships in the family combine with those of the community and work to make women and men socialists or join trade unions? How have women of different classes seen their potential liberation? How have socialists regarded housework, woman's control over her own fertility, the education of the young? Have their attitudes affected what they did in their own lives as well as for the socialist future? What differences are there between public programmes and personal practice within the socialist and labour movements?[16] These questions involve not only a reassessment of how the history of the left is seen. They are pointing towards a re-evaluation of what kind of contemporary socialist movement we need. They are inseparable from more general problems of how we understand class, kinship, community and consciousness.

For of course none of these political and cultural attitudes existed in isolation from the wider movement of society. For instance Joanna Bornat in 'Home and Work. A New Context for Trade Union History' focuses on men and women who entered the woollen manufacturing industry, in Colne Valley, West Yorkshire between 1900-1910. She shows how they experienced home and work in their lives and how it affected their trade unionism. She points out that the conventional approach to trade union history only looks at work and the official version of activity, it draws attention away from the interrelationship between home and work in real life.

To say that capitalism needs the family is not the simple story of the exploitation of its members. It is also the story of how those members learn to survive and support one another within the constraints of the wage labour-capital relationship.

She says she is 'arguing for an approach which seeks to understand men and women, their institutions and self-conceptions in terms of their living and working relationships'.[17] She therefore examines the interconnection between class relations and 'dependency' by which she means 'the unequal relationship between men and women maintained through social and economic means within the capitalist mode of production'.

This criticism of the artificial separation between work and everyday life is consistent with a general tendency in radical history away from the assumption that workers' consciousness can be simply equated with the views of people at the centre of institutions – either trade unions or political parties. This is clearly most relevant for women, who have only rarely taken part in central organizational leaderships.

There has been a cumulative movement in Britain, roughly since World War Two, which has been undermining and overturning many over-simplified approaches to history among socialists: for instance E.P. Thompson's *The Making of the English Working Class* examined how people experience themselves as part of a class through politics, community life, work, culture, and religion. Though he touches on family relationships these are less developed. The topics which have come up in the 'History Workshops' and appear in the journal of the same name, explore further similar areas of experience. Working-class childhood, school strikes, relationships in the family, imperialism and motherhood, control over fertility are some examples. Attention is not only directed at heroic moments, the 'peaks' of confrontation but how the rest of life itself gives rise to opposing consciousness. Several strands apart from the New Left and the CP have contributed to this process of re-examination. The Solidarity group, for instance, has been involved in a sustained critique of Leninist interpretations of the socialist past; and some Labour Party and IS historians have begun to open up a less dismissive approach to syndicalism. For example, despite a tendency to isolate work as a source of consciousness, James Hinton's *The First Shop Stewards' Movement* provides us with an understanding of how changes in the labour process meant syndicalist ideas made sense to a particular section of the working class. These approaches to history have been affected by contemporary politics. 'Rank and Filism' can contribute to making radical historians suspicious of using only the official documents of trades unions. Faction fighting may make yet others distrustful also of the official versions of socialist organizations' past. Oral history and personal papers might tell a different tale from the socialist newspapers and journals. Official organs could be revealing only what the editors think, not the movement. (The same is true, of course, of feminism.)

Socialist historians have become very wary of presenting the past of radical movements as a smooth progress towards a contemporary notion of enlightenment. If we approach the question of working-class organization by asking when have large numbers of women become involved, it is particularly evident that we do not see a steady march of enlightenment towards either Marxism-Leninism or the Labour Party. We can see instead a complicated process of loss and gain. Dorothy Thompson, for instance, comments on the participation of women in the early years of Chartism in the early 1830s. Towards the late forties they had disappeared and their involvement had been forgotten. She suggests part of the answer was a changing ideal of feminity which affected skilled working-class women, but also:

> in moving forward into mature industrial capitalist society important sections of the working class developed relatively sophisticated organizations, trade unions, political pressure

> groups, co-operative societies and educational institutions... In a variety of ways they were able to find means of protecting their position within an increasingly stable system. They left behind the mass politics of the early part of the century, which represented more of a direct challenge to the whole system of industrial capitalism at a stage in which it was far less secure and established. In doing so, the skilled workers also left behind the unskilled workers and the women, whose way of life did not allow their participation in the more structured political forms. These forms required both regularity of working times and regularity of income for participation to be possible.[18]

The trauma of Stalinism within the socialist movement has undoubtedly contributed to this wariness of a crudely progressivist picture in which the working class guided (of course) by correct ideas and the Party moves inexorably forward towards the sunset. This has made radical historians sensitive to understanding the meaning that ideas had for people in their own time, rather than imposing our 'answers'. But it is clear from the feminist experience that ideas can have various meanings for different groups even within the same movement. By focusing on the specific relationship of women to radical organizations and thus readjusting how we see men's position as well, socialist feminism can bring out the complexity of these different meanings.

But both the movement within radical history and the questions of socialist feminists remain curiously remote from much of the history which Trotskyist groups present as background to education articles or exposures of contemporary follies. I think this is less true in the Communist Party now, though I suspect that popular versions of history still retain some of the 'sunsets' of Stalinist days. But certainly it is still possible to find among Trotskyists an assumption that class consciousness comes solely from the experience of work. There is still a preoccupation with the moments of confrontation –

1917 or the betrayals of the TU leadership aided by the CP in the General Strike, for instance. The problem of why workers accepted such leaders is evaded. The interior reality of socialist organization is rarely touched. The pastime of fishing for a pure Marxism-Leninism with the last word on all subjects is still with us. Leninists have the fish and know the fish, they just need to haul it in. So it becomes inconceivable that the Leninist approach to 'the women's question' jettisoned many important understandings about prefigurative change, for instance, present within utopian socialism. It becomes absurdly hard to acknowledge that under Marx and Engels' influence communists dismissed crucial questions about sexual oppression, control over fertility and the cultural subordination of women as a sex which other contemporaries in the socialist and feminist movement recognized. This is not to dismiss the inspired leaps made by Marx and Engels theoretically or to forget that Lenin was more sympathetic than some of the Bolsheviks towards women's emancipation. It is not to deny that Trotsky paid more attention to cultural aspects of subordination though he stopped short at sexuality. But they were not omniscient. There is no reason to see them as the bee's knees in every subject. It is worth noting the points at which the social democratic and Bolshevik approaches to 'the woman question' brought them into conflict with the incipient socialist feminism of the period 1890-1920s. It is also worth exposing the over-simplified caricatures of 'bourgeois feminism' which concertina-ed several kinds of feminism into one grotesque creature. Social-democrats, communists, anarcho-syndicalists and anarchists all had their own versions of these caricatures. They have been taken too much at face value by socialist women writing history. (I include myself here.[19]) They leave us with an unchanging polarity between bad 'bourgeois feminists' and good working-class women. This means we fail to recognize that there are different kinds of 'bourgeois feminism', that some working-class women and men supported 'bourgeois feminist' campaigns, just as many middle-class men and women became socialists.

Any sectarian blunders of socialist organizing is completely obscured by the enormity of the crimes of 'bourgeois feminists'. Conflict between working-class men and women appears as occasional prejudice. Its sources remain ideological rather than part of the material circumstances of their lives. This is not to say we should never look at feminist movements critically or that there were not real class differences in the way women saw their liberation. But we do not get to these by ignoring sex conflicts within the working class or by simply posing socialist women against feminists, by extracting only the conservative features of the feminist movement and implying that socialists had all the answers in particular conflicts with feminism.

This uncritical view of the socialist, labour and feminist past only serves to confirm contemporary complacencies. If Marxists knew best not only now but in the past, we only need to provide a few modifying footnotes. The truth is already known, it just tends to get misplaced now and again. Once this is assumed, badly thought out actions in the past are passed on as issues of principle. This tendency already present within the Second International appears in the Third International, to reach the most paralysing proportions under Stalin. But it is not only a feature of Stalin's rule. It lingers even in the anti-Stalinism of the Trotskyist groups and the contemporary Communist parties.

So it is not really surprising that there has been a muffled combat going on since the women's movement emerged in the late sixties between socialist feminists and the purveyors of orthodoxy in left groups about history. For the way the feminist movement is seen, the relationship of feminism and socialism historically, the actual similarities and differences within the working-class and middle-class women at various periods have a close bearing upon many of the arguments we have today.

We can develop our own understanding of our politics through a living relationship with the past. But not if we search for points of conflict which can be raided for a 'history shows us' article or speech from which a fixed set of rules about how to organize now can be extracted.

C. The Power of Definitions and Icons

With this manipulative approach to history goes the power of definitions in left groups. I don't mean by this the necessary effort we all make to define and distinguish different aspects of reality. I mean the false power which avoids and actually prevents us thinking about the complexities of what is happening by covering it up in a category. All references have to be in terms of the categories. Once named, historical situations and groups of people can be shuffled and shifted into neat piles, the un-named cards are simply left out of the game. They don't exist. The named are branded 'ultra-leftist' or pensioned off as dozy but harmless 'progressive peoples'. Guilt is by association – the Stalinist use of 'social fascist' is the most notorious – but Trotskyists have their own hold over names. The game is rigged to dispose of the 'baddies'. The slots for those labelled only come in certain shapes. So criticism of particular forms of organization has to be disposed of down one slot marked 'anarchism', questioning of a particular idea of leadership goes down into 'spontaneism', some baddies are stricken with a terrible hereditary disease and called 'middle class'. They have only one chance of survival – join the something party. It all sounds absurd when it is put like this. It is an absurd activity. But nonetheless the power of naming is a real force on the left today. It deflects queries about what is going on. It makes people feel small and stupid. It is a part of the invalidation of actual experience which is an inhibiting feature of many aspects of left politics now. Part of its power is in the strange lack of self-consciousness which the left has towards its own values. The power of defining is reduced as soon as it is itself described. But the silences within the Leninist language of politics make it impossible to expose these hidden sources of power. They also make it hard to see that behind, for example, the Trotskyist approach to history, there is a personal vision. It is this vision which sustains certain concepts of consciousness, leadership, and the form which it is assumed that the struggle for socialism will take. It is a self-confirming system which is why it is peculiarly difficult to oppose within its own terms.

Individual intention is constantly overridden in practice and sustained by the organization. These choices are rarely stated, the opponent is dismissed as 'backward' or 'opportunist' or whatever or becomes caricatured as morally evil behind the phoney objectivity of 'reformist', 'centrist', etc. This is a language you learn. It is part of the training about how to organize. The words are some of the tools of the trade. The names do have a fascination when you try to see through them to the diverse realities which they encapsulate. But even this delight is a trick. It channels the imagination and keeps thought straining between closely defined points. It has the pleasurable intensity of theological disputes over doctrine. The game is to see how deviously you can stretch the finite bits of elastic. But absorption in the game makes you deaf to the experience of other people and blind to their capacity for self-activity. This vesicatory rigour intimidates opposition and actually contributes to the fears we all have in a competitive capitalist society about our incapacity to think and act.

Although the Leninist left eschews discussion of its personal values and self-image, it nonetheless carries a version of what it means to be a socialist in images and assumptions. All kinds of dusty icons lurk behind the public face. We need to bring them to the surface. Once we have them out in the open we can examine whether this really is how we want to be and whether it is likely to make most people want to become socialists. For example, what about all those comparisons to nineteenth-century armies marching in orderly formation and retreating smartly at the officer's command? Why is there such a horror of cosiness, as if cosiness were almost more dangerous than capitalism itself? Now it may well be true that at certain times we will all practise drill and that cosiness is inappropriate for some of the circumstances of conflict. But there seems to be an imbalance in the contempt it evokes.

The fear seems to be that cosiness means people get cut off from the 'real' politics. I think this should be put the other way round. If a version of socialism is insisted upon which banishes cosiness, given the attachment of most people, working-class men and women included, to having a fair degree of it around in their lives, this socialism will not attract or keep most people. Why should the ruling class have a monopoly of cosiness?

> During the strikes against General Electric (GEC) in 1974, women at Heywood, Lancashire, made themselves a picketing base by occupying an empty house owned by the firm just outside the factory, putting in carpets and cooking apparatus and even decorated the mantlepiece with flowers. They inhabited the picket.[20]

It can after all make our conditions in life and in politics more warm and loving as the early socialists recognized in their fellowship evenings.

Values are carried not only in implicit attitudes but through the dark shadowy vision of the individual revolutionary. This individual militant appears as a lonely character without ties, bereft of domestic emotions, who is hard, erect, self-contained, controlled, without the time or ability to express loving passion, who cannot pause to nurture, and for whom friendship is a diversion. If this is our version of what it means to be a socialist, it implies that we see socialism as limited to a professional elect who can muster these eccentric qualities. Membership of this elect will for a start be predominantly male, for if it attracts a minority among men, it fits even fewer women. Left to carry the burden of a higher consciousness, members of this elect will tend to see the people around them as, at worst, bad, lazy, consumed with the desire for material accumulation and sundry diversionary passions; at best, ignorant, needing to be hauled to a higher level. In the hauling the faint-hearted fall by the wayside, the cuddly retire into cosiness and all the suspicions of the elect are confirmed. Being an elect they can rely on no one and being an elect means they have to do everything. And always the weight of the burden of responsibility, the treachery and insensitivity of everyone else is bearing down on them.

It's a stark, bleak vision of sacrifice and deprivation which when stated explicitly appears to be a caricature. Nonetheless it strikes some chords of recognition on the contemporary left. It surely owes something to the strange things done to little boys in preparing them for manhood in capitalism. More particularly it presents in cameo a nostalgic and romantic yearning for the pristine clarity which is seen as 1917. How often do we need to say we are not in Russia in the early twentieth century before it becomes a felt reality? The Tsar is dead!

That the imagery and icons of Bolshevism should be particularly precious to Trotskyists is not surprising. This historical placing of self was important for lonely fighters against both Stalinism and capitalism to hold close to a lived experience of revolutionary process. They would perish in the cold wilderness without it. Within Trotskyism the desire to return to the molten heat of the early Russian revolution has all the intensity of the need for survival itself. For the Communist Party it is different. Until recently their past was so cauterized by the revelation of the horrors of Stalinism, that they became historically benumbed. But Trotskyism stalked the crimes of Stalinism acutely aware of the need to hold the strategic entrances to the past. The years of betrayal sound their knell 'In the year... and again in... and again in... Stalinism betrayed the working class and again the betrayers of the working class in...' Until in an eerie way the heroic conscience only comes to exist as the opponent of the bad man. Ironically the historical preoccupation with the failures and treacheries of Communist Party leadership echoed the Communists' own denunciation of the same aspects of social democracy.

Even the anarchists and anarcho-syndicalists have clustered round these high points where power is seen by them as becoming coercive. They have been more concerned with the corruption of the powerful – including the Communists and Trotskyists and their suppression of popular resistance. But in this critical emphasis on the leadership and on their moments of confrontation, they have nonetheless excluded most people, including most women from their version of history. The dramatic instances of conflict are extracted from their longer term context, the to-ing and fro-ing of resistance which is so evident when you focus on women's lives.

So the women's movement is contesting not simply at the level of programmes and constitutions, which is why we could never find adequate words to meet the aggressive question from men in left groups in the early days: 'Well what is it that you want?' The dispute is about an idiom of politics. (in this sense it is not only a dispute with Trotskyism.) It is about how we think about what we are doing; how we situate ourselves historically; how we see ourselves and one another in relation to the movement for change and how we see the forms in which we resist capitalist society. These open up fundamental disagreements about how you organize for socialism and what is the relationship of parties to other movements. They involve the power to define what is politics. Are left politics the preserve of professionals who hold the crucial interconnecting points? Have the rest of us merely to file under like in the game of 'oranges and lemons'?

II

A. The Problem of Democracy

If there was an ideal equal relationship between organizations and movements we should just pool our strengths and weaknesses and get on with it. Unfortunately it is not that simple. Bolshevism has a particularly long and sinister record in these matters which I think it's too easy to foist off onto Uncle Joe. More immediately the left groups have often been wrong in the last ten years or so but this seems only to make them more certain they hold the most complete understanding. This absurd paradox might begin to be cleared but for an enormous reluctance at the centre of organizations to say simply that they were wrong, that they have learned this or resisted that out of fears and misconceptions. These seem obvious enough things for human beings to say, not as a great beating of breasts and tearing of hair but as a basis for working together as equals. But it seems to me that a Leninist approach to organization (and here the name is important) is inconsistent with such equality, regardless of the intention of individual Leninists.

For although Leninist and Trotskyist groups acknowledge the need to learn from the working-class movement, I think that secretly they feel deep down they already know better? What else could distinguish the member from the 'contact'? Along with this inner assumption there is an acceptance of hierarchy within the organization itself. If members know better than non-members then the leaders know better than members and the world is felt to be an orderly place. Why else would they be leaders – mere staying power? The thought brings a rash of intolerable anxiety. Away with it – such psychologizing leads into the black holes of cynicism.

But there is democratic centralism, that wonderful device without which it would be impossible for everyone to do everything at the same time. We know the enemy all right. Here is real socialist democracy, none of your liberal nonsense. And haven't we learned from the crimes of Stalinism? Don't we allow factions even. Don't we just!

Democratic centralism was one of the issues raised in 1956 by the men and women who left the Communist Party to form the New Left. They argued that it was inherently undemocratic. Behind the versions of democratic centralism in the Trotskyist groups and the neo-Trotskyism of the SWP now is the conviction that it is a neutral form which can be adapted in a non-Stalinist context. With this goes the belief that the basic problem of making socialism is primarily the making of a leadership through the creation of an 'efficient' organization.

Richard Kuper in 'Organization and Participation' questions the separation between efficiency and democracy. He pointed out the way in which Leninist groups still tend to reduce the criteria of success to an old-style managerial concept of efficiency at the expense of democracy, long after the real managers have caught on to the 'efficiency' of limited forms of participation.

He believes that 'it is ludicrous to believe that we can reduce the goal of the party to a simple formulation about a decisive act – the conquest of state power'.

As for the 'efficiency' of democratic centralism he says that the question of the degree of centralization we might decide is necessary, depends on our assessment of the nature of the task in hand. It requires also that we have a very general kind of agreement. If that is not present 'democratic centralism' is merely a tool to quell opposition. Richard Kuper argues that when it is presented as an absolute rule the concept itself tends to provide a structure which is 'uniquely vulnerable to a certain kind of degeneration and one extraordinarily difficult to regenerate'.[21]

Whether we argue for a more generous or a more scrupulous interpretation of democratic centralism, or a more relative concept of the relationship between centralism and democracy, or whether we believe with Ralph Miliband that it '. . . has always served as a convenient device for authoritarian party structures'[22] and should be simply dumped, we have to concede that the evidence of this century indicates that it is not a 'neutral' form. There has been something very funny indeed about it in practice. This has not only been a feature of Stalinism but of the more recent experience of the Trotskyist groups in the last decade. For instance it is a curious fact that the hard core of the leaderships of these groups, despite a series of palace revolutions, manage to tuck themselves into the centre into perpetuity and that bits of broken-off leaderships resurface within the splinters. They have a permanent advantage against all incipient oppositions because they are at the hub of communication and can organize to forestall resistance quicker than people who are scattered in different branches and districts. Also they are known – and better the devil you know!

Even if it gets a bit hot at the top now and then, there is a loophole. The members – poor old things, tramping around getting sore feet on their paper sales up and down all those concrete council-flat steps, getting calloused hands lassoing elusive 'contacts' over the balconies. Well they have a tendency to get routinized. Not the leadership. It is up to the leadership to spot when this is happening and leap out towards 'the class' to knock the members into shape. Whoosh – Superman! Poor old members they look on with awe. Some get a bit grumpy. Why isn't democratic centralism binding on the leadership? Because the leaders know best. How else could they possibly be leaders? Whoosh goes Superman again, only doing his duty. How does Superman leadership know when to go whoosh towards the advanced sections of the class? Because he is leader of course. Pop go the poor members. The cosy ones fall by the wayside to seek comfort in discussion circles while the neurotic ones disappear to be cuddled in therapy groups. The intransigent form a small splinter replica. And the leaders go whoosh, whoosh all the way back to the centre.[23]

Soon they are safely ensconced again with the added authority of the patent they have out now on 'the class'. No wonder leaders of Leninist groups have staying power. They are further legitimated by the respect in Leninism due to leaders and by the assumption that just as the members know better than non-members leaders know better than opposing members. The factions can stand up democratically and be counted. They can thus be rapidly isolated. But even if the opposition is based within a campaign, a movement, a trade union or community activity, there is a strong possibility that the leaders' position will prevail. The individual member will face a split loyalty between a commitment to an autonomous group and the organization. The theory says the Party must be more important. The choice is either to get out of the organization (which seems from within to be leaving socialist politics itself), to ignore the centre (in which case democratic centralism has proved unworkable), or to accept the line. So however unsectarian this socialist may be, he or she has very stark choices and a political ideology which sanctions accepting party discipline more than helping to develop the self-activity of other people.

I am not trying to assert against this that the women's movement has found the answer about how we should organize.

Though it is certainly worth noting that the women's movement has found a means of remaining connected while growing for a decade, and that shifting and spontaneous initiatives have been taken by an extremely large number of women within the movement. But I am arguing that the form in which you choose to organize is not 'neutral', it implies certain consequences. This has been a growing recognition on the left since the late sixties. If you accept a high degree of centralization and define yourselves as professionals concentrating above everything upon the central task of seizing power, you necessarily diminish the development of the self-activity and self-confidence of most of the people involved. Because, for the women's movement, the development of this confidence and ability to be responsible for our own lives was felt to be a priority, this became part of the very act of making a movement. The enormous weight of the inner passivity which was the result of the particular nature of the subordination of the women who became involved meant that the effort to struggle, both against the personal forms of men's control and our oppression within capitalist society, became inseparable from the struggle against the ways in which these had become internalized. We had to learn to love ourselves and other women so we could trust one another without falling back on men. We inclined consequently towards small groups, circles rather than rows, centres as information and research services, open newsletters. The attempt to avoid individual women being isolated as exceptions, either as spokesperson or as freak, the need for our own movement and the feeling of sisterhood came from this understanding.

I am not suggesting that such concerns are unique to women or that such forms are biologically determined. Indeed I believe that the problem of how people can overcome the passivity, self-hatred and lack of trust which is peculiar to modern capitalism is crucial for making a socialist movement – which is not to say that recognizing this as central solves the problem of how to do it.

Basically the women's movement accepts a form of

'participatory democracy' which has a long tradition from democratic religious groups to the American New Left of the late sixties and the anti-authoritarian currents in the student movement. The problems about participatory democracy are evident. If you are not able to be present you can't participate. Whoever turns up next time can reverse the previous decision. If very few people turn up they are lumbered with the responsibility. It is a very open situation and anyone with a gift for either emotional black mail or a conviction of the need to intervene can do so without being checked by any accepted procedure. Participatory democracy only works if everyone accepts a certain give and take, a respect for one another's experience, a desire and need to remain connected. If these are present it can work very well. If they are not it can be a traumatic process. We have lived these difficulties in the history of women's movement conferences and the arguments about the Workshop Centre and Women's Day March. Despite obvious inadequacies though, 'participatory democracy' does assert the idea that everyone is responsible equally and that everyone should participate. It concedes no legitimating respect for permanent leaders or spokespeople.

It has been modified in the practice of the women's movement by women bringing in other concepts of how to organize from tenants' groups, trades councils, trade unions or from the Labour Party, the CP and from Trotskyist and Maoist groups. Sometimes these have been met with a defensive suspicion and dismissed simply as male dominated. But in cases when the women's movement has been stronger and more confident we have been able to meet these ideas and recognize the validity of some of their criticisms. The resilience of the women's movement has been partly because of this openness. In practice what we have been doing is adapting several forms of organizing to fit the particular circumstances we are engaged in. This does not remove the dangers of 'substitutionism', or centres losing contact with local groups, or small groups of people doing all the work, or people not knowing what other people are doing.

All the problems of democracy do not magically disappear. But it does make for an approach to organization which is prepared to test forms and discard or select according to the situation rather than asserting a universally correct mode. It also means that the ' movement' is perpetually outwards. As women encounter feminism they can make their own kinds of organizing depending on their needs. It is this flexibility which it is extremely important to maintain. It means that, for example, groups of women artists or groups of women setting up a creche or on the subcommittee of a trades council can decide for themselves what structure is most useful.

The women's movement shares with the 'anti-authoritarian' movements of the late sixties a commitment to a notion of democracy which does not simply recognize certain formal requirements of procedure. Obviously the danger of this is to reject completely any understanding of how these formal procedures have historically come to be used. When the dust of the first rush of enthusiasm settles it is often handy to have them. But if we simply respond to this by dismissing 'anti-authoritarian' movements as naive and just ignorant of the 'correct' political procedure, we miss an insistence which carries a deeper meaning of democracy. Faced with the opposition of women and workers in Lotta Continua, an Italian revolutionary organization, Adriano Sofri, its founder and undisputed leader, made a self-criticism. He said democracy involved not only formally contesting theories of organization which left politics to the professionals. It involved examining his own inner sense of being a professional. It meant uncovering in public his own capacity to survive and not be frightened by political opponents. He could no longer take refuge in the objectivity of the socialist theoretician. His desire for power could no longer assume a paternal legitimation in a sense of responsibility. There was a strange sense of history repeating itself. He compared the confrontation that he faced to his own opposition, with others, to the Communist Party leadership in 1968. This was 'not a conflict over political line, but a conflict over what politics was all about'.[24]

The encounter of the left groups with women's liberation, gay liberation and men's groups in Britain over the slower time scale of a decade has also been such a conflict and has assumed a particularly sharp form in relation to the political assumptions of Leninism held by Trotskyist groups.

B. Leaders and Cadres

Feminism has implicitly questioned the whole notion of the professional revolutionary who is cut off from other people and the training of revolutionaries which has been a feature of Leninism and Trotskyism. It is evident that if politics are to be the domain of professionals, most women will be excluded. The emphasis on training professionals has been particularly important in the Trotskyist groups presumably because their isolation was so extreme that for a long time they could do little else. But it was important in the early days of the CP and persists still in the upper ranks of the Communist Party. Within Leninism there is a tension between the concept of leadership as the training of political administrators or theoreticians and leadership as a process of learning the ability to act in local and immediate struggles. Both the Communist Party's general approach in Britain and IS/SWP now place greater emphasis on the creation of a leadership through practical experiences than the orthodox Trotskyist groups. But despite this organizational power still tends to accrue with the political administrators at the centre of parties who are necessarily cut off from the immediate local problems of political agitation.

There was an awareness of the problems of permanent leaders in the pre-Leninist socialist movement which seems to disappear in the 1920s or become implicit. *The Miners' Next Step* (1912), for example, listed what could be the immediate short-term advantages of leaders but pointed out how the acceptance of permanent leaders also took away from people their capacity to develop initiative and responsibility.

I think it is foolish to deny that you must train people in particular skills or that certain kinds of knowledge which we need take time to develop. We need also to recognize the value of experience in agitation in which individuals can have decisive effects and of differences rather than inequalities in our abilities to do various things. But the recognition of the whole range of capacities for leadership people can develop is not the same as training leaders.

Members of Newsreel described their approach to this in the context of a film collective:

> The problem politically... Is how to separate bourgeois notions of 'skill' and 'talent' – which are always used to divide people, to create hierarchies, to make some people feel superior or to assume more power than others – from the very real differences of skill and experience and inclination which we do have that aren't only expressive of our conditioning, but of our individual creative selves which need nourishing...

But they also said:

> ... we recognise different capacities as skills which go entirely unrecognised in the bourgeois media; the ability to relate to people, to express feelings directly; to recognise and express differences and personal needs; to take care of one another. These skills are often also unrecognised on the left.[25]

When you bring in this much wider concept of political ability the Leninist notion of training becomes absurd and even the definition of learning through agitation appears too narrow.

Opposition to individual leaders emerging in the women's movement has come from the same understanding that the rank and file trade unionists who wrote *The Miners' Next Step* in 1912 expressed as the danger of passivity. Women, having such a far-reaching struggle against the hold of men's authority have been loathe to circumscribe this within a new female hierarchy. Also women's liberation recognized from the start the impossible pressures on a woman acting as an individual. Individual women could be both absorbed as exceptions and devoured as victims. Sisterhood extends the notion of collectivity which is present in solidarity, it's not merely the public act of being together consciously, it is the personal care and love without which growth and creativity are impossible. The women's movement in recognizing it was not just what you said and did but how you said and did things which transmitted your politics, extended the scope of practice. Within this approach to politics the significance of a training for leaderships shrinks. The capacity to initiate such a myriad of transformations can be encouraged, tended, reared, nurtured, developed but not simply trained.

The problems which have arisen out of this resistance to making a movement with no clear hierarchy are well known. The danger of informal leadership structures has been much discussed in the women's movement internationally. The fraught relationship between collective sisterhood and individual self-expression has been a paralysing and sometimes agonizing experience. There is also a more personal, informal, female version of leadership through an oppressive kind of mothering which smothers rather than smashes opposition.

Despite these real difficulties, the women's movement has still created ways of organizing in which leadership has been much more widely dispersed than in left organizations. Groups of women have taken initiatives but these have varied considerably in the decade or so of our existence. Individual women have synthesized ideas but the sources of these ideas have been innumerable discussions and the shared experience of hundreds of women. These initiatives and ideas have flowed and combined in countless shapes and forms which make it impossible to locate a single leadership of the women's movement. It has meant that the women's movement has been able to grow organically in areas of life in which it is difficult for Leninist groups to 'inject' themselves into. It implies a politics in which the very process of radicalization carries the necessity of taking initiatives in many aspects of our lives, If this is not to be an impossible and soul-breaking ideal it requires the conscious creation of cultural forms and a personal vision of politics. I think the women's movement experience of this spreading and transformation of the idea of leadership is vital for the making of socialism.

C. *The Leninist Sleight of Hand*

Values, attitudes and forms of organizing are thus carried and recreated by people in the ways in which they associate. We learn not only from what is said or what we read but from our relationships with other people. This process does not mysteriously stop when we desire to associate in order to create a socialist society.

Our encounters with other people in capitalism are not free, open and equal. But there are different degrees of inequality, distance and coercion involved. These differences in degree make it possible to imagine how things might change. They force the cracks which open to illuminate the soul.

If our imagination is to be sustained by our associating, the ways we meet and co-operate and feel towards one another must develop not from our experiences of the most repressive and authoritarian encounters, but from our understandings of more loving, free ways of connecting to others and acting.

A vital feature of Lenin's concept of the Party is based on its supposed capacity to bring together, spread and transcend the limited, uneven notions and experiences of an alternative to capitalism which are present in the various sections of the working class and among the groups of people who support them. Now this is obviously a real and enormous problem. We are limited and cut off by our specific experiences of oppression and by the conflict of interests between us. The disagreement is about how this can best be overcome.

Let's pretend for a moment that there was a revolutionary party in real life which did bring together all the elements most 'advanced' or developed in their opposition to capitalist society. Why does it follow from their bringing together in this pretend ideal party that their limitations are transcended rather than partially reflected and reproduced? If there is no conscious acknowledgement of the need to create and develop political forms which seek to overcome inequalities, and release the full potentialities of all socialists, what is there to prevent power consolidating with the powerful but moral strictures? How can the real antagonisms which are the source of division between oppressed people in capitalism disappear within the Party? Isn't this assuming that the Party is an island?

If we descend from the ideal party in the sky to more earthly groups and parties, the prospect is even more gloomy. Central committees scurry like a lot of white rabbits through a series of internal and factional documents and the smaller the party the greater the hurry. In such circumstances the pressures to neglect inequalities within the organization in pursuit of the ultimate goal are great. But the theory of what a Leninist Party should be leaves hardly any space to help people participate more equally much less to develop their potential. Without any theory or structure it seems to me idealistic folly to expect 'the Party' to overcome rather than simply reflect and harness these inequalities of power which we are opposing in capitalism.

The argument used against these criticisms is always to deny that 'the Party' or 'parties' should be places where people experience anything other than the relationships which dominate capitalism. This gruesome state of affairs is presented as being necessary for the working class to take power. Though it is not the working class who are to be relied on to reach this conclusion but 'the Party', which by a process like apostolic succession inherits Lenin's words. The criticisms he made of the non-Bolshevik strands in the Russian revolutionary movement are cited as vindication. These sources of dispute were undoubtedly present in the whole process internationally of Bolshevization which brought the new Communist Parties into line with Lenin's concepts of organization. And these arguments about the nature of political organization were certainly there in conflict between the Communist Party and some members of the left of the Independent Labour Party between the wars. Ironically the original Trotskyists in Britain were perhaps closer to the left of the ILP in their criticism of the CP than Trotskyist groups would now acknowledge.[26]

This issue has involved a continuing argument between anarchists and communists. It was present in different ways in the New Left after 1956 and in the libertarian Marxism of the early 1970s. The black, gay and women's movement have been bringing the criticism more closely home, because they have raised inequalities actually within Leninist organizations. They have demanded that changes have to be made now. These changes involve examining how real life inequalities as opposed to ideal interpretations are disregarded and perpetuated within socialist parties. They have argued that it is not enough to declare that people should not be 'prejudiced'. The socialist organization has to create forms of associating and relating which actively seek to overcome the sexism and racism within it. It has become more and more difficult to dismiss these demands as 'utopian'. Not only do they involve a loss of membership, but they come up again and again.

Now the problems of relationships within the Party have been discussed by Leninist organizations in the past though not in these terms. They have been seen as particular deformities which arise and have to be dealt with as they emerge. The emphasis in the Communist Party historically has been on the relationships between workers and middle-class intellectuals (mainly men). More recently it has been a tortured and painful area in the Socialist Workers Party, because of the effort to change the class basis of this organization. Both the Communist Party and the Socialist Workers Party have relied formally upon political education and informally upon guilt to try and curb the confidence of middle-class intellectuals. Sometimes it has been used by one group of middle-class administrators against another, or by the permanent administrators against intellectuals who might challenge the central bureaucracy. It has also been used, more understandably, by working-class people as a defence against being made to feel ignorant and humiliated by the intellectuals' use of theory as a form of power against them. But whatever the reasons this negative control through the public orchestration of personal guilt has a terrible record and disastrous ramifications. It is certainly not caused by Leninism. For instance, guilt between blacks and whites, women and men, gays and heterosexuals bedevilled the American New Left in the late sixties and early seventies. Leninism serves in fact to hold the extremes of this negative response to power relations at bay. But this is not the same as providing a solution by going directly to the sources of the antagonisms producing guilt and allowing them free expression which implies trusting the imaginative capacity of human beings to enter one another's predicaments and learn from the attempt.

The inequalities between men and women within 'the Party' have not been given the same continuing scrutiny as class or race. But the whole issue of relationships of the sexes and the position of women within the Party were the subject of debate in the Soviet Union and in the International Communist Movement in the 1920s and early thirties. These were far-ranging in their implications despite the tendency to dismiss sex-gender conflicts as cultural or superstructural problems.

But the outcome of the debate around the organizational power of women's sections in Communist Parties had been partly pre-empted by the approach which had prevailed from the 1890s in the Second International towards the women's movements of the day. The oversimplified and sectarian dismissal of all autonomous forms of feminism with the insistence on the Social Democratic Party as the only place for women's agitation isolated many socialist women from the more radical currents within feminism.[27] This necessarily curtailed their capacity to question the Marxist theory of the 'woman question' or to challenge the hegemony of the male leaderships of the Social Democratic Parties. The tighter discipline of the Bolsheviks and the acceptance of democratic centralism cut off the possibility of appeal outside the parties. Under Stalin of course all forms of inner party democracy in the Soviet Union perished and with them the women's section. This had international implications.

The position of gay socialists has a much murkier record. A formal tolerance has been the best response. Homosexuality and lesbianism have either been defined as personal questions or regarded as diversionary decadence before the emergence of the recent movement for gay liberation. On this point the educators really had to be educated.

Not until the 1960s when the black question was raised by the growing militancy of American blacks and revolutionary movements in developing countries was the power relationship between autonomous movements and socialist organizations seriously contested. In the course of this confrontation the need for autonomous movements of self-definition was clearly asserted. This was to be a decisive influence on the emergence of the women's liberation movement.

We have no clear alternative of how to combine the advantages of autonomous movements with the strengths of a more general combination. But at least we must now recognize it as a problem to face. Leninism does not 'know' the answer. It merely asserts an ideal transcendence.

There remains then no effective guarantee within Leninism that the groups who are in a dominant position in capitalism won't bring their advantage into 'the Party'. Worse there is an effective sleight of hand which conceals this inherent tendency in the assertion of the ideal of the Party transcending the interests and vistas of its sections.

This does not imply that we should deny that people can become stuck in their own grievances and not see the wood for the trees. There is always the temptation to attack the people in the same boat as you, as this takes the least effort and involves the least risk. The argument is about how to overcome this. We need a form of organization which can at once allow for the open expression of conflict between different groups and develop the particular understandings which all these differences bring to socialism. For if every form of oppression has its own defensive suspicions, all the movements in resistance to humiliation and inequality also discover their own wisdoms. We require a socialist movement in which there is freedom for these differences, and nurture for these wisdoms. This means that in the making of socialism people can develop positively their own strengths and find ways of communicating to one another what we have gained, without the transcendent correctness which Leninism fosters.

The attitude towards power relations within socialist organizations has an important bearing on how such an organization will relate outwards.

Indeed opposition within the Communist Party was caught within this dilemma. Trotskyism was born in the realization of the need to combat Stalin's silencing of democratic criticism among the grass-roots of the Bolshevik Party. But Trotsky retained the assumption that the reconstituted (Trotskyist) Communist Party must be the hegemonic authority. Though both Lenin and Trotsky argued at various times that the Communist Parties must learn from workers' struggles, this was still in the terms of the director consulting the workforce. The heresy of Trotskyism, like the more conservative branches of protestantism, was limited to the claim of being the rightful church. The vital issue of democratizing the relationship between the reconstituted 'Party' and other left groupings and popular movements was not made. Though this has been a rumbling subject for concern among breakaway libertarian currents within Trotskyism it has never been resolved because Trotskyism has been confined to a minority sectarian tradition. The clash between the contemporary women's movement and the Trotskyist groups has again brought this whole issue to the surface.

III

A. Autonomy and Power

I think there is a certain tension inherent in any encounter between a group of people who are organized for a particular purpose and people who are less clearly associated. Thus a movement like women's liberation can be viewed suspiciously by groups of women involved for instance in a strike or a community project because they might fear that their needs will be used by a political organization and consumed in slogans with which they do not agree. But this distrust can be made worse or diminished depending on how it is approached. I know this is individually understood and acted upon by many members of Leninist and Trotskyist groups. But I also think that there is a general tendency within the Leninist approach to organizing which is inclined to dismiss these recognitions of their own members and an inclination to look elsewhere for 'mistakes'. So it is mysteriously someone else who is responsible for 'substitutionist' politics which deny the validity of actual struggles.

It has been an issue of great contention in the conflicts between the women's movement and left groups (particularly with the Socialist Workers Party in the National Abortion Campaign). It has been a source of considerable rancour between the left groups and a whole series of newspapers, journals and single issue campaigns in the last decade. I don't think it can be seen only as a feature of our recent experience or explained away as the peculiar aberrations of the contemporary left. I believe that the Leninist tradition, with its emphasis on the intervening role of the Party and the superior understanding of the Party has historically intensified these weaknesses in the left. A conflict has been built into the very way the Leninist Party functions, quite regardless of the individual militant's intention. This approach is like insisting on scaling a mountain up its sheer face instead of finding an alternative route and then explaining away any casualties as unfortunate accidents.

The power relationship between 'the Party' and other movements has a particularly vexed history within the Bolshevik tradition. The dire circumstances of the Soviet revolution obviously contributed to this. But I think it is too facile to say this has only been a feature of the Stalinist distortion of Leninism, which lets Trotskyism too neatly off the hook. There is certainly an instructive tension within Lenin's and Trotsky's writing in which the starting point is circumstance and both a movement towards the centralized control of the Party and awareness of the danger of substituting the Party for working-class activity are present. But in practice it has been impossible for the Communist Parties to maintain the precarious balance necessary for this dialectical transformation. Trotskyism has had a tinier practice within which it has preserved a Leninist concept of 'the Party' like a pickled onion in a jar. But jars can get left on dusty, unused shelves. Criticizing Mandel's *The Leninist Theory of Organisation*, Paul Thompson and Guy Lewis say in *The Revolution Unfinished?*: 'It never situates relations between party and class in changing conditions of struggle, but rather in absolutes of consciousness, spontaneity, the party and the like.'[28]

Granted that times have been hard but surely one of the points about a theory of organization is that it must find ways of surviving the bad times? Perhaps it's not that the Leninist theory of this relationship has not been practised or interpreted in its full complexity but that the approach itself is flawed?

The problem for feminists and men affected by feminism is that none of the various left traditions which have been critical of Leninism are concerned specifically with the significance of sex-gender relationships. So they have not worked through the implications of the need to transform these for a theory of organizing. The anarchists have certainly held a commitment in principle to connecting a critique of authority relations in the family to society and to the forms of organization for change. But as anarchist feminists have recently pointed out, the personal practice of these interrelationships of power for women have proved more complex.

Moreover, as Temma Kaplan has shown in her study of anarcho-syndicalism in Spain, within this particular strand of anarchism there has been a further tension which relates closely to the involvement of women. There was a persistent pull in the anarchist movement in the 1880s between communalist forms of resistance which implied making prefigurative forms for everyday life like utopian socialism and the emphasis upon the union (syndicate) which was restricted to workers' control over production.[29]

I think that the emphasis upon trade unionism, workers' control and the stress on work as a source of dignity rather than upon the values of a co-operative social life or upon a general concept of human creativity was becoming more marked in anarcho-syndicalism in the early years of this century. The preoccupation with direct action focused on work and the general strike of wage-earners was the main revolutionary tactic. The relations of production were certainly the central issue for both those left groupings in social democracy which were later to develop theories of Council Communism and the Workers' Opposition in the Bolshevik Party. They believed that a general release of self activity would follow from strengthening workers' control over production. This meant that factory councils were seen not only as a necessary defence but as a prefiguration of future relationships. So they did not equate workers' consciousness and power with the central authority of the Bolshevik Party. On the other hand the shift to the organization of production made this area assume a priority which had not been present in libertarian forms of Marxism like the Socialist League in Britain in the 1880s or the Anarchist-Communism of Emma Goldman in America.[30]

It was as if the actual development and consolidation of capitalist society actually wrenched apart and shattered earlier visions of the transformation of life itself. For though there are interesting historical connections between these dissident traditions of the early twentieth century and socialist women – for example Elizabeth Gurley Flynn, who worked with the American anarcho-syndicalists the 'Wobblies',[31] Sylvia Pankhurst, who Lenin berated for 'infantile leftism', and Alexandra Kollontai, who was part of the 'Workers' Opposition' – the theoretical integration of socialism and feminism remained barely developed. Kollontai especially made a valiant and remarkable effort in opposing the deterministic emphasis in contemporary Marxism upon objective scientific laws of change and also in realizing the need to develop the idea of workers creating a new culture beyond work into every aspect of social and political life. She saw communal housing, sexual unions in which women retained an autonomous identity, co-operative nurseries, as forms through which people could begin to experience truly democratic communist relationships. But not only was she in a minority in this emphasis in the Bolshevik leadership, she did not clearly question the sexual division of work between men and women. The implications of this for a challenge to all kinds of hierarchy and coercion which has been so important in the politics of the women's movement in the last decade were crucial absences in her thought. She struggled, just as we have struggled, for a language to describe the sexual and personal forms of men's control over women. She stumbled towards trying to connect these to the need to release all human beings' 'potential for loving'.[32] She glimpsed the extraordinary transformation of consciousness which this would require and the consequent need for multiple cultural transitional forms. She also noted that the oppressive atmosphere which was beginning to stifle debate in the Bolshevik Party was bound up with personal political behaviour. It was transmitted and sustained through apparently trivial incidents and encounters. She wrote in the document *The Workers' Opposition* for the 1921 Congress, 'If only comrades would cease to consider it necessary to jump heavily on anyone who says anything that is at all new, would cool their "polemical" ardour somewhat, and stop building every molehill into a "deviation" or "principled difference".'[33]

The contemporary women's movement has begun to uncover the pattern of similar tiny moments of constraint in resisting women's subordination. But Kollontai's remarkable if fragmented vision flickered into darkness as the Bolshevik revolution was tragically overwhelmed by its enormous internal problems and its isolation in a hostile capitalist world.

Certain historical connections also existed between this

syndicalist influenced left and those socialist feminists who argued for women's control over their sexuality and fertility before the First World War. Margaret Sanger, who was influenced by the American Left Syndicalists, the Wobblies, as well as the anarchist-communist Emma Goldman, argued for birth control in the same terms as workers' control. Similar arguments were later used by Stella Browne in Britain. They have also appeared again among socialist feminists now.[34] The problem is that this sets up as significant two poles of struggle, production (economic) and reproduction (biological) which become the keys to workers' and women's emancipation. This misses out the ways in which these are inseparable from political, legal, cultural and ideological forms of struggle. It creates again a primacy of particular spheres of activity and it assumes that workers are all men and that men have no relationship to reproduction. It makes it possible to see the inadequacies of a simple base-superstructure model. But it is difficult within the terms of this polarized connection of workers' control and feminism to present a different view of how we come to consciousness.

Anarcho-syndicalists and left-wing communist tendencies were inclined to be more dismissive of attempts to change laws in capitalist society than both social democrats and Leninists. Indeed this was the source of Lenin's irritation with what he called 'infantile leftism'. This meant that within the parties of the Second International the 'right wingers' were sometimes more sympathetic to working with autonomous feminist organizations for the suffrage than the lefts. So precisely those anarchist and left socialist women who were prepared to argue for workers' self-determination or woman's control over her body tended to become isolated in practice from the more radical currents within feminism.[35] This made it even harder to transcend the detachment of the relations of production from a critique of social relationships as a whole.

As an undercurrent alternative to Leninism ideas of workers' control have had a strong influence on the left in Britain.

When the Communist Party was formed, syndicalism and the decentralized approach of the Guild Socialists were significant influences. In the 1920s and thirties there were various kinds of rank and file movements. Since 1956 there have been a series of reassessments on the left of the ideas of workers' control which have contributed towards the formation of the Institute of Workers' Control, the emphasis placed by the International Socialists on linking to shop stewards and on rank and file movements, and Big Flame's analysis of the changing role of shop stewards. After May 1968 in Germany, Italy and France there was also a great revival of interest in non-Leninist traditions on the left. This undercurrent of syndicalist-influenced leftism with its stress on grass-roots struggle against bureaucracy has coincided with the growth of the women's movement, indeed they have certain things in common. Both emphasize autonomy against the central control of the Party (or parties) and self-activity against a leadership. Both are asserting the need to make some changes now. There are obvious parallels with the period before the First World War.

But again feminists have often found themselves at odds with the stress on workers' control. For it obviously excludes women working in the family just as it excludes other groups who are not on the cash nexus, children or old people for example. It also tends to disregard areas of life which are crucial in women's lives, around welfare legislation for instance, or around personal and sexual relationships. It does not illuminate the interconnection between different forms of power which men's groups, the gay movement and women's liberation have begun to discover. It leaves us with a very limited understanding of how we come to be critical of our situation in the world. By focusing on class struggle at work other aspects of power relationships become of secondary importance. There is also a tendency to see workers possessing a true consciousness intact underneath the encrustment of treacherous leaders and the beguilements of the leaders. (This can be transplanted to women.) Once the crust is cut off the true consciousness becomes apparent. This implies that the people cutting the crust off are somehow not part of the problem.

Feminists have pointed out that not only does the emphasis on work exclude women but that the whole approach is presented in terms of the male workers' situation and that the attempt to argue for women's liberation in terms of a syndicalist stress on production sets up a split between the 'real' world of economics and the 'unreal' sphere of consciousness. The latter is always secondary. Even the modification which argues for women's control of her body along with workers' control only attaches a 'biological' material struggle to the economic.

Many feminists in rejecting the inadequacies of the syndicalist approach have sought an answer in an assertion of an orthodox Leninism or accepted Leninism with various additions, particularly Gramsci's concept of hegemony and Althusser's notion of the relative autonomy of the superstructure.

Several practical implications follow from this. It appears that a solution to the questions raised by the women's movement about the role of the Party and about consciousness already almost exists. We need simply a more sophisticated version of Lenin which we can find, it is argued, in more orthodox Trotskyism, in the Communist Party, or, vaguely, in an imaginary 'Party'. The stress on self-activity shared by the new left, by libertarianism, and by the syndicalist influences upon IS/SWP, as well as the women's movement, is obscured again. The emphasis on our personal involvement in making ideas and understanding movements fades in the face of 'a science'. This means we cannot become self-critical about our own partialities. We are no longer open to the wider movement of society which might make us discard our theories and rediscover a new means of abstracting upon our reality. 'Theory' is once again asserted as 'above' experience rather than as an integral part of it. If the notion of a true consciousness beneath the crust is avoided, it is at the expense of a picture of human beings, who are merely the sum of the functions they perform for capital or 'patriarchy'. Hopelessly entrammelled in capitalist and/or patriarchal ideology we are helpless again before the ascendent sometimes even imaginary 'Party' and the 'Theory' it has tucked safely away in some inaccessible and lofty pinnacle.

The variations on this approach do not reveal, much less solve, the actual problems of power, they merely lead us back to the Party as the 'answer'. The understanding of the inadequacies within the syndicalist opposition to the central authority of the Party is accurate. But the elaborate evasion presented as an answer defuses the implications of the women's movement on the left groups.

This is perhaps one of the reasons that feminists within the International Marxist Group and the Communist Party have had much greater scope for manoeuvre than women within the Socialist Workers Party. But the conflict has been postponed, not removed.

Eurocommunism has opened up the issue of autonomy in a different context from the classic stress on the Party in Leninism. Its supporters stress the need to make alliances rather than the vanguard role of the Party. This expresses actual changes in practice of which the British Road to Socialism was a part. It involves a different approach to the transition to socialism.[36] This means that many feminists in Britain regard their membership of the Communist Party and the women's movement as less contradictory than belonging to either Trotskyist groups, who believe (with tact or without it) that they should play a vanguard role, or to the Socialist Workers Party, whose version of the vanguard amounts to themselves plus a well-screened working class in struggle. I think the radical importance of Eurocommunism is that it opens up the possibility of rethinking together a strategy for socialism in advanced capitalism which includes members of the Communist Party. But I don't think feminism can be grafted onto it. There seems to be little explicit recognition within Eurocommunism, either of the nature of sex-gender relations or of the need to challenge the forms of relationships within the Party as a central part of the process towards the transition to socialism.[37] The view of how such a transition will occur does not involve a real transformation of the institutions of power relations. As an alternative to Lenin's strategy of conquering them, Eurocommunism aspires to move in and inhabit them. The practice of politics seems to move even closer to the bourgeois parties in accepting the existing terms of power within capitalism. True, there is the promise of a more equal relationship between the Party and autonomous movements. But what are the guarantees for us non-Party masses? What if the Party line changed in the course of the transition to the transition? As the saying goes, 'the proof of the pudding will be in the eating'. But we would look well to be extremely wary as we munch. The leadership of Communist Parties are tough, well-seasoned cooks who do not give much spare change away in the pud. It seems unlikely that they would concede to an autonomous women's movement the power they have withheld from several generations of workers.

However it is over simple to assume that the ascendency of 'the Party' and the view of consciousness which this involves are simply imposed by the leaderships. This would imply that if feminist women gained the leaderships the problem would be solved. In fact personal ways of seeing, assumptions about organizing and political attitudes are part of the culture which people make within political organizations. Feminists within left groups and parties have thus been engaged not only in an argument about the policy of leaderships, about what is said in programmes or even what is done, but how things are done.

For example it is interesting that IS/SWP should have had the most stormy relationship with the women's movement because in certain ways IS/SWP was itself critical of how things were done in the Communist Party and the Trotskyist groups. They were opposed not only to the manipulation of announcing popular fronts or rank and file movements, which you made sure you then controlled, they were suspicious of paid professional trade union officials and critical of sham 'labour movement' shells which failed to express spontaneous movements. They also believed that intellectuals should have no special privileges. Indeed quite the reverse – they should do more of the donkey work as their jobs were easier. There could not be separate spheres for intellectuals and workers. Thus the fact that they denied that the Soviet Union was a socialist or even a workers' state gone sour was based on the relations of production. And this difference led implicitly to the possibility of holding other assumptions about relations within our own socialist movement. These involved the self-image of being above sectarianism.

But these assumptions stopped short at certain points and the women's movement was one of them. Conflict was more immediately in the open because there was no internal organizational means of holding the movement at bay.

In the case of the International Marxist Group, it was possible to draw on Leninist ideas, while the Communist Party had a historical practice which included considerable experience in keeping uppity movements in their place. This allowed feminist women a little more space to argue. But it did not mean that the organization saw itself being transformed by the women's movement. It was clear (to both the IMO and the CP) that sectional movements do not hold general briefs on how to organize. So the argument has tended to be more within the organizations in which feminist women have demanded a different, more democratic relation to an autonomous movement. They have argued the need for the left groups to learn from the women's movement.[38] This has both contributed towards and been strengthened by a genuine concern among the membership, particularly in the Communist Party, not to repeat the disastrous record of the past. However it has not seriously rattled the leaderships into changing their concepts of a socialist organization and questioning their own roles within it. Nor has the influence of the women's movement on the left extended into a critique of all the areas of inner personal and political practice which are part of the cultural life of organizations.

Oddly enough, the whole issue has loomed a bit closer since most of the left became rather ominously polite to the women's movement. Now I know that after all these years we should resist the temptation to a wry 'that we should be so lucky'. I mean, I know it's an 'advance' even though it feels like so many years. But I don't think we should be satisfied. We don't want a limiting kind of acceptance which would be a new keeping us in our place, do we?

It would be ironic, wouldn't it? The autonomy of the women's movement and gays might be recognized, the right to have gay and women's caucuses on everything granted, the specifics of sexual politics could be allowed more regular space in left papers. But the ideas of what socialism is and the relationship to these ideas would remain the same.

Bob Cant noted this in his talk for the conference of ex-IS members:

They have failed to understand that sexual politics is not just about sexual practice but is also intermeshed with questions of power, ideology and culture.[39]

This failure, which is not of course peculiar to IS/SWP, seems to me a refusal to learn openly from the last decade. It means that dogmatism has found a reasonable face because the pressures from feminists, gay people and men affected by feminism have become impossible to ignore. It is harder to explain such suspicions. It seems to many people, even those profoundly affected by sexual politics, that you are never satisfied. The discontented are left muttering and cantankerous. But this is not perversity, because the disagreements are about the power relationships within the movement for change. They do not only involve the acceptance of sexual politics. They require a different kind of socialism.

Fernando Claudin in his book on Eurocommunism pointed to the tendency in the Communist Party and other left parties:

> to regard overall political action as a private reserve and to try and restrict other organisations – the trade unions, organs of grass roots democracy, the women's movement etc. – each to their own 'specific problems', preventing them from taking initiatives in relation to major general questions.[40]

B. Vanguards and Consciousness

It is not difficult to demonstrate that Lenin's notion of the vanguard was not devised to give comfort to bossy socialists but to illuminate the strengths and weaknesses of the forces of resistance to capitalism. In theory, it provided a means of channelling for the greatest effect all the elements in struggle, not only the economic conflict of workers against employers but all the experience of social and cultural struggles. The idea was to bring the strengths of the most 'advanced' to the assistance of the less developed through the Party.

According to one current version of this Leninist intention, 'advanced' consciousness by definition finds its way into 'the Party'. This internal definition of the vanguard tends to be a characteristic of Trotskyism. It becomes a tautology. The 'Party' is the expression of advanced consciousness therefore advanced consciousness is to be found in the Party. The circle is unbroken by reference to actual circumstances and it is difficult to break once the Trotskyist group has announced its coming out as the 'Party'. Though under pressure individual members in more open groups like the IMG will concede in broadminded moments that owing to the imperfect confusion of the times some bits of advanced consciousness may go astray and lurk temporarily in movements, before mouldering into centrism, or even find a berth through some gross misunderstanding among the rank and tile of the Communist Party. But the force of their thinking is still towards vanguardism assuming primacy.

In the attempt to break with this narrow and internal idea of the vanguard various attempts have been made to locate the vanguard in struggles outside the Party. This was an argument internationally within Trotskyism after the Second World War. On the Italian left after 1968 some socialists argued that the workers in struggle are the vanguard rather than the Party. In America by the early 1970s the vanguard was up for grabs. Everyone claimed to be the vanguard – blacks, women, gays. In fact they all fell out with one another over this.

This notion of the vanguard assumed it applied to either

the most oppressed or the most foolhardy and illustrates the problem in defining the vanguard in terms of whoever is struggling.

In Britain the Socialist Workers Party has evolved its own peculiar combination of these. There seems to me to have always been considerable tension within the theory of IS/SWP between the feeling that the membership are the most advanced elements – else what are they doing joining? – and the conviction that the working-class in economic struggle is the vanguard. This tension partly comes from the awareness both of the dangers of self-appointed vanguards and out of an understanding that the act of struggle in itself is not automatically going to be for socialism, or even for the working class as a whole. In practice though this IS/SWP notion of class struggle has tended to be narrower than that of either the US libertarian Trotskyists or the Italian socialists who stressed a wider concept which involved more aspects of everyday life.

Criticisms of the Leninist idea of the 'vanguard' have tended to assume that the attempt to assess consciousness itself was at fault. I think this needs shifting into a different area of dispute. The argument is really about who has the power to define how the estimation is made and the acknowledgement that none of us are the embodiment of the pure abstract reason of correct ideas. Our estimation will be affected by our own circumstances. Another source of confusion in any discussion of the Leninist concept of the vanguard is that there are several interpretations current on the left at present, quite apart from the cruder forms of practice which are based on a 'we knows you know' attitude rather than Leninism.

So in reaction against Leninism there was a tendency in both the American New Left and among British libertarians to dismiss the very attempt to assess consciousness as inherently elitist. Less clearly this dismissal of the problem has been present in the women's movement.

The trouble is that if you disregard all attempts to work out who is likely to stick their neck out in particular circumstances and who can sustain attack in particular places you are left wide open. Without any historical and social estimation of different kinds of consciousness you are left with only static categories of the oppressed. You have no means of deciding how various sections are likely to respond to change. As your oppressed constituency is both enormous and inert and as there is no difference between the oppressed category and conscious politics there is nothing to stop you acting on their behalf. There is not even the awareness that is present within Leninism of the dangers of 'substitutionism'. Here a sleight of hand appears in an over-generalized concept of a static condition of oppression. A politics of example by self-appointed small groups has often been the undemocratic consequence of a critique of differentiation as elitist. This has bedevilled anarchism historically and was a paralysing feature of libertarian Marxism in the early 1970s. It has been a rumbling source of confusion in the women's movement.

Instead of examining the actual social composition of our movement and the forces and experiences which have radicalized certain groups of women, the feminism of the women's liberation movement can be presented as the consciousness of women in general. This makes it impossible to begin to work out the relationship of the movement to women not already involved. Their absence is in fact being dismissed and explained away. They need simply to be reached and enlightened by the propaganda of the movement. Any opposition they might make is because they have been hopelessly brainwashed by men. Under a 'false' non-feminist consciousness sits a 'true' natural feminism in every woman. Feminists just need to plumb the depths of this well of common sense to reach what every woman knows. It is true that every woman knows but we happen to know somewhat differently depending on our circumstances and the openings created by the process of change. We need to examine what is specific as well as what is shared by women in differing situations. If circumstance and consciousness are concertina-ed we fold an abstract category 'Woman' into a particular historical movement which has emerged out of changes in the lives of some women.

Thus if we are to distinguish the various ways in which women approach their situation we need to understand the different nature of the power relationships which enmesh us. This means that we do not present relations in the family simply as the equivalent of relations on the cash nexus, or assume that the condition of a sex is the same as class relations. It also means we need to assess very carefully changes in class composition and their impact on women's consciousness.

Some socialist feminists in America have been drawn to analyses of class in which professional, service, administrative and communications workers are equated with the working class. This recognizes the emergency of new kinds of work closely connected to the welfare of people and the communication of values which have become crucial areas in modern capitalism. It also focuses on the radicalization of men and women in these jobs. But it makes it difficult to understand the specific ways in which changes in class composition have affected various groups differently. In Britain the emotive force of class has led to similar elliptics in practice. For example the IS Rank and File groups and Working Women's Charter tended to emphasize the similarity between white collar trade unionists and manual and lower-grade service workers. They were all trade unionists. This was important to assert against the traditional suspicion in the trade union movement of white collar workers and the dismissal on the left of women. But this meant that other important power relationships were dismissed. These were in fact vital to an understanding of consciousness which could avoid fatalism, a notion of an intact true consciousness or an external vanguard bringing understanding. The 'Red Collective' pointed out in a criticism of the Charter in 1974 that the simple assertion of a common trade unionism denied '... the experiences that brought these women into women's liberation, and the difficulties they must meet in their jobs as "handlers" of people which ought to make them aware of other divisions, based on a hierarchical division of labour'.[41]

While resistance to 'handling' was certainly part of the personal experience of women in local Charter groups and also in the rank and file of 'Rank and File', it was not accepted as part of the theory of organization and consciousness of the IMG and IS who had hegemonic positions in these groupings. So individual understandings were passed over as by the way. But in fact the women's movement and the whole process of radicalization among people in these jobs were providing vital clues to the puzzle of how to oppose modern capitalism and how to go about a more complex assessment of consciousness.[42]

The women's movement has broken the circle in the concept of a vanguard Party by questioning the criteria used in assessing the meaning of 'advanced' and 'backward' and arguing that this assessment is not a neutral and objective process but a matter of subjective interest. This argument in Britain has meant a particularly acute confrontation with the SWP because their definition of class struggle has emphasized production and until recently dismissed serious consideration of feminism by concentrating on women as workers or the wives of workers. Although there was never complete acceptance of these priorities it was more difficult for those IS women, who accepted the basic terms of reference of their organization, to contest them than for women in the IMG or the CP.

The dispute between women's liberation and the IS/SWP came to be polarized as economic versus personal struggles. Even though many women in IS/SWP pointed out that women workers or the wives of strikers might also be people who were overwhelmed and lonely in the home, struggling to assert themselves in sexual relationships, troubled by how to relate to their children, these dilemmas remained by-the-way. Similarly the development of a wide range of campaigns within an increasingly activist women's movement in the mid-seventies did not crack this polarization. It was sustained by the self-image of IS/SWP as the people who were really doing something. It has made for a particularly fraught encounter between feminism and the organization which potentially held a more open concept of the vanguard role of the party.

Women in IMG and the CP could invoke the need to regard the vanguard as encompassing the broad movement of what Marxists call 'layers'. Women could be accommodated then as a significant layer and even allowed a few of their own peculiarities because of the effect on them of a floating monster called 'ideology'. Within the Communist Party a strong sense of past crimes with a tendency for a low-key approach to the vanguard Party gave feminists considerable scope.

So the same polarization has not occurred with either the Communist Party or the International Marxist Group. But nonetheless suspicion still festers between them and the women's movement and the full challenge of feminism is muffled rather than resolved.

The women's movement's criticisms of the ways in which the Leninist left assess activity and the manner in which consciousness changes have come not from a completed theory of organization but from the experience of a particular group of women's lives. The wide-ranging areas of women's oppression, the complexity of the subordinated relationship with men, and the deep personal hold of women's sense of secondariness have combined with significant changes in class composition and social relations.

It is not enough for left groups to simply widen the range of subjects which can be discussed in their publications or meetings – the crucial question is what significance is given to these subjects and how is that estimate reached? If a political or economic scale is used the same judgements of advanced and backward forms of consciousness can be retained with a few sexual political frills. But if you take into account other kinds of struggle like resistance to the domestic control of the state which has been part of a wide range of community politics or the emotional personal challenge to sexual domination, the old scale of measuring consciousness becomes ungainly because you are moving in several dimensions at the same time. People can be so backward and so forward at the same time that the scale won't work anymore. There is no way of marking consciousness off on a straight line to assess it in this clear and simple way.

Of course Leninism recognizes that consciousness is uneven. But this still assumes that it can reach one level. The notion of the vanguard suggests a tough poky thing moving in the same direction at the same time. The approach to consciousness in the women's movement has uncovered many aspects of experience neglected by socialist politics but it also has the awareness that formal theoretical or practical public abilities are not the only important areas of growth. Our personal relationships with our families and friends, how we connect to other women in the movement and our inner spiritual and sexual life are never separate from our feminism, indeed as we resist subordination most strenuously in one area it has a way of creeping up on us from some completely different direction. The feminist approach to consciousness perceives its growth as many-faceted and contradictory. The model of the vanguard doesn't fit into this way of thinking. It's not even like trying to put a square peg into a round hole, it's like dropping it down a well. The criteria used for 'advanced' and 'backward' elements can no more be applied to this more complex view of political consciousness than a spirit-level can be used for assessing an electrical current. This does not mean that we should abandon the attempt to estimate the consequences of different forms of consciousness at various times. But it means we need a much more delicate kind of socialist theory to gauge them. The Leninist approach simply blots out immense but fragile processes of transformation.

Left organizations, particularly since the Bolsheviks, have assumed a kind of pyramid of levels of activity. Near the top are struggles for political power and conflict at the workplace. Community struggles follow, traditionally seen mainly as the housing question and tenants' movements. After them education, welfare and cultural issues may be considered with an optional cluster of sexual politics, ecology and what not under a rather dusty heading of 'quality of life'.

Feminists have criticized these levels, arguing particularly against the over-emphasis on wage work, which excludes many women. (In Britain this argument has been mainly with the SWP but it has arisen with other left groups as well.)

The problem can't be solved by recognizing demands for a changing quality of life and just widening the areas of activity. Both the IMG and SWP for example are quite prepared to do this. We also need to challenge the notion of consciousness which is behind this approach to activity. For consciousness is also being chopped up into categories of significance. The women's movement has enabled us to understand that such divisions do not reach the roots of oppression. Presenting consciousness in the compartments of political, economic, cultural, social, personal, makes it impossible to begin to see how the different forms feed and sustain one another. Feminism has shown how consciousness spills over these boundaries. I don't think this need imply that particular groups of socialists should not make certain forms of activity a priority given resources of time, energy and skill, and the forces of opposition. For example it would be evidently absurd to expect that the possibilities present for women in a democratic capitalist society would be the same as the narrower options for resistance under fascism. It is not an absolute moral principle which is involved but the power to challenge the criteria in which priorities are decided.

IV

A. Where Does Consciousness Come From?

Lenin argues in *What is to be Done?* (1902) that the working class, bogged down in their day-to-day economic struggle and without culture (in the sense of education and knowledge) could not understand and act upon the interconnection between their exploitation at work and the political form which secures this, the state. So he maintained that,

> Class political consciousness can be brought to the workers only from without, that is, only from outside the economic

struggle, from outside the sphere of relations between workers and employers.[43]

The Party, as vanguard, is presented as the means of combining the revolutionary potential of the working class and the scientific knowledge necessary to plan revolution, which is to be brought into the Party by the intellectuals.

Carmen Claudin-Urondo sums this up in her book *Lenin and the Cultural Revolution.*

> This vanguard, the Party, thus realises, in the persons of its 'professional revolutionaries', its 'full-timers' in the service of the revolution, the symbiosis of social being of the proletariat and its consciousness, and embodies the reconciled identity of the historical class and the class as a concrete reality.[44]

Lenin was arguing against a reliance on the working class becoming spontaneously revolutionary in the context of a period of Tsarist repression and he was to shift the emphasis between party and class later. Indeed the Bolsheviks had great difficulty in even keeping up with the working class in the making of the revolution. But he did not fundamentally reformulate the theory of consciousness present in *What is to be Done?* This theory is an essential part of the case for a Leninist Party. The polarization is presented as being between the conscious knowledge of the Party and the 'instinctive urge' or the 'elementary instinct' of the workers in movement.[45] This may change the immediate course of action chosen by the Party but it still cannot (within the terms of Leninism) fundamentally transform the nature of the revolutionary organization itself.

The issue of the ascendency of the Party and conflict between the Party and autonomous movements of workers and of women had arisen within the Second International. The conflict itself was not created by Lenin. However, Lenin's emphatic assertion of central direction over self-activity and self-direction gave the concept of the monolithic Party a much greater authority because the Bolsheviks had led a successful revolution. Fernando Claudin in *The Communist Movement* traces how this emphasis was put into effect internationally and how it was to harden under Stalin.

The claim that the Party 'knows best' persists even when it is said that the Party (or parties) must learn from autonomous movements. There is still the belief that it is the Party, itself, which will decide what it wants to learn. The Party is presented as soaring above all sectional concerns without providing any guarantees that this soaring will not be in fact an expression of the particular preoccupations of the group or groups with power within it. It is claimed that the Party is separate from the relations within capitalist society merely by being the revolutionary Party. Yet it is also claimed that any attempt to change relations within the Party is utopian. So how do they become separate and distinct? Or what makes Leninists different from other people? Within Leninist terms it is a closed debate. Leninists are different because they are members of the revolutionary Party. The Party is ascendent because it holds the correct scientific understanding. (Other Leninist parties are not ascendent because they are only pretending to have the correct ideas. They will be found out in time.) Now correct ideas can certainly be tested in practice to make sure that they are correct and may need a few hasty adjustments en route to the conquest of state power. But they are basically there (but only in the revolutionary Party).

So where did they come from in the first place? Lenin and the Bolsheviks? They must have got them from their own lives and times. So personal and historical factors creep into scientific understanding. What else creeps in? Kautsky, the German social democrat hovers in this dawn of revolutionary science.

For, like Kautsky, Lenin saw socialist consciousness as essentially the knowledge of certain theoretical truths with which the Party educates and trains its members. Although the test of this knowledge/consciousness is the experience of agitation and class struggle it cannot be derived from experience. The notion of agitation is also narrow in scope. It does not touch inner subjective forms of consciousness.

When it comes to the personal hold of ideas, Lenin and Trotsky recognized there was a problem but presumed emotional responses will change after socialism.

There was disagreement among the Bolsheviks about the need to make explicit the creation of new forms of organizing to meet the problem but these took place after the revolution. They were not seen as part of the transition to socialism.

For Lenin the lessons of consciousness through struggle remain generally subordinate to the leadership of the Party. Here he broke with Marx's view of consciousness and adopted the position of the German social-democrat Kautsky who argued that socialism and class struggle arose side by side. He went on from this historical observation upon the circumstances of the late nineteenth century to announce this as a 'law' of Marxist organization, which Lenin accepts. According to Kautsky: 'Modern socialist consciousness can arise only on the basis of profound scientific knowledge.' He goes on to say it was the bourgeois intelligentsia who possessed this knowledge/consciousness, not the working class.

> Thus socialist consciousness is something introduced into the proletarian class struggle from without and not something that arose within it spontaneously. . . The task of Social-Democracy is to imbue the proletariat [literally saturate the proletariat] with the consciousness of its position and the consciousness of its task.[46]

But where then does this consciousness of the bourgeois intelligentsia who join the Party come from? It is in fact a circular argument. Their consciousness comes from knowledge. So the consciousness of the intellectuals comes not from their lives and relationships like other people but from the pure development of Thought. By possessing these intellectuals (suitably tamed to make sure the development of Thought does not go against the interests of the working class, as defined by the Party), the Party possesses Thought. The working class cannot become the revolutionary class without this superior knowledge which the Party possesses. Crudely then the Party has to nab the intellectuals, discipline them and guard the working class from any contenders who might mislead them with incorrect thoughts (variously defined at different times as bourgeois feminism, syndicalism, anarchism, Trotskyism, centrism, etc.).

Carmen Claudin Urondo points out in *Lenin and the Cultural Revolution* that this 'makes class consciousness dependent necessarily on socialist theory and the latter a pure product of culture'.[47]

Culture is defined here in its narrow sense of high culture. This means that organizational forms workers create only have a revolutionary validity when they are under the authority of the Party. Anarcho-syndicalist arguments contested this. But they do not raise the question of the relationship of the Party to other autonomous movements which arise, for example, among black people, women, and gay people. The emergence of these movements has called into question the whole relationship of the Party and autonomous movements and with this the view of how consciousness is formed. Equally the experience of Stalinism has made thinkers and historians within the new left tradition re-examine the differences between Marx's view of consciousness and Lenin's theory. It was no longer possible to simply equate the consciousness of workers with the revolutionary political organization.

Fernando Claudin, for example in *The Communist Movement* points out that Lenin was forced to quote Kautsky because he was breaking so decisively from Marx.[48] Marx had not argued that consciousness and knowledge could be equated in this way as if socialist thought was the sole source of wisdom. He believed that we make our consciousness in the process of making ourselves and changing the world, within the limits of the particular historical circumstances in which we find ourselves. A dogmatic adherence to Leninism has effectively blinkered many socialists not only to Marx's views but to unfolding contemporary understandings. E.P. Thompson shows in *The Poverty of Theory* that Marx's view of consciousness has since been developed in relation to particular historical contexts and within non-capitalist societies. Thus historians and anthropologists working in the Marxist tradition,

> ... have insisted that ideas, norms and rules be replaced *within* the mode of production, without which it could not be carried on for a day; and on the other side by cultural materialists who have insisted that the notion of a 'superstructure' was never materialist enough.[49]

This exposes the model of a tidy trade union consciousness arising from the economic struggle as both mechanical and unreal. It simply does not fit our understanding of reality. For in the last decade the process of both women's and men's involvement in trade unions had not been simply a response to conditions at work but part of a wider process of radicalization. It also makes nonsense of the view that socialist theoretical consciousness is derived purely from an objective scientific knowledge. The people doing the deriving, however intellectual they might be, are still people expressing in various ways their understanding of the world in which they find themselves. In Leninism thought comes from thought which means there is no room to qualify certainties with the historical experience which might reveal how actual people arrived at Leninist ideas or might lead them to seek alternatives. By disguising the process which went into the creation of ideas they are protected by a timeless inviolability. The clear separation of the Leninist Party from everyday consciousness can be artificially secured and the Leninist concept of the Party can thus hold out the trump card of being the only means by which the particular experiences of exploitation and oppression can become generalized. But the trump card is part of a neat confidence trick. Again we can question this with reference to the process through which many people have become radical in the last few years. In the case of the women's movement, for example, many women have become involved in socialism through feminism without, indeed often despite, the intervention of parties. Equally many socialist women have come to shed the assumption that they already had the answer by the questions raised by feminism and the experience of being in a movement which is continually pressing against and dissolving removed ideas which pretend they do not have people inside them or behind them.

E.P. Thompson also argues that there is a missing dimension. Marx neglected the particular ways in which we not only handle our experience through our consciousness but through our 'culture'. Culture is being used here in the broad sense in which intellectual culture combines with 'a vocabulary of norms, values, obligations, expectations, taboos, etc.'[50]

There is thus not a simple opposition between the theoretical knowledge which is the monopoly of the Party and an undeveloped instinct for rebellion among workers (or other subordinated groups). There is another significant aspect of people's consciousness.

> They also experience their own experience as feeling and they handle their feelings within their culture, as norms, familial and kinship obligations and reciprocity, as values or (through more elaborated forms) within art or religious beliefs. This half of culture (and it is a full one-half) may be described as affective and moral consciousness.[51]

This restores real men and women, the relationships in which they find themselves, and their efforts to change these and their feelings about their situation, themselves and other people. It connects theoretically to movements which have been concerned to change feelings and desires, gay liberation, feminism and the black movement.

The implication of these views of consciousness is to dislodge the superior relationship of the Party to the movements of the working class and to other radical autonomous movements. They also break down the separation between movements and the monolithic concept of 'the Party'. It becomes impossible to regard 'the Party' or socialist organization as a kind of red zone from which professional revolutionaries sally forth with a superior knowledge untouched by culture themselves to insert, inject, imbue or saturate and drown other movements. Even Gramsci's version of this relationship which stressed the need for working-class intellectuals within the Party and the existence of forms of leadership within 'spontaneous' movements is also being contested. For he still assumed that these leaders within spontaneity were necessarily confined within the dominant assumptions about the world. Without the Party, and hence theory, they could not transcend 'common sense'. But the women's movement, gay liberation or the cultural self-definition present in movements of racially subordinated groups have required that changes in feeling and desire become part of the movement of resistance. They have been assailing those elements within the 'common sense' of society which deny and oppress them. This process of transforming what is taken for granted has come from the interior. 'The person', to echo Bea Campbell again, has become a 'political problem' – including persons within the revolutionary parties. The 'lived relation of subordination' is to be contested wherever it is to be found.

B. How Does Consciousness Change?

How then do people come to see the possibility of socialism? How do we conceive and imagine a completely different society, involving not only change in the external structures but an inner transformation of our consciousness and our feelings? How do we begin to connect our own experience to other people's? There is no clear simple 'theory' of how such changes might take place. There is no straightforward, complete alternative to Leninism as an organizing idea and as a historical practice. But it is possible to open up certain entrances which people have made in other movements. They have become rather silted over and unfrequented but they are still there.

Historically many radical movements in the past have raised the connection between changing our consciousness and making a new culture with opposing values. This was a vital aspect of Owenite socialist feminism, for example. In attacking the hold of religion the Owenites began to make their own marriage ceremonies. In contesting the values of capitalism they created their own schools. Similarly the Chartists called their children after radical heroes. *The Morning Chronicle* commented in 1849 that in Middleton, Lancashire

> ... a generation or so back, Henry Hunts were as common as blackberries – a crop of Feargus O'Connors replaced them, and latterly there have been a few green sprouts labelled Ernest Jones.[52]

In the late nineteenth and early twentieth centuries socialists understood this need for a protective culture. They extended the ideas of the labour movement, of 'brotherhood', 'solidarity', 'fellowship' and 'comradeship' into their relationships within socialist organizations. 'Brotherhood', though gender-bound, has a warmth which 'comrade' with its echoes of commissars and ice picks lacks. 'Solidarity' carries most immediately the strength of being solid. But it has also had an interpretation which involves conscious individual commitment. In the words of *The Miners' Next Step*, the document produced by South Wales miners, influenced by revolutionary syndicalist ideas, in 1912, 'Sheep cannot be said to have solidarity'.[53] Workers had a vision of a new kind of community, which was partly sustained by their resistance to capitalism but also moved towards the future co-operative commonwealth. It helps to remember that there were these other kinds of socialism, as well as anarchism, which stressed the transformation of values and relationships in the process of making the new world, We need to be able to learn what we can from them just as much as from the Bolsheviks. And on the creation of a new culture as part of the transition to socialism they have more to say than Leninism.

Discussion of the quality of relationships was common in the early British socialist movement. Becoming a socialist meant for many people a spiritual rebirth. Socialist culture, particularly in the Socialist League, the Clarion cycling clubs and choirs and the Independent Labour Party, but even at a local level in the Social Democratic Federation, was a means of sustaining the faith as well as transmitting socialist values. People used the word 'fellowship' to describe their sense of community within the socialist movement. These understandings of the personal, spiritual meaning of becoming a socialist were quite alien to Leninism. The growth of the Communist Party as the revolutionary party meant that such discussions were no longer central to the socialist experience. I don't think they ever died out altogether, even in the Communist Party itself. They ceased however to be explicitly recognized and accepted. They did not belong to the new pantheon of 'correct' ideas which Leninism brought as a theory of organization. Instead they lived on as part of a twilight oral tradition which was passed on by working-class socialists. I think that the shock of 1956 and the post-war disintegration of older forms of working-class politics in both the Communist Party and the Labour Party weakened this oral tradition of the personal meaning of socialism. From 1968 many of the informal links of communication were severed. For the post '68 generations on the left it seems that these old understandings have little resonance. This was just at the moment when an awareness began to grow that the personal meaning of socialism needed to be recreated anew.

I feel sadness at this apparent loss. But I know too that there is a false security in sentimentalizing the demise of all aspects of this culture. While implicit values are an important means of surviving in a hostile world, without becoming theoretically explicit and part of a new order they are forced to seek some form of accommodation. So although the labour movement has carried an implicit opposition to reproducing hierarchy and a partial assertion of different forms of relationship these have coexisted with less democratic values. Not only have the terms in which they could be expressed been predominantly male, reflecting the importance of workers in jobs like mining and the docks in the labour movement, but a vital source of working-class male dignity has been bound up with having a skill. Although revolutionary socialists have always opposed craft elitism in theory, the reality has been that these workers' resistance to economic threats to skill have often also vitally contributed to the political vanguard organization of the working class against capitalism. Thus the destruction of skills, an important area of creativity allowed to some workers, has been countered by a passionate assertion of manhood within the cultural assumptions of the labour movement. Economic militancy, class pride and confidence, political involvement in revolutionary and shop-floor organization have combined to make workers like printers and engineers 'advanced' in the Leninist sense. But groups like these have also been extremely suspicious of the threat of women and the unskilled generally.

In one sense the militancy of skill is a vital opposition to the degradation and paralysis of exploitation. But it also contains our perception of dignity as a characteristic of masculinity and skilled work. It closes in on itself and becomes exclusive. Not only does this vision of militancy fail to reach most women as workers, as they are mainly among the unskilled, but it cannot reach beyond the confines of wage work to question the apportioning, scope and circumstances of our whole lifetimes. In relation to the family it has a paternal conservatism, it implies that the man must be the sole provider for the family, pass on his trade to his son and keep a stern eye on his apprentice. Responsibility merges with possession and authority. The exclusive, conservative features of this concept of militant dignity have become clearer because it has not only been under attack because of the influence of feminism. Within capitalism the continuing dissolution of the older forms of craft skill and the imperatives of inflation which require the exploitation of both men and women's capacity to labour have combined with changing ideas of how men and women, young and old should interact personally. No one is completely certain any more that a man should be master in his own home, it has been difficult for Leninists to grasp the significance of these developments because of the lack of attention to personal responses and the implicit nature of the dignity carried within this male class pride.

The terms in which consciousness and culture have been discussed in the contemporary women's movement do not provide an intact alternative organizational model to set against the 'partial' view of the male-dominated labour movement. But the particular circumstances of the women who have become radicalized by feminism in the last decade contribute towards connecting certain aspects of consciousness. Splits between work and home or between the very process of their partial dissolution. Young women swept into the educational expansion, thrown out into the expanding welfare service sector in significant numbers were cut off from the lives and values which most of their mothers had known and communicated to their daughters in western capitalism. This was intensified by the startling intervention of technology in women's biological destiny. Despite the real problems about the coil and the pill they did mean that women could with much greater reliability for the first time in history assume that heterosexual intercourse did not mean they chanced getting pregnant. This represented a most dramatic break with the past experience of women of their bodies. Yet these changes coincided with the growth of media stereotypes of femininity and an ideological emphasis on the family and the psychological responsibility of the mother for the child. Women found themselves vulnerable in the public world of work and then expected to readjust to the private sphere of isolated child care as many nurseries had been closed after the war. These uneven and awkward shifts which appeared in modern capitalist society were factors in forcing a new feminist consciousness which questioned the demarcations set by men upon the personal and the political. For example it is evident that our views and feelings about trade unions come from our home, our sex, our community, from the media, from legal judgements as well as from our work and class. Equally it is clear that our vision of sexual relationships comes from the personal lived relationships we have with our family, our friends as well as our class or our knowledge of other times and other societies. For women, quite unrevolutionary steps like speaking at a meeting, writing a pamphlet, joining a union or even a football team immediately open up other wider issues of authority. They question the relation of public and private spheres. They involve immediately notions of gender and concepts of human nature. Apparently straightforward actions are easily seen to relate to deeper power relations. They extend the immediate issue into a myriad of questions about human existence and the society in which we live. The women's movement has never been comfortable with only demanding more or simply equality with men, in the sense of equal rights, or even accepted the terms in which Marxists saw the 'woman question'. Instead it has probed the relationship of power which exists between the sexes. It has thus helped to extend our concept of how power is passed on and held in a crucial area of everyday life. The personal is political here in the sense that the dominant male definition of 'what is left politics?' excludes crucial aspects of this power struggle between the sexes.[54]

A complex understanding has grown up through the practice of the women's movement of the interconnecting nature of different forms of power relationships. For instance the campaign for a woman's right to choose freely whether to have an abortion or to have a child raises immediately control over her own fertility and maternity which leads to the more general issues of man's sexual hold over woman, of human beings' relationship to their bodies and the importance of sexual pleasure. All four aspects of the question have been neglected by Marxism. But the campaign also involves an argument about laws and parliament, about a democratic and social medical service, an extensive system of childcare facilities, about the power of the state to determine population policy, about how decisions about investment in contraceptive technology and medical research are made and in whose interests. It implies a discussion about the strategy of a campaign both to pressurize Parliament and to transform the relationship to the body.

I think the implicit recognitions about how our consciousness emerges from the interrelationship of the power relationships which have come from our practice as a movement are actually more complex than the concept of 'oppression' can express. When the black movement in the late sixties, followed by women and gay people asserted the idea of oppression which could include the cultural and personal experience of being subordinated as a group as well as economic and social inequalities, it was an important corrective to the emphasis within the left on class and economic exploitation. When all these movements went on to argue for autonomy and the people involved insisted that they understood their own situation best, this was an essential form of resistance to oppression being reduced by the left to an economic or equal rights issue and spoken for by 'professionals' who claimed they knew better than the people involved in the movements. But arguing in terms of a series of separate 'oppressions' can have an ironic consequence. We can forget that people are more than the category of oppression. 'Each of us lives these conditions but is at the same time more than them.'[55] Movements which initially stressed self-activity and self-development can come to distrust their own origins and reduce human potential to a total, determining, fatalistic state of oppression if this is ignored. We thus have the means of seeing people as victims but not the means of seeing the sources of power which all subordinated groups have created. Equally we do not experience a single defining relationship of subordination in our lives any more than we possess trade union consciousness. We live within a complexity of relationships. This means we have certain sources for comparison and contrast. We can imagine how relationships might be different. We are capable of myopia about other people's culture and experience. But we are also able to extend our understanding and feelings towards others in the past as well as the present.

Zillah Eisenstein in *Capitalist Patriarchy and the Case for Socialist Feminism* describes how Marx's theory of alienation could provide us with a more dialectical approach to women's subordination.

> The theory of alienation and its commitment to 'species life' in communist society is necessary to understanding the revolutionary capacity of human beings... Reality for Marx is more than mere existence. It embodies within it a movement towards human essence. This is not a totally abstract human essence but rather an essence we can understand in historical contexts... Without this conception human beings would be viewed as exploited in capitalist relations, but they would not be understood as potentially revolutionary... When extended to women this revolutionary ontology suggests the possibility of freedom exists alongside exploitation and oppression, since woman is potentially more than what she is. Woman is structured by what she is today – and this defines real outer limits of her capacities or potentialities. This of course is true for the alienated worker... By locating revolutionary potential as it reflects conflicts between people's real conditions (existence) and possibilities (essence), we can understand how patriarchal relations inhibit the development of human essence. In this sense, the conception of species life points to the revolutionary potential of men and women.[56]

If we think about our experiences in the light of these ideas we can grasp the actual complexities of how we develop a critical consciousness about our predicament, how we imagine alternatives and relate these to other people's lives as well as our own. I know from my own political experience that innumerable men and women have in fact changed as part of such a process in the last decade or so. This has sometimes been outside political parties, sometimes within one organization or several. But it has not been the work of any creature called 'the Party' for the simple reason that no such creature exists.

More particularly, for several years I have taught a Workers' Education Class in social history. At various times we have drawn upon our own experience and members of the class have talked about how they became interested in socialist or radical politics and how the women's movement has affected them. The extraordinary diversity of influence upon even people within roughly the same age group, the combination of private and public experience which had brought them together even simply to study the history of radical movements, was a salutary lesson for anyone attempting the history of a social movement. They made nonsense both of the mechanical notion of trade union consciousness and the static categories of certain limited forms of oppression. In fact we all have some such experience and understanding in our lives but it is always difficult initially to hold on to these and put them against a 'theory'.

The recognition which was present within pre-Leninist radical movements of the importance of making values and culture which could sustain the spirit and help to move our feelings towards the future, has been reasserted by the women's movement. This means we can begin to think again about the problem of how we move towards socialism. Leninism has been particularly weak in relation to the actual transition to socialism. Although Eurocommunism raised the problem of the transition, it is not preoccupied with the creation of new forms of power and consciousness but of how to occupy and inhabit the existing institutions. The experience of sexual political movements suggests that not only can gains we make shift the balance of power relationships significantly but that the existence of radical movements concerned to make a new culture and to release and develop the potential of subordinated groups, can also touch and begin to transform not only the ideas and feelings of people within them but of those outside. They bring with them different ways of interpreting, and perceiving the world.[57]

They also reveal a dimension of consciousness which has been missing from socialism and certainly from Leninism. We can recognize and comprehend intellectually without wanting something to change. We can be opposed to hierarchy and elitism and yet feel superior. We can oppose men's control politically and then feel deserted when it is not asserted in our own lives. We can resist being treated as an object and yet still want to be desired in this way, as this remains our means of valuing ourselves. These dimensions of transformation have been a vital part in the practice of the contemporary women's movement.

Sarah Benton in 'Consciousness, Class and Feminism' in *Red Rag* describes how the women's movement has approached our emotional resistances to changes which we may consciously desire.

> It's not enough for the individual woman to 'know' she is possessed or dominated; in order not to be possessed or dominated, indeed in order not to want to be, there must be an alternative culture in which such values are seen to be dominant and to be practised (in however erratic a way) in relation to which she can define herself.[58]

This understanding has been central for women because of the circumstances of our particular oppression as a sex. But its implications are not limited to the politics of the women's movement. This personal approach to consciousness is relevant in the ways in which dominance appears in left organizations and to limitations present in the contemporary labour movement's resistance to capitalism. For example, a middle-class man who becomes a leading theoretician may also be quite inept at relating openly to people. Indeed he may have become a theoretician initially out of this shyness and loneliness. But the psychology of theoreticians does not come within the scope of Leninism! In time indeed isolation will be increased by responsibility for other people. It will be encased within this concept of the role of a leader. The justification of such a personal distance will always be of course service to the Party. It will be further accentuated by his need to be invulnerable because he expresses only what is objectively true, not what he personally feels. But this necessarily restrains his relations with other people. A sure sign of a leader of a Leninist political group is a tendency to look past your eyes and over your head when they talk to you. Either they are taking a long objective view which does not involve encountering you, or they are looking for more prestigious 'contacts' in the shape of a shop steward or so. They quite forget how to meet person to person because they always have a thick wadding of more important purposes stuffed under their belts. This does give them an unreality but it also gives a certain power. They are untouchable and apart. This is of course just like leaders in the public world of government and institutions like the trade union movement. The pattern is reproduced. There are informal cultural correctives to this process in the labour movement But men who are shop stewards and convenors can become locked and isolated by a sense of their need to prove their manhood which removes them from other people, excludes women and makes co-operation between people as equals difficult. These personal characteristics of organization may be privately noted by Leninists but they do not belong to the public discussion of politics. In a consciousness-raising situation (or in a radical therapy group) this source of power in removed objectivity is dissolved. It becomes irrelevant and the personal unhappiness behind it can be revealed. The idea (though it hasn't always been the reality) of a consciousness-raising group is that you can be vulnerable and open without being destroyed because you are protected by the group. Feminists have called this sisterhood, which carries a more intimate notion of democracy than the trade union 'brothers (and sisters)'.

In fact the very act of me writing this has been affected by such a personal tremor in the pattern of feeling – my own involvement in a women's group formed to discuss our relationships and feelings towards our fathers. I struggled against the hold my father had over my life desperately and when he died twelve years ago I was still too scarred to open up to my feelings about him. Over the last few years I have been searching to understand and know him as a person rather than as the projection of my resistance to his authority. I saw obscurely that unless I could spiritually meet my own father person to person, I would continue to simply react against and oppose all forms of authority rather than confront and contest them in the open. Talking and listening to other women in a consciousness-raising situation has helped to shift some of my fear. As I was able to open to some of my affectionate feelings towards him and to respect him within his own life and times rather than in his disastrous relating to me, he became not an object of dread, anger and humiliation but a muddled and unhappy human being. This has released a source of courage and made it possible not to evade the authority and dread which the ones of organization have always held for me. It has become possible to translate the general understanding within the women's movement, that we are all equally responsible for making ideas and ways of resisting a society we oppose, into thinking critically about theories of organization which have always held a particular terror for me.

V

Prefigurative Political Forms

It has become evident that the power of capitalism to survive cannot be challenged only by demanding gains of quantity, or even simply questioning the quality of life. We need political forms which consciously help people to overcome the continual mining of our capacity to resist which is characteristic of modern capitalism. Socialists have been learning this in the last two decades but it goes completely against the grain of a Leninist approach to socialist organization. How can we struggle for prefigurative changes through an organization which reproduces the relationships of power dominant in capitalism?

The right, being part of how things are, often grasps the significance of the connection between areas of control more thoroughly than the left. In education, for example, left groups have supported comprehensive schools and opposed streaming and authoritarian teaching methods, but also have been quite capable of using exactly these authoritarian approaches to their own ideas of political education and propaganda. Similarly, sections of the left have developed a theory which is critical of bureaucracy within the trade union movement while remaining blithely unselfconscious about the effects of bureaucratic power in revolutionary organizations. Force of circumstance in modern capitalism has been bringing socialists into confrontation in areas of control which throw into question the internal relationships within left organizations. This process is making it harder to caricature the struggle to make new kinds of relationships which can be the means of growth and transformation in the making of socialism, as a mechanical and arbitrary utopianism. We do not seek isolated and impossible alternatives to the way of the world. We need to strengthen and give space and substance to the positive understandings which come from all our experiences of resisting capitalism.

The slogan 'the personal is political' has been important in the women's movement. Its appearance indicates how shifts in the relationships of gender have affected the terms in which notions of individual identity can be seen in modern capitalism. These are shifts which socialists need to explore more fully. Specifically in relation to the question of organization though, the slogan implies a very different view of practice and consciousness than is current on the left. This involves both the forms of activity which are regarded as important and our approach to relationships within the movement for change.

Two obvious examples of forms of activity which have been important in the women's movement are consciousness-raising groups and self-help groups of various kinds like women's health, Women's Aid, Rape Crisis centres.

The consciousness-raising group assumes that our consciousness is changed in the realization that we share a common predicament, this has been the aspect of consciousness-raising which the left groups are now prepared to accept and in the case of the IMG extend to men. But the other aspect of consciousness-raising is that we experience a different kind of relationship with other women than we knew before. The ideal is an openness and trust, a recognition of other women's experience as well as our own. In practice we know consciousness-raising groups can become frustrating, as for example it is difficult sometimes to make general connections from personal experience. People feel other women know more than them, and are holding back. Mysterious silences appear in the meeting. It is sometimes hard to assert individual personal experience against a collective consensus which may appear because of hidden power structures. There are unstated ideological assumptions or an emotionally terrorizing morality. So consciousness-raising groups, like other political forms, are not magic. But they are still part of a crucial process of learning and feeling towards alternative relationships from those which predominate in capitalism. I know I really do feel a closeness and love towards women I have known within women's group situations which is quite different from the experience of socialist branch meetings. This collective experience has been a vital force in the women's movement's strength. I see no reason why it should be gender bound.

Self-help groups emerged in the community politics of the New Left in America and have become an important form of organizing in the women's movement.

Linda Gordon and Allen Hunter comment on the American experience:

> The model of collective self-help, while not in itself a socialist strategy, strengthens the connection between personal and social change. In the best of cases, self-help groups combine consciousness-raising with material aid and an opening to a new community of people; thus providing not only the ideas but some of the conditions for adopting a less passive stance towards the world. The self-help model is a way of dealing with the fact that politics often becomes a part of one's life only when a political problem is directly experienced.[59]

Everyone knows there are enormous problems involved in doing this. Nonetheless the political experience gained from these very diverse activities is a crucial part of learning to resist in the process of changing ourselves. The Rape Crisis Centre in Britain for example is concerned with providing practical help to raped women. It is also a collective effort to overcome the fears within women and a sense of ourselves as victims. They point out that a raped woman has been victimized but 'this is not her total identity, she does not remain the "passive subject of attack" as implied by the word "victim"'. One of the aims of the Centre is 'to help ourselves, as women, to become aware that we do not have to accept the identity given to us by the society'.[60]

One of the objections which the CP and the Trotskyist groups made to self-help projects as they first emerged in the women's movement in Britain, with close political links to libertarian Marxism, was that they evaded the necessity of making demands on the state. They eased the pressure on the social provision we had to force out of capitalism. They were middle-class projects, not popular demands. Supporters of self-help projects replied that making demands on the state did not leave you with control over the kind of social provision you needed. This issue of control has been very important in women's health groups against the bureaucratic formality of the National Health and against a male-defined concept of medicine. It has also come up in the question of nursery provision. How could we simply demand nurseries when we were insisting on the need to transform gender relationships from the beginning? In certain areas of women's health and in the growth of community nurseries this has been a really fruitful collision in which two quite different assumptions of organizing have learned from one another. For example the Tower Hamlets abortion centre which is part of the National Health System is sensitive to the needs and feelings of women and firmly committed to women's right to control their own fertility. Here the health workers themselves have been influenced by the women's movement. Community nurseries allow for more democratic participation from parents, are committed to non-authoritarian non-sexist childcare and are partly financed by the council. A Hackney mother describes the effect on her of the local community nursery:

> I found attitudes at the nursery were very different from those of the school. Everyone was encouraged to take an interest in how it was run – for the sake of the children. At that time I didn't understand that our nursery was different from any other nursery, such as those run and controlled by the council. Now of course I realized the nursery *was* different and it was up to us – the parents – to take all decisions about how the place was to be run. Problems were met and overcome not by them, but by us. Gradually I was drawn into helping. I liked the idea because I am a very independent person.[61]

I am not suggesting that the idea of mutual self-help is new or limited to the women's movement in the last decade. Indeed it has an ancient genealogy from the creation of friendly societies and co-operatives to the cycling clubs, Workers' Esperanto groups, nurseries and Socialist Sunday Schools of the late nineteenth and early twentieth century. Mutual self-help was an integral part of the creation of a new culture of fellowship in the movement towards a Socialist Commonwealth. Moreover there has been a recent growth of an enormous variety of forms of self-help which relate to personal and social problems, like playgroups, One o'Clock clubs, Gingerbread, Parents Anonymous, Alcoholics Anonymous, Stigma along with voluntary organizations from the Samaritans, Citizens Advice to radical therapy and co-counselling. There has been a similar development of community projects, the law centres for example. These movements assert the possibility of people changing themselves, and helping one another through co-operating. They are concerned about our social lives. Some carry an alternative to the monopoly of the state over welfare and question the partiality of the law. Some of the forms of organizing in the women's movement relate to these self-help groups and can best be seen within this more general context. I am not suggesting that we can evolve to socialism through self-help or that all forms of self-help are necessarily radical or that self-help cannot coexist with a new form of labour reformism. It is evident that the coercive power of the state must be contested, that several class interests can use similar forms of organizing and that some strands of the right can assert self-activity as well as the left. With the active support of working-class people in a community, mutual self-help forms provide a potential means of distinguishing between the coercive aspects of the state machinery and those activities of the state which are necessary to people in their everyday life. They raise the possibility of welfare control. Self-help community activity is not a substitute for the equally important radical struggles within the welfare state sector. But they can indicate ways of questioning the role of professionals and the means of creating more direct forms of control over welfare resources.

There is of course a very old argument between anarchists and socialists about how we regard the state and whether we should make demands on the state. In one sense it is obvious that we cannot ignore the power of the law or the need for welfare provision. On the other it is true that laws which workers or others have fought for can be interpreted against them, that welfare reforms which were the result of past victories can circumscribe resistance. In one sense there is no absolute solution within capitalism.

But it is possible to approach the problem without simply falling into the acceptance of either polarity, if the anarchists close their eyes and wish the state would float away, Trotskyists present the state as a big balloon. If we all blow hard enough it goes pop. When it does not go pop the answer is we must blow harder. The trouble is we tend to burst before the state, which is nowadays a most wiggly and wily, stretchy monster. More dialectical dealings are suggested in the recognition that past gains need not simply contain present militancy and that they have contributed to important shifts in power within society. These shifts allow people to develop the confidence and the space in which mutual self-help groups, therapy and community politics have grown. The women's movement itself has emerged partly out of certain fissures in the relationships of power.

Within the women's movement self-help forms can be seen to be directed towards several aspects of resistance. Some are specifically against men's hold over women as a sex and the consciousness which this relationship of inequality and possession generates. Women's Aid Centres and rape crisis centres are two examples. They provide a means of protection against women's encounters with male violence and a means of sustaining our resistance. Though they are in practice also linked to work and housing conditions, to the law as well as to our ideas of sexuality and of masculinity and femininity and are thus issues which must affect men as well as women. Other forms of self-help organizing are not aimed against the hold of men as a sex but primarily against the power of the state to determine and distort work and kinship relations, for example claimants' unions and community nurseries. Indeed men are involved in these as well as women. The struggles against men's hold over women and against the state are not identical. Different forms of power relationships are involved. The state in capitalism still basically expresses the power of an elite of ruling-class men. From this power their women derive a certain though not equal privilege. Nowadays the ruling class in the modern state in order to retain this power have had to make concessions to pressure from workers and other subordinated groups including women. Feminism has been a force along with the labour movement in the making of the welfare state. But of course there remain great inequalities in people's power to define and secure welfare, as well as differences of interest within the working class between men and women, black and white, skilled and unskilled, because of their differing social circumstances. However men as a group do not have equal degrees of power over state policy.

The struggle for welfare rights and legal changes cannot be seen as primarily against men. Indeed as in the work situation there are shared interests in combining resistance.

It has been the strength of feminism that in beginning with the particular circumstances of everyday life it is possible to move towards the interlocking relationships of power which contain not only women but men as well. This is certainly limited by the particular class composition of the women who have been most radicalized by changes within relations in capitalist society and by the absence of a mass socialist movement in Britain which can complement the organizational initiatives and activity of an autonomous movement. Nonetheless this has been a significant and valuable breakthrough which urgently requires a more general means of development.

Feminism has also been the main organizational form through which the idea of prefigurative politics has begun to influence the contemporary left. Consciousness raising, therapy and self-help will imply that we want change now. They are involved in making something which might become a means of making something more. They do not assume that we will one day in the future suddenly come to control how we produce, distribute and divide goods and services and that this will rapidly and simply make us new human beings. They see the struggle for survival and control as part of the here and now. They can thus contribute towards the process of continually making ourselves anew in the movement towards making socialism.

The women's movement has played a vital part in challenging the politics of deferment. From the start feminists have said some changes have to start now else there is no beginning for us. This was not initially expressed as a theoretical position but as a practical need. For example, women in the student movement in the late sixties pointed out that the structure of meetings made it impossible for nearly all the women and many men to participate. Women with children said, 'We want creches at meetings otherwise it is impossible to come'. Women's liberation also involved obviously changing relationships at home. Feminist consciousness was not seen as isolated from how we make love or from our intimate selves. It was not merely an item to be included in a programme.

It was harder to go on from the practical need to its full implications. This has been a problem in the women's movement, and has perhaps contributed to the recent interest in theories of consciousness which emphasize the strength of the hold of circumstance against the earlier stress on voluntarism. 'I will change and no one shall stop me' has shifted to 'Why do I change so slowly?'

There is not a simple one to one connection between various forms or power. Our consciousness of ourselves in fucking cannot be neatly transferred to our activity in a union branch, any more than change in the mode of production automatically changes men's attitudes to women. We have to struggle in several dimensions, which involves a fundamentally different attitude to ourselves in relation to other people and thus to our politics. This is a long-term project!

But to say that change is more complicated does not mean that we have to accept a fatalism that denies personal change is possible. The personal is political even though people are more personal than any form of politics can express.

On the left the slogan 'the personal is political' has become rather an embarrassment as if everyone had heard it all before. But hearing and doing are different matters. The questions remain. How do the form of meetings reflect much deeper relationships of power for instance? How can we confront these not by merely altering the forms but changing the relationships? For example the creche might appear nowadays but remain a child-parking place. It is not necessarily seen as a living part of the political practice of socialism or, sadly, always of feminism. Nonetheless all these creches have had and will have an influence on how our children experience the socialist and feminist movement. This is as important at least as what happens in most meetings. But it is rarely acknowledged as part of the main business of socialism or even feminism. Theoretically the connection between changes in power relationships in the family and within left groups has remained sotto voce. In the left there are still plenty of Dads who rule OK, and remain relatively unruffled. I mean not the fathers of children but the founding fathers of left groups. Feminism is rather more vigilant but we all carry a Dad and Mum boss in us. In other words, the implication of challenging sex-gender relationships has only partially become a critique of power relations within radical organizations and movements.

It is important that we remember radical politics are also personal affairs. Feminists have argued that the personal is political and that this has implications for how you organize. It is possible however for socialists to interpret this narrowly. Under pressure 'personal' subjects like rape or abortion can be taken up but in the terms of an existing public politics. The forms of organizing around these issues are simply transplanted from the parliamentary pressure groups, the factory meeting or the committee room. Not that these experiences are invalidated. There are certainly strengths and resources which left groups can bring to feminist campaigns. But the exchange has to be between equals and the learning process two-way. The strangled antagonism which appeared in the National Abortion Campaign came out of this feeling in the women's movement. It was nonetheless difficult to assert the unspoken understandings about organization and the lived encounter we knew with a different kind of politics when the public world of politics loomed so large and men and women in left groups saw the argument in terms of efficiency (themselves) versus inefficiency (the women's movement). Feminists responded by being suspicious of NAC because it included men.[62] There has been an obvious difference between the relationship of men and women in left groups to the women's movement, and this has influenced how they work politically. There is an immediate link between left group women (Leninists included) and feminists because they are all affected by their social predicament. Socialist women have been changed by feminism. Nonetheless, I think it cannot be seen simply as a male/female split, but is in fact a political argument about organizing. Some men feel as alienated as many feminists from vanguard assumptions of organization. There are also many socialist women who believe in the Leninist approach to organizing.

There is a missing element here. It goes beyond simply applying established forms of organizing to the areas of personal oppression which feminism has revealed. We need also to question the approach to what the left defines already as public politics. I think it is hard to see this from the vantage point of either the women's movement or the male-dominated left. It emerges from the politics of men who have been both driven and encouraged by feminism to explore and expose the areas in which men of different classes and races are reared for various forms of domination and submission. This means disentangling the distortions in how men reach manhood which contributes, for instance, to the appeal of fascism, or to soldiers' obedience to their officers even when it means killing someone of their own class, or makes it possible for a trade unionist to be economically militant yet look down on labourers, blacks, apprentices and women. To bring it closer to home, it also involves looking at how people relate personally to left groups. The connection of personal and public politics involves not only making personal questions political, it means approaching 'public' politics personally as well.

A negative short-term consequence of the resistance of socialists to sexual politics has been to alienate many men from all existing forms of left politics. This has tended to leave men's groups stranded within purely personal forms of politics. Socialist men have been caught between two stark options in ways that socialist feminists have been able to avoid through the women's movement. The only compromise possible has been individual participation on the left combined with a separate existence in men's groups. But this reinforces the existing male split between public and personal. An example of the different political predicaments of men and women affected by feminism has been the experience of radical therapy. It has been easier for women involved in Red Therapy to go outwards through the connection with the women's movement. There has been a much greater gap and in some cases strong hostility towards both men's and mixed consciousness-raising and therapy groups in the socialist movement. This enforced isolation breeds its own kinds of paralysis and defensiveness.

Nonetheless the positive potential of the sexual politics which has radicalized men as well as women lies in developing an understanding of how our personal experience of gender is bound up with the politics of class and racial struggles and indeed in our very assumptions of what it means to be a socialist. The inspiration for this understanding was feminism. But such an integration cannot obviously be the work of the women's movement alone.

CONCLUSION

It has required a big argument on the Leninist left to take up even one aspect of 'personal' power relationships – the question of inequality between men and women within socialist organizations themselves. The feminist movement has challenged this reproduction of inequality within the left. After nearly a decade sexism (like racism) is now admitted to exist even within left parties themselves by most organizations on the left. This used to be denied or it was said that it was utopian to expect anything else until after socialism. The ground has shifted because men and women affected by sexual politics have been saying both inside and outside socialist groups that we can't wait. We have to find effective ways of struggling against these inequalities for they are not only wrong in themselves, they paralyse many socialists and restrict our communication with many people who can see little difference between socialist and right-wing organizations. They also block understandings vital for the making of socialism.

However the implications of this recognition are still not followed through. The assumption within left groups has continued to be that the remedy for inequalities was the exhortation to improvement. It is presumed that within the organization itself change can be a result of an effort of pure reason. It is true that we can change our minds when confronted with 'facts' and argument. But they are inadequate on their own to touch the full extent of the problem. This emphasis on reason and will is the reverse side of the coin to the fatalism which denies the possibility of prefigurative change before socialism. Leninists are saying at once no change is possible and yet all changes necessary can be made by political education in the Party.

Feminists have been urging the need for a form of politics which enables people to experience different relationships. The implications of this go beyond sex-gender relationships, to all relationships of inequality, including those between socialists. Leninist organizations have made piecemeal concessions to the women's movement and the gay movement under pressure. They have been affected also by the contradictory pulls in modern capitalism which have led to questioning certain areas of control in everyday life. But they have resisted the implications of these social changes and movements as a more general challenge to their notion of politics. The notion of organization in which a transforming vision of what is possible develops out of the process of organizing questions some of the most deeply held tenets of Leninism. The weight of Leninist theory (Gramsci apart) and the prevailing historical practice of Leninism is towards seeing the 'Party' as the means by which the working class can take power and these 'means' have a utilitarian narrowness. Other considerations consequently have to be deferred until the goal of socialism is reached. But socialist feminists and men influenced by the women's movement and gay liberation have been saying that these are precisely the considerations which are inseparable from the making of socialism. These involve considerable disagreement about the meaning of socialist politics and what it means to be a socialist.

So I don't believe it is a matter of adding bits to a pre-existing model of an 'efficient' 'combative' organization through which the working class (duly notified and rounded up at last) will take power. You need changes now in how people can experience relationships in which we can both express our power and struggle against domination in all its forms. A socialist movement must help us find a way to meet person to person – an inward as well as an external equality. It must be a place where we can really learn from one another without reference or resentment and 'Theory' is not put in authority.

This will not just happen. It goes too deeply against the way of the world. We really cannot rely on commonsense here. We need to make the creation of prefigurative forms an explicit part of our movement against capitalism. I do not mean that we try to hold an imaginary future in the present, straining against the boundaries of the possible until we collapse in exhaustion and despair. This would be utopian. Instead such forms would seek both to consolidate existing practice and release the imagination of what could be. The effort to go beyond what we know now has to be part of our experience of what we might know, rather than a denial of the validity of our own experience in face of a transcendent party. This means a conscious legitimation within the theory and practice of socialism of all those aspects of our experience which are so easily denied because they go against the grain of how we learn to feel and think in capitalism. All those feelings of love and creativity, imagination and wisdom which are negated, jostled and bruised within the relationships which dominate in capitalism are nonetheless there, our gifts to the new life. Marxism has been negligent of their power, Leninism and Trotskyism frequently contemptuous or dismissive. Structuralist Marxism hides them from view in the heavy academic gown of objectivity. For a language of politics which can express them we need to look elsewhere, for instance, to the utopian socialists in the early nineteenth century, or to the Socialist League in the 1880s, or Spanish anarcho-syndicalism. We cannot simply reassert these as alternatives against the Leninist tradition. There are no 'answers' lying latent in history. But there is more to encourage you than meets the Leninist eye. We have to shed completely the lurking assumption that

Leninism provides the highest political form of organizing and that all other approaches can be dismissed as primitive antecedents or as incorrect theories.

it has been difficult in the last decade for us to bring together our political experience. The versions of Leninism current on the left make it difficult to legitimate any alternative approaches to socialist politics which have been stumbling into existence. These Leninisms are difficult to counter because at their most superficial they have a surface coherence, they argue about brass tacks and hard facts. They claim history and sport their own insignia and regalia of position. They fight dirty – with a quick sneer and the certainty of correct ideas. At their most thoughtful intensity they provide a passionate and complex cultural tradition of revolutionary theory and practice on which we must certainly draw. Socialist ideas can be pre-Leninist or anti-Leninist. But there is no clear post-Leninist revolutionary tradition yet. Leninism is alive still whatever dogmatic accoutrements it has acquired. The argument is about the extent of its usefulness for making socialism now.

I know that many socialists who have lived through the complicated and often painful encounters between sexual politics and the left in the last few years believe we must alter Leninism to fit the experience gained in sexual political movements. I have been edged and nuzzled and finally butted towards believing that what we have learned can't be forced into the moulds of Leninism without restricting and cutting its implications short. Moreover the structures of thought and feeling inherent in Leninism continually brake our consciousness of alternatives, if Stalinism made it impossible to challenge aspects of Leninism, the growth of Trotskyist and neo-Trotskyist groups since 1968 has postponed this by appearing to provide the solution. I don't see the way through this as devising an ideal model of a non-authoritarian organization but as a collective awakening to a constant awareness about how we see ourselves as socialists, a willingness to trust as well as criticize what we have done, a recognition of creativity in diversity and a persistent quest for open types of relationships to one another and to ideas as part of the process of making socialism. In the long term I think we need new forms of socialist organizing which can grow from such a practice and bring together these efforts towards a different politics. The spirit in which we could make such an organization (or organizations) cannot be the distinguishing correctness which Leninism has fostered; I find the spirit of *The Miners' Next Step* more appropriate. The authors said the pamphlet was 'the best product of our time and thought, which we freely offer as an expression of our oneness of heart and interest as a section of the working class. Do what you will with it, modify or (we hope) improve, but at least give it your earnest consideration.'[63]

Notes

1. E.P. Thompson, 'Outside the Whale', *The Poverty of Theory*, Merlin Press, 1978, pp. 312
2. Martin Shaw, 'The Making of a Party?', *Socialist Register 1978*, Merlin Press, p. 110.
3. Grace C, Lee, Pierre Chalieu and J.R. Johnson, *Facing Reality*, Correspondence Detroit, 1958, pp. 130-1.
4. Two books which deal with the history of this period do not disentangle the similarities and differences. David Widgery's *The Left in Britain 1956-1968*, Penguin, 1976, has an implicit movement within it towards the emergence of International Socialism as the hidden denouement of the left after the book ends. Nigel Young's *An Infantile Disorder? The Crisis and Decline of the New Left*, Routledge and Kegan Paul, 1977, contrasts the American and British New Left. He assumes that all aspects of Marxist politics before 1956 in Britain belonged to the dark ages, and sees the fact that the British labour movement had survived during the fifties as a disadvantage which prevented the emergence of a genuinely 'new' left. He appears to have little sense of political ideas developing through the clash and interconnection of different traditions in which people can learn to respect one another's cultural political heritage.
5. Jan O'Malley, *The Politics of Community Action*, Spokesman, 1977, pp. 25, 29-32.
6. See, for example, Conference of International Socialists on

Revolutionary Unity Documents, February 1978. Two of these were published: Richard Kuper, 'Organisation and Participation', *Socialist Review*, July/August 1978; Julian Harber, 'Trotskyism and the IS Tradition'. *Revolutionary Socialism*, no. 2; Richard Gombin's *The Origins of Leftism*, Pelican, 1975, is useful to compare the British left groups with France.

7. Shaw, 'The Making of a Party', p. 107, op. cit.
8. See Rose Shapiro and Tricia Deardon, 'No Leaders, No Dogmas: Getting Personal about Politics', *The Leveller*, no. 14, April 1978.
9. See, for example, Fernando Claudin's account of the Communist International, *The Communist Movement: From Comintern to Cominform*, Peregrine, 1975.
10. E.P. Thompson interviewed by Terry Ilot, 'Recovering the Libertarian Tradition', *The Leveller*, no. 22, January 1978, p. 20.
11. For a discussion of Trotskyism as an identifiable political tradition see Geoff Hodgson, *Trotsky and Fatalistic Marxism*, Spokesman Books, 1975. Jim O'Brien's summary of the histories of American Leninist groups makes for an interesting comparison with Britain. Jim O'Brien, 'American Leninism in the 1910s', New England Free Press, 1979. (This article originally appeared in the November 1977/February 1978 issue of *Radical America*.
12. Rosalind Petchesky, 'Dissolving the Hyphen. A Report on Marxist-Feminist Groups 1-5', in Zillah R. Eisenstein (cd.), *Capitalist Patriarchy and the Case for Socialist Feminism*, New York, Monthly Review Press, 1979, p. 386. (For discussion of these problems see the *Feminist Review*, *Red Rag* and *Scarlet Women*.)
13. Felicity Edholm, Olivia Harris and Kate Young, 'Conceptualising Women', *Critique of Anthropology* (Women's issue), Vol. 3,nos. 9 and 10, 1977, p. 126.
14. Bea Campbell, 'Sweets from a Stranger', *Red Rag*, no. 13, p. 28.
15. W.B. Yeats, *Memoirs*, London, Macmillan, 1972, p. 192.
16. On women's consciousness and relationship to radical organizations in the past see, for example: Barbara Taylor, 'The Woman Power', in Sue Lipschitz, *Tearing the Veil*; Gail Malmgreen, *Neither Bread nor Roses: Utopian Feminists and the English Working Class 1800-1850*, PO Box 450, Brighton, Sussex BNI 8CR, John L. Noya; Ingrun LaFleur, 'Adelheid Popp and Working Class Feminism in Austria', ***Frontiers***. A Journal of Women's Studies, Vol. 1, no. 1, Fall, 1975, University of Colorado; Jill Liddington and Jill Norris, *One Hand Tied Behind Us*, London, Virago, 1978; Temma Kaplan, 'Other Scenarios, Women and

Spanish Anarchism', in Renate Bridenthal and Claudia Koonz (eds.), *Becoming Visible: Women in European History*, Boston, 1977; Anne Boboff, 'The Bolsheviks and Working Women, 1905-1920', *Radical America*, Vol. 10, no. 3, May-June 1976.

17. Joanna Bornat, 'Home and Work. A New Context for Trade Union History', *Radical America*, Vol. 12, no. 5, September-October 1978, p. 54.
18. Dorothy Thompson, 'Women and Nineteenth Century Radical Politics', in Ann Oakley and Juliet Mitchell (eds.), *The Rights and Wrongs of Women*, Penguin, 1974, p. 137.
19. I think now that *Women: Resistance and Revolution*, in asserting the existing involvement of women in revolutionary movements tends to dismiss the various currents within feminism from the late nineteenth century as well as the involvement of women in non-revolutionary organizations like the Independent Labour Party or the Women's Co-operative Guild. So while it challenges women's position in socialism, it does not raise the relationship of socialist organizations and the feminist movement. Also, because it was written just as the women's liberation movement was emerging in Britain (1969-71), it inclines towards seeing the particular understandings of the new contemporary movement as a synthesis with answers that evaded movements in the past. Ten years after, the strengths of pass movements are more apparent and it is possible to have a perspective on the modem movement which enables us to see our weaknesses as well as our gains. A much dearer example though of the uncritical acceptance of a simple polarity between socialism and feminism appears in an otherwise useful introduction: Barbara Winslow, *A Short History of Women's Liberation Revolutionary Feminism*, (USA, Hera Press, no date). Although recently reissued the bulk of this pamphlet dates from the early period of the women's movement too. For an example which rushes enthusiastically into the same trap see Anna Paczuska's 'The Cult of. Kollontai', *Socialist Review*, December l978/January 1979. This eccentric effort purports to be attacking a 'cult' which is the creation of the author's own imagination, while herself adopting an uncritical stance to Kollontai's sectarian approach to feminist organizations.
20. Bea Campbell and Sheila Rowbotham, 'Women Workers and the Class Struggle', *Radical America*, Vol. 8, no. 5, September-October 1974, p. 63.
21. Richard Kuper, 'Organisation and Participation', *Socialist Review*, July-August 1978, p. 36.

22. Ralph Miliband, 'The Future of Socialism in England', *The Socialist Register 1977*, Merlin Press, p. 50.
23. For a recent example of whooshing see Chris (Super) Harman, 'For Democratic Centralism', *Socialist Review*, July-August 1978, p. 39.
24. Adriano Sofri, *Italy 1977-78: Living With an Earthquake*, Red Notes pamphlet, no date, p. 95. See also the criticisms made by women in Lotta Continua of the leadership's response to feminism.
25. 'Newsreel Five Years On', *Wedge*, no. 3, Winter 1978, p. 41.
26. See Reg Groves, *The Balham Group: How British Trotskyism Began*, Pluto Press, 1974.
27. See, for examples of this, Hal Draper and Anne G. Lipow (eds.), 'Marxist Women venus Bourgeois Feminism', *The Socialist Register 1976*, Merlin Press, 179-226. Draper and Lipow seem to be unaware that the political contribution of the women's movement and the work of feminist historians can enable us to unravel various strands of feminism and quite different relationships between women and radical movements which do not involve setting the leading women in German social democracy upon a pinnacle of correct socialist consciousness. The documents they translate are nonetheless useful for tracing how Marxist positions on 'The Woman Question' emerged.
28. Paul Thompson and Guy Lewis, *The Revolution Unfinished: A Critique of Trotskyism*, Big Flame pamphlet, 1978, p. 23.
29. See Temina Kaplan, *Anarchists of Andalusia 1868-1903*, Princeton, 1977, pp. 86-7, 136-67. On the contemporary relevance of anarchism for feminist organizing see Lynn Aldenon, 'Anarchism and the Women's liberation Movement', *Catcall*, Issue 6, July 1977.
30. See E.P. Thompson, *William Morris: Romantic to Revolutionary*, Merlin Press, 1977, and Emma Goldman, *Living My Life*, Dover, 1971.
31. See Elizabeth Gurley Flynn, *The Rebel Girl: An Autobiography*, New York, International Publishers, 1973.
32. Alix Holt (ed.), *Selected Writings of Alexandra Kollontai*, Allison and Busby, 1977, p. 208.
33. Ibid., p. 215.
34. See Linda Gordon, *Woman's Body, Woman's Right*, Penguin, 1977, chapter 9, on birth control and American socialism and syndicalism, and Sheila Rowbotham, *A New World for Women: Stella Browne, Socialist Feminist*, Pluto Press, 1977. Veronica

Beechey in 'On Patriarchy', *Feminist Review*, no. 3, points out this dualism in some contemporary uses of the word.

35. See, for example, Emma Goldman, 'Woman Suffrage', in *The Traffic in Women and Other Essays on Feminism*, with a biography by Alix Kates Shulman,US,Times Change Press, 1970, pp. 51-63; Lily Gair Wilkinson, *Revolutionary Socialism and the Women's Movement*, SLP,c.1910; and *Women's Freedom*, Freedom Press, c.l914; Bruce Dancis, 'Socialism and Women in the United States 1900-1917', *Socialist Revolution*, no. 27, Vol 6 no. 1, January-March 1976; Alexandra Kollontai, 'The Social Basis of the Woman Question', in Alix Holt (ed,), op. cit.
36. See Sam Aaronovitch, 'Eurocommunism: A Discussion of Carillo's Eurocommunism and the State', *Marxism Today*, July 1978.
37. See Carl Boggs, 'Marxism, Prefigurative Communism and the Problem of Workers' Control', *Radical America*, Vol 11, no. 6 and Vol. 12, no. 1, November 1977/February 1978.
38. On the need for the organizations on the left to learn from the women's movement see: Margaret Coulson, 'Socialism, Politics and Personal Life', in ibid.; Frankie Rickford, 'The Development of the Women's Movement', *Marxism Today*, July 1978; Celia Deacon, 'Feminism and the IS tradition', Conference of International Socialists on Revolutionary Unity Documents, February 1978. The East London Socialist Feminist Group Conference Paper 1978 discussed the need for us to also look at general problems of socialism, not only women's issues,
39. Bob Cant in Documents, op. cit.
40. Fernando Claudin, *Eurocommunism and Socialism.* New Left Books, 1978, p. 125. Margaret Coulson makes the same point in criticizing John Ron's article on 'Capitalism, Politics and Personal Life'. He confines women's liberation to a social sphere, trade unions to the economic and politics to the revolutionary party. She says, 'his formula blocks us off from understanding the processes involved in the development of politics'. (Margaret Coulson, 'Socialism, Politics and Personal Life', *Socialist Woman*, October 1978.)
41. Red Collective, 'Not So Much a Charter, More a Way of Organising', mimeograph, 1974. (The Red Collective were a small group of men and women concerned to relate socialism and sexual politics.) This statement is quoted in Barbara Taylor, 'Classified: Who Are We? Class and the Women's Movement', *Red Rag*, no. 11, p. 24.

42. See for example, *Case Con*, Women's Issue, Spring 1974, and *London Educational Collective in Women and Education*, no. 2, 1973-4, on Rank and File's resistance to taking up women's subordination in education.
43. V.L Lenin, *What is to be Done?* quoted in Carmen Claudin-Urondo, *Lenin and the Cultural Revolution*, The Harvester Press, 1977, p. 69.
44. Ibid, p. 71. See also Lindsay German, 'Women and Class', in *Socialist Review*, no. 5, September 1978, and the reply by some Hackney Socialist Feminists, 'Feminism Without Illusions', in *Socialist Review*, no. 7, November 1978.
45. V.L Lenin, *What is to be Done?* quoted in Carmen Claudin-Urondo, *Lenin and the Cultural Revolution*, The Harvester Press, 1977, p. 70.
46. Ibid, p. 70.
47. Ibid, p. 72.
48. Claudin, *The Communist Movement*, p. 630, op. cit.
49. E.P. Thompson, *The Poverty of Theory*, p. 352, op. cit.
50. Ibid., p. 364.
51. Ibid., p. 363.
52. Dorothy Thompson, 'Women and Nineteenth Century Radical Politics', op. cit., p. 122.
53. Unofficial Reform Committee, *The Miners' Next Step*, 1912, Pluto, 1915, p. 27.
54. All the left organizations have sought to encapsulate the implications of the women's movement within the terms of equal rights or concrete demands and campaigns, 'issue politics'. They were distrustful of the emphasis upon challenging and transforming relationships and upon the consequences of this approach to politics. They preferred the language of 'rights' and 'discrimination' to that of 'liberation'. Liberation has tended to be suspect and has been sorted away under 'culture' which has dubious middle-class connections and might even be a mere creation of an overheated feminine imagination! I think these anxieties have affected not only the leaderships of left groups but socialist women within and without them. Personally it has been the continuing practice of the movement which has helped to shift some of the nervousness for me. Amanda Sebestyen makes a similar point in *Cat Call*, Issue 3, July 1976.
55. Paul Atkinson, 'The Problem With Patriarchy', *Achilles Heel*, no. 2, 1979, p. 22.
56. Zillah R. Eisenstein, 'Developing a Theory of Capitalist

Patriarchy', in ed, Eisenstein, *Capitalist Patriarchy and the Case for Socialist Feminism*, New York, Monthly Review, 1979, p. 7-8.

57, See Vic Seidler, 'Men and Feminism', *Achilles Heel*, no.2.

58. Sarah Benton, 'Consciousness, Classes and Feminism', *Red Rag*, no. 12, p. 27.

59. Linda Gordon and Allen Hunter, 'Sex. Family and the New Left: Anti-Feminism as a Political Force', *Radical America*, Vol 11, no. 6; Vol. 12, no. 1, November 1977/February 1978. (This article is also available in pamphlet form published by the New England Free Press, 60 Union Square, Somerville, Mass. 02143.)

60. Introduction, *Rape Crisis Centre First Report*, p.1.

61 *Not so much a Nursery* ..., Market Nursery, Hackney, London, 1977, p. 22.

62. On NAC see Ruth Petrie and Anna Livingstone, 'Out of the Back Streets', *Red Rag*, no. 11; Roberta Henderson, 'Feminism is not for Burning', 'Speculations', in *Cat Call* Issue 2, April 1976; *NAC and its Lessons for the Socialist Feminist Movement*, document, Socialist Feminist Conference.

63. Unofficial Reform Committee, *The Miners' Next Step*, p. 12.

After this was finished I read two articles which are arguing along similar lines from rather different starting points. If you are interested in following some of the ideas through either in terms of the strategy of the women's movement and socialism or in terms of working-class community organizing, see: Nancy Hartsock, 'Feminist Theory and the Development of Revolutionary Strategy', in ed. Eisenstein, *Capitalist Patriarchy and the Case for Socialist Feminism*, op. cit, and Kathy McAfee, 'City Life: Lessons of the First Five Years', *Radical America*, Vol. 13, no. 1, January-February 1979.

A LOCAL EXPERIENCE* (1979)

Lynne Segal

Certain political ideas and experiences are always more fiercely and critically debated than others on the left. The debate is usually confined within certain orthodox frameworks of discussion. The need for a revolutionary party and programme, the relation between party and class, and the nature of the working-class road to power, are among these classic debates. As the theses pile up on these important debates, the actual experiences of people as they consciously, and less consciously, participate in the struggle for a better life can disappear from history. And that is most unfortunate.

I believe we can learn useful, if limited, lessons from the activities of a group of people struggling for socialism, fighting for feminism, within their own small groups in one local area. I am writing as a woman with a libertarian feminist history, living in Islington since 1972. Islington is an inner suburb of London. It does not have any large industrial base, workers are mostly employed in the public sector, or in small factories. Like me, many people who live in Islington don't work there. My political experience has been as a community activist; it is not based on the workplace.

I will be trying to draw on my experiences in the last seven

* This article was originally based on a talk given together with Sheila at the Islington Socialist Centre in August 1978. Since the first edition of *Beyond the Fragments* I have rewritten sections of it. The sympathetic comment and criticism of the first edition by my friends and comrades in Big Flame and by other independent socialist feminists have been of invaluable assistance to me in clarifying some of the ideas which appeared rather sketchily in the first edition. I am very grateful to all those who participated in this learning process with me.

years, not just in the women's movement, but also as part of the libertarian left in London. It is a subjective account, but I hope it will raise general issues concerning women and revolutionary politics and the problems we face. I was lucky in that I wasn't around in England in 1969 and 1970 when the reaction of the whole of the left to women's liberation was derisory and dismissive. Though I do clearly remember Sheila's books being dismissed by left colleagues of mine at work, and declared both diversionary and reformist.

In 1970 a group of women organized a demonstration against the Miss World contest; some were arrested, and they later produced a pamphlet which explained what they had done. And this was just one of the things I remember that influenced and inspired me in 1972 – because that pamphlet *Why Miss World?* not only talked of the humiliation of women as sex objects, but also of the lack of confidence and fear these women felt mounting the first protest against their own oppression. It wasn't just that women felt frightened to protest politically, but that most of us found it difficult to speak publicly at all; we were used to relating passively and dependently to the world as presented to us by men. We were used to being dominated by men: it was hard not to want to be. And it really hasn't been easy to change this, either then or since.

Libertarianism

For me, in many ways the ideas of the libertarian left and feminism did seem to be in harmony. I will try and explain this. First of all, they both seemed new. The libertarian politics of the seventies did not really owe much to the anarchism of the past. Though anarchism has a very long history, as old as Marxism, the student radicals of the 1968 generation were in the main not radicalized through the efforts of the 'organized' libertarian and anarchist groupings. I know this also from personal experience as I was a student anarchist in Australia in the early sixties but it took me a few years to begin to understand the political ideas that came to prominence after May 1968.

Libertarian politics were more of a genuinely spontaneous

upsurge of ideas which drew their inspiration from many different thinkers, from Marcuse, Che Guevara and the early Marx, to Laing and Vaneigem.[1] This upsurge was a product of capital's period of boom, when everything did seem possible, when in the Western world capitalism's main problem seemed to be how to keep buying all the goods it could produce. This led to the reaction against pointless consumption; 'consume more, live less'. The emphasis was on the quality of life in capitalist society and this is why psychological writings seemed important, as did those of the young Marx when he spoke of the effect of alienated labour on the individual spirit and saw the division of labour itself as a stunting of human potential.

To those who had become active in 1968 it seemed a time when anything could happen. Looking back on it, we could say that from Vietnam we drew the lesson that American imperialism, despite its technology, was not invincible. Though I'm not sure that we were aware of this at the time, we only knew whose side we were on. We certainly felt politically inspired seeing a small nation fighting 'the Beast' to the death. From the mass workers' struggles which occurred throughout France in 1968 and in Italy in 1969, people drew the lesson that the working class was prepared to fight for a better life, and that it had not been bought off by consumer durables. Students, for example, were inspired by the thought that they had a political part to play, and could act together with industrial workers, as happened in the worker-student alliances of May 1968, and the worker-student assemblies in Turin in 1969. So class struggle was once again on the agenda, and the class militancy which continued in Italy and in Britain in the early seventies showed how difficult it was for the ruling class to keep a grip on the situation in a period of economic boom. That the optimism of the early seventies and the militancy of workers' struggles which inspired us then, have not been able to survive the capitalist economic recession of the mid-seventies is something I will return to later on.

After 1968 the emphasis among the new largely ex-student libertarian left centred on the following issues. First, autonomy

– which is not the same as individualism, but meant to us taking control over your own life. Libertarians believed that people could act to change the quality of their own lives; they were more than just the passive tools of historical forces. There was a deep suspicion of any organization that claimed to do things for or in the name of the people. 'Power to the People' was one of the slogans we were chanting, as we watched our friends arrested on demonstrations, or were hauled off ourselves. As we saw it, we were the people, up against the repressive forces of the state, in our attempt to change our lives now. This meant that we were slow to form any alliances with others in our struggle, whether it was to seek support from the organized labour movement or the organized left, or progressive forces in local authorities or the left of the Labour Party. We saw them all as intrinsically reformist and hostile to our attempts to control our own lives. This wasn't inconsistent with their response to our activities.

Secondly, personal relations – you've got 'to live your politics'. We argued that our social relations now must reflect or 'prefigure' the social relations we want to create after the revolution. We said that the desire to change your own life and the world about you now is an important part of building for socialism in the future. So we opposed the Leninist position that you couldn't change anything under capitalism, you could only build an organization to overthrow it. We thought that there would be little reason for people to join a revolutionary movement unless it brought an immediate improvement in the quality of their lives, as against those who believed that you could make a split between public politics and private life. We were critical of those who might participate in some form of socialist politics and yet remain authoritarian and uncritical of their relation to their wives or their children at home, or to others in their work situation. We had in mind, for instance, the male militant who left his wife at home to mind the children while he did his 'political' work. We wanted our political activity to make room for those with children, and also to include the children.

Thirdly, you organize around your own oppression. You begin from your position as a woman, a squatter, a claimant, etc. This was linked to attacks on the nuclear family. We read both Laing and Reich, and were quite certain that we could never return to the restricted and restricting lifestyle of our parents. We saw that oppression, the power of one person to dominate and control the life of another, could be as much a part of personal social relations as of economic social relations. This led to an emphasis on collective living, collective childcare, and the setting up of nurseries.[2] The family was seen as the producer of neurosis and 'the policeman in the head' which leads people to collaborate in their own oppression.

Fourthly, the rejection of vanguards and any hierarchy of struggle. We rejected the idea that the industrial working class must be the vanguard of revolutionary struggle. Libertarians argued that all areas of life were of importance to revolutionaries. The traditional left was seen as only concerned with people at the workplace, not in the community. But libertarians always argued that people who worked at home, minded the kids, etc., were doing as important work as that done in the factories. This was expressed theoretically in a rejection of the Trotskyist left's permanent illusion that capitalism was on the point of collapse, saved only by props like the 'permanent arms economy', as IS used to suggest.[3] We felt this under estimated the role of the state in stabilizing the economy, not just through economic measures such as investment policies but through the hegemony of state ideology, and ideas expressed at every level. We saw the capitalist state as far more resilient and flexible than much of the left had previously argued. So libertarians developed richer theories of the role of the state, and its hard and soft forces of repression, not just through the police and the army but via education, health, sex role conditioning, etc.[4]

Before most of the left we emphasized work with youth. Though left groups did have their youth sections, libertarians were interested in practical work, setting up youth houses, youth newspapers, adventure playgrounds and free schools.

This youth work was not only practical but also prefigurative in its stress on young people being able to experience a different situation and develop a sense of self-determination.[5]

We worked mainly in community politics, starting community papers, squatters' and claimants' groups, and trying to organize around housing. 'Decent homes for all' was the slogan we used, aiming in particular at the failure of local authorities to provide housing for single people. The squatting movement was reduced in strength as people could no longer bear to keep on moving, keep on facing the bailiffs, as they were bought off by councils with licensed short-life houses, and the number of empty houses declined. But it did nevertheless win certain limited victories. In Islington it eventually forced the council to change its policies and begin providing housing for single people; It introduced the notion of 'shared singles' to the housing bureaucracy, to add to their 'family units'. (This can't simply he dismissed as 'reformism' since struggles were not fought in a reformist way.)

This was the time of the 'gentrification' or middle-class takeover of working-class housing in inner city boroughs like Islington. Landlords conspired with estate agents like Prebbles to 'winkle' tenants out of their homes. There was a campaign against Prebbles by the Islington Tenants Campaign which picketed Prebbles' office for many months until a historic high court judgement against them ruled that all non-industrial pickets were illegal. We did extensive research on the activities of the big property sharks like Raine, Freshwater and Joe Levy, and how the housing system worked in general until we felt we could understand what was going on.

We resisted all notions of revolutionary leadership. Living our politics meant sharing skills and breaking down all authoritarian relations now. We emphasized the creative aspects of politics, that it should be fun, and not dreary. All bourgeois social relations around work, the family, 'pleasure', possessions and relationships were challenged. This was perhaps why we supported those most oppressed by bourgeois society, prisoners, the homeless, claimants, etc., and believed that you could only fight back if you shared the material situation of the most oppressed. 'When you've got nothing, you've got nothing to lose' the tough ones sang along with Dylan. But misery does not always equal militancy, and those most oppressed are sometimes so smashed that it's hard for them to fight back at all.

Feminism

Many of these issues which I've described as central to libertarian thought were also central to feminist thought.

First, the autonomy of the women's movement was the crucial issue for women. Though left groups saw this as divisive, we were aware that their programmes of formal equality for women could conceal the actual subordination of women in their own organizations. Women had to organize their own fight against male domination; it could not be done for them.

Secondly, feminists always emphasized the importance of the personal and the subjective, the need for a total politics. By this we meant a politics that saw the links between personal life and the oppression of women at home, and the exploitation of men and women in paid work. Women demanded changes in the social relations between men and women now. We wanted to help to break down the isolation of women in the home, and to begin to change ourselves. We had to change ourselves, because the whole ideology of sexism ensured that we had always seen ourselves, and were seen by men, in ways which made us feel inferior and allowed men to dominate us. We spoke of our sexuality being defined and controlled by men, as well as the suppression of women's sexuality in most heterosexual relationships. We supported the demands of lesbians, and the importance of women exploring their own sexuality. We knew that women's sexual passivity and sexual objectification by men was linked to our feelings of powerlessness.

Thirdly, as feminists we organized around our own oppression. We also criticized the nuclear family, seeing it as the seat of women's oppression. But we were not simply concerned with the repressive ideological role of the family but saw it as the place where woman do unpaid work, thus creating the basis for our social subordination in general. We argued that the way in which domestic labour, childcare and work are organized today will all have to be changed before there can be any real liberation for women. We saw that the Marxist analysis of capitalism and class struggle had not proved itself an adequate theoretical tool to conceptualize these changes. While the traditional left was slow to realize the anti-capitalist nature of women's liberation, feminists were able to show how it was the unpaid work done by women in reproducing labour power and servicing the work force that was essential to capitalist social relations. 'Women in labour, keep capital in power' was one of the slogans painted on the wall at the first women's liberation conference held in Oxford in 1970.

More thoroughly than the libertarians, women developed new theories of the welfare state.[6] Women as mothers came into contact with the state more directly than men, in the form of welfare, nursery provision, education and health services. So it was more urgent for us to analyse the control of the state over our lives. We were aware that it was the inadequacies of these social services that created the burden borne mainly by women today. And we were aware that the provision which was available to us was not what we wanted. For example, women took up many issues in the field of health care. We demanded control over our reproduction. We exposed the way that doctors, who are mainly men, treat women's specific illnesses with contempt. We publicized the way millions of women are regularly prescribed tranquillizers and other drugs by doctors instead of them examining the social causes of many women's problems. Indeed, feminists were able to establish that the medical profession saw femininity itself as in some way pathological.[7] The feelings of passivity, dependence and powerlessness, felt by most women today, are rightly seen by psychiatrists as opposed to mental health. But instead of these aspects of feminity being attributed to the oppressive socialization of women, reinforced in everyday life, they are wrongly seen by most doctors as natural to women.

These are only a few of many such issues.

Fourthly, the women's movement also rejected 'stageism' – the idea that women's liberation could be put off until after the revolution.[8] We argued that our struggle against male domination, or patriarchy, was as central as the struggle against class oppression.[9] We said that women's oppression could not be reduced to class exploitation, that though interconnected with it, it pre-dated it and could continue after the smashing of capitalist class relations.

It was women who not only introduced many new issues into socialist politics, but also developed new forms of organization – ones which would enable us all to participate more fully in revolutionary politics. We introduced consciousness-raising groups, where all women could learn that their misery, isolation and feelings of inferiority were not simply personal problems but common to nearly all women and the product of material and ideological conditions. We introduced the small group as a more supportive and equal way of discussing things and working together. We wanted the experiences of all women to be respected and the movement to grow on this basis rather than through following general principles. We criticized the formal public meetings of the labour movement and the left where inexperienced and less confident women (and men) felt unable to contribute.

We were opposed to all forms of leaderism, and struggled for equality in all our social relations, because we were aware that the forms of dominance and subordination we were fighting could easily remain invisible, as they had been before. We knew that our struggle began with the need for women to believe that what we could contribute was important and valuable. Through writing, poetry, music and film we began to create a new feminist culture, as a part of changing our consciousness and because we knew that men have dominated every aspect of our life, including all areas of culture. We worked locally in the community, at a time when most of the left, apart from the libertarian left, was not interested in this.

Many of these ideas on the form and nature of political activity and organization can be illustrated by looking at some of the things which the women's movement initiated in Islington in the early seventies. In August 1972, a group of women opened the first local women's centre in York Way. This was one of the first women's centres anywhere in England. The idea of having a centre was in itself different from the way in which most of the left organized. A leaflet from Essex Road Women's Centre explained:

> The Women's Centre grew out of a need to meet and talk to other women about the particular problems that we all face. Many of us feel anxious that we alone are responsible for the problems we have – like loneliness if we're stuck with our kids all day and can't get out, finding a decent place to live, worrying about our health and our kids' health, or worrying about work and keeping a home going as well
>
> By meeting and talking to other women we found that we are NOT alone in our problems. And when we find that we do share experiences, it's not only a big relief, but it makes it easier to try and change things that need changing – whether it's the planning of the street you live in, or whether it's about contraception or childcare, schools, problems at work, etc. We think that women are in a really strong position to change things – because they are close to the root causes of the problems of day-to-day living, both in the house and at work.

So the idea of the centre was, firstly, as a place to meet and give real support to any women who were in some way trying to break out of their isolation, and, secondly, to allow us to build our confidence and strength that we as women could change things.

At York Way we began one of the first women's health groups, taking up many of the ideas of the women's health movement in the States. We were also active in the family allowance campaign, demanding that it be increased and paid directly to women. At about this time the Wages For Housework campaign was started and began to demand wages for women working in the home. We agreed that it was valuable to emphasize that domestic work is work, important work which is undervalued and invisible because it is unpaid. All this was a revelation to some people on the left.

We too saw woman's unpaid domestic labour in the home as central to her oppression, and also central to the reproduction and maintenance of the workforce (labour power) and thus to the maintenance of the capitalist social formation. There was a theoretical debate here, though we were not all aware of it. Wages For Housework, following the analysis of Mariarosa Dalla Costa,[10] argued that women's work at home was not only essential to capital as we said, but it also produced surplus value – that is, it directly added to the profits which capitalists could make out of their labour force. Because if there were no housewives male workers would have to pay someone to look after them, and thus would demand higher wages. We thought that this whole debate was perhaps not important, because whether or not housewives and other domestic workers produced surplus value, we were equally concerned to challenge the division of labour which consigned women to the home.

It was the pressures of housework, the double shift for 'working' women, and our general servicing role which were the major causes of women's isolation and exploitation at home and at work, as well as of our low self-evaluation and status. So the Wages For Housework campaign seemed wrong at a practical level, because their solution would institutionalize the division of work in the family. (There are now ideas to implement such a suggestion in Italy and Canada.) It also seemed wrong at a theoretical level being simply the other side of the economism of traditional Trotskyism, which sees the only way to get power in the class struggle as that of fighting for more and more money, through a wages offensive.

We began to argue generally for the socialization of

housework, for more nurseries, playgrounds, and so on. Here it wasn't just that we widened the areas of political activity in which the left had been active, in order to include women's needs. There was also the recognition of the need to have control over any gains we might make. For instance, in the demand for nurseries, we didn't just demand money from the state for more nurseries, but helped to create more community-based, non-authoritarian, non-sexist relations in the nurseries we helped to establish. Val Charlton describes this in her account of the Children's Community Centre in North London which was opened in 1972 after feminists had successfully battled for council funding:

> We are trying to break away from the traditional authoritarian mode of relating to children and are attempting to offer them as many choices as possible and as much independence as they can cope with. All activities are made available for children of both sexes but it's not simply enough to treat all the children equally. The boys have frequently already learned their advantage and are quick to make capital of it. There has to be positive support in favour of the girls, who are generally already less adventurous.[11]

Also in 1972 a women's Holloway Prison Support Group was set up, to campaign around women prisoners. We picketed Holloway Prison saying 'Free our sisters, free ourselves'. In 1973 we protested over the death through fire of Pat Cummings in Holloway Prison. We knew that most women are not in prison for crimes of violence. Petty crime, SS fraud, prostitution, etc., are the main reasons for women being sent to prison – often simply attempting to fulfil their social role of caring for their families on inadequate means. Yet, women prisoners are notoriously violent, mostly self-destructively violent – cutting themselves up and smashing their cells. Used to providing the caring and affection for just a few people, women in prison face the possible break-up of their families and loss of their children.

Women face this more than men because women tend to support men more than men support women.

In this vulnerable position, official ideology can easily work to persuade the woman in prison that she is not so much 'criminal' as maladjusted or sick – another role which women in our society, through powerlessness and training into passivity, are more likely to accept. In line with this, we tried to expose the fraud behind the rebuilding of Holloway Prison as more of a hospital, creating even greater isolation for the women inside. Over 50 per cent of women in Holloway are on drugs, indeed drugs are the only provision which women can freely obtain in Holloway. The new Holloway Prison, which places even greater stress on the therapeutic rehabilitation of women, simply encourages them to blame themselves for the predominantly material problems which landed them in there in the first place.

But York Way was not a good site for a women's centre. It closed in 1973, and in February 1974 we opened a new women's centre in Essex Road. Many women's groups, campaigns and activities started at that women's centre. The most successful was probably the health group, which produced literature on women's health, did pregnancy testing, provided a woman doctor for advice sessions, learnt self-examination, took health classes with school children, collected information on doctors and their treatment of women, provided information on abortion facilities, and, more generally, argued for the importance of preventive health care rather than simply curative medicine. Less successfully, we wrote and distributed leaflets on housing conditions and the isolation of women at home with children. We supported women's struggles for better housing, and some of us were active in squatting struggles.

By 1975 many campaigns were being co-ordinated by groups originating from the women's centre. 1974 was the beginning of the various cuts campaigns against the ever-increasing public expenditure cuts. We began campaigning to prevent the closure of our local Liverpool Road Hospital, and fought hard for it to be kept open as a community health resource. Some of us were active in the Islington Nursery Action Group, visiting nurseries to help unionize workers and also successfully pressurizing the Council into abandoning its attempts to make cuts in nurseries, showing how the cuts hit women hardest.

The campaigns for 'more and better services' emerged at the same time as the government pressure for cuts. It was in November 1974 that the first government circular came demanding cuts. And that's when a general cuts campaign started in Islington, with its first meeting held in December of that year, initiated by a group of militants, some inside and some outside the Labour Party. As a broad front campaign it was supported by community groups like the women's centre, tenants' groups, public sector workers and, in particular, by the many council-funded community service groups like law centres, Task Force and the Neighbourhood Forums. This was perhaps the first time that we got some relationship developing between the libertarian and feminist milieu and the labour movement. But at this time it was an uneasy alliance. It was never given any real support by the Trades Council, which even came out and attacked the campaign after it had held a day of action. This campaign did not last. Today with the left in a stronger position in Islington there is more hope for the new anti-cuts campaign which is being formed.

The National Working Women's Charter Campaign was also started at this time, holding its first delegate conference in October 1974. It was never very popular with us at Essex Road. This was because of the dominance of the organized left in the Charter and their wrangles over leadership, and also because it was very schematic, being simply a list of demands, and because it was concerned primarily with women in the workplace. Marxists had always argued that woman's liberation would be achieved through her full participation in waged labour. In this way they were able to subordinate women's struggles to class struggle. And it was also in this way that they were able to dismiss the importance of organizing with housewives or the struggles of those many women marginal to the wage system, for example, prostitutes.

The Working Women's Charter, a list of ten demands which would improve women's situation in paid work, was originally put together by a subcommittee of the London Trades Council. It was seen by some women in left groups as an adequate basis for socialist feminists to organize from. Though the demands did include ones around contraception, abortion and nurseries it was not an adequate platform for the socialist feminist current of the women's movement to base itself on. (And there have always been socialist feminists in the women's movement despite the different setbacks we have faced in our attempts to organize ourselves.)

The Charter's inadequacy stemmed from its orthodox reflection of the position that women's oppression is due to her unequal share in class struggle. The demands did not even criticize the sexual division of labour, which is central to male domination. It is this sexual division of labour which ensures that even if women can go out to work they will in general have the lower-paid jobs and the lower-status jobs. The point is not just that women happen to be low paid, it is that they are overwhelmingly concentrated in 'women's jobs'. And these jobs which are available to women are low in pay and status precisely because they are 'women's jobs'.[12] The threat to male workers of more women entering a particular career, is that by their very presence in any large numbers, they lower the status of that work. The best-known example of this was the change over from male to female secretaries at the end of the nineteenth century.[13] So even at work women are oppressed as much by their sex as by their class position.

The Working Women's Charter was basically a trade union response to feminism, and it was good to get some response, but it shared the inadequacies of trade unionism towards women. Some of us did however support the Working Women's Charter activities, although in fact local Charter groups interpreted and used the Charter in quite different ways – in Islington, women were involved in the local Nursery Action Group, in the Liverpool Road Hospital Campaign, in attempts to unionize workers at Marks and Spencers and elsewhere, and organizing a general meeting on women in Islington sponsored by the Trades Council. There were, however, many aspects of feminist struggle that the Charter could not incorporate. In 1975, the Working Women's Charter was rejected by the Trades Union Congress conference. It had fallen between the two stools of feminist and labour movement politics, and in the end could not survive.

In 1975 a local NAC (National Abortion Campaign) group was formed to fight James Whites's anti-abortion bill. NAC was also organized as a national campaign. But once again many women were suspicious of the national structure, saying that it was not feminist. They saw it as dominated politically by the International Marxist Group (IMG), and objected to its main focus for activities being that of lobbying MPs, seeing this as reformist. Feminists often felt that any national campaigning structure gave

women in left groups an advantage over them, in terms of determining policy, as they were more experienced in that form of centrally organized politics. This has always been a problem in the women's movement, and one of the causes of the deep tensions between women in left groups and non-aligned women, even in the socialist feminist current of the movement. Outside of left groups we moved more slowly, each of us puzzling over the pros and cons of particular tactics, particular slogans, etc., most of us frightened to push ourselves forward, and therefore hostile to those women who already seemed to have all the answers on the questions of tactics and organization. Today I feel that, difficult as it is, we must all learn to overcome our fear of political differences and be prepared to argue through our politics.

But many women did become involved in local activity against the threatened restrictions on women's access to abortion facilities, with stalls in the local market and elsewhere. We also organized colourful public protests against the Miss

Islington beauty contest, describing the degradation, violence and restriction on women's lives created by our status as sex objects for men. It was especially when we challenged this area of men's control over women, speaking of the daily rape and violence against women that we were most ridiculed in the local press and elsewhere. For it was here that we were most directly challenging the central ideology of male domination, a sexist ideology which not only attributes certain particular characteristics to women that enable men to dominate us, but also belittles and degrades those characteristics it sees as feminine.[14]

Together with the Arsenal Women's Group and others we held a local conference to try to organize the women's movement on a local area basis. We were also actively involved in all the early socialist feminist initiatives at organizing in the women's liberation movement. Many consciousness-raising and study groups started at the centre, and a women's self-help therapy group was formed, partly as a support for some women who had suffered severe emotional crises, but also because all the women involved saw mental health as an important issue. We saw that many of our deep anxieties and fears were a reaction to our powerlessness, and often because we could not receive any adequate nurturing from men. We were used to providing emotional support, but not to demanding and receiving it. This is behind the current emphasis on feminist therapy, and the creation of a Women's Therapy Centre in Islington. We talked on women's liberation at schools like Starcross, a local school for girls, and some women ran classes on women's liberation for schoolgirls at the centre. A literacy class was set up for women. There was a group for women working in traditional men's jobs, and, in fact, so many groups that I can't remember them all.

But, despite all of the creativity and energy which originated from the women's centre, it was always hard to keep it open to all women for more than a few hours a week, on Saturdays and Wednesday nights. And many women were only active in the centre for about a year, and would then drift off. It was often hard to get the new women who came along involved in the centre, and it was difficult to keep up any good communication between the different groups which did meet there.

Some of us wanted to obtain money for a paid worker at the centre in order to keep it open to co-ordinate and plan activities. But others rejected such an idea out of hand, believing it would be 'selling out' to obtain money from the local council or the state, paving the way to our co-option by them. Women also feared that a paid worker would create a hierarchical structure. The first point came from our analysis of the state, which led us to see social workers, for instance, as the repressive 'soft cops' of the system. There seemed to be a contradiction between our emphasis on self-help and collective activity and the idea of state funding. Wasn't the role of the social worker or the state-funded service centre to prevent people taking collective direct action to solve their problems by holding out the false promise of there being some individual solutions for people's problems? But weren't we just unpaid radical social workers anyway?

At that time we were less aware of the radical potential for militancy in the state sector workers, living out the contradictions of trying to provide a service for human needs while employed by a state tied to the profitability of capitalism. Many of these workers are very frustrated by the futility of their attempts to meet their clients' needs. Some social workers, for instance, were already referring people to squatting advisory centres and other groups committed to building struggles around particular issues. It is in the area of social services and the state that the threat to jobs through cuts and closures and rationalization can be most easily linked to wider possibilities for anti-capitalist struggles, because they raise the question of people's needs. Many health workers, teachers, etc., are aware that it is not just lack of resources that makes their jobs unsatisfactory. It is also the formal hierarchy and the rigid rules through which the state is organized that makes their jobs so difficult.

The current attack on the funding of so-called voluntary groups, for example, law centres, housing aid centres, and other radical advice centres is precisely because they have been able to provide the space for and have been effective in helping to organize struggles around people's needs. The money that is being saved by such cuts is often quite negligible, the motivation for them is political. It may be true that these voluntary groups provided new jobs mainly, although not only, for the 'radical professionals', but I think that at Essex Road we were not as aware as we might have been of the contradictions over funding, and the possibilities of using it to 'bite the hand that feeds you'.

With others I have thought more recently about some of these problems and think they need more analysis. The modern state is such a huge and complex organization, the situation being quite different from that in 1917 Tsarist Russia, from which so much revolutionary strategy derives. Then the state's role was purely repressive, defending the interests of the ruling class. But the modern state has been formed by the on-going compromise between the working-class movement channelled into reformist political strategy and the capitalist class. The state spreads its tentacles throughout society. Nationalization, health care, education, care of the young and old, research, funding of the arts are some of the ways in which the modern state interpenetrates society in a way it never did before 1945.

For libertarians and many feminists, instances of the creeping hand of state control were everywhere, from community festivals to nurseries and old people's homes. We tended to argue that the whole system was rotten, and it was useless to tinker with it. We were not wrong to emphasize the extent of this state control over our daily lives, but we were wrong to see the state in all its ramifications as a monolith, and not see that there could be contradictions in its development. This is particularly clear now that the Tory government is trying to sell off state services to the private sector as fast as it can – continuing the attacks on state welfare already initiated by the previous labour government. Today it should be clearer that we must defend many existing state services, from the National Health Service (NHS) to school crossing patrols. It's no longer simply a question of the overthrowing of the state, but of a strategy which fights for an expansion and transformation of the services it provides – not necessarily in a centralized form. This raises the whole issue of the nature of a socialist state, which we all need to think about, and which is crucial for us as women fighting the sexual division of labour which is basic to women's oppression.

Today we need a more sophisticated analysis of reformism and the state, which, on the one hand, is not based on the traditional social democratic idea, and in a different way on the Leninist model, which sees socialism as nationalization plus state planning, nor, on the other, one which turns its back on the need for struggle to expand state provision. This means a strategy which both defends the welfare institutions of the state when they are under attack while arguing the need to go beyond them. On a small scale this strategy can be illustrated by the 160 women's aid refuges that have been set up over the last few years to enable battered women to escape from violent husbands. The National Federation Of Women's Aid was able to obtain local state funding for refuges while insisting that the refuges should be run by and for women and should encourage self-help and independence. Similar examples, as Sheila shows, can be given of nursery victories where funding was provided and the people who fought for it retained control over the nurseries.[15]

But to return to my story, when our women's centre was forced to close in late 1976, we had sufficient anxieties over whether we were going about things in the right way that few tears were shed. One woman, involved from the start, said, 'That's good, now we can start again, and build up another women's centre'. But we never did. For the next three years there was no broad-based open women's liberation group in Islington, though we did have a national Rape Crisis Centre, women's refuges, a NAG group, and other groups organized around particular issues as well as women's consciousness-raising and study groups. Today there is a new women's centre in Islington, but there is little continuity between our old women's centre and the new one which is being opened. It is as though things are all starting again from scratch and I'm not sure that any lessons have been learned, or could have been learned, from which this new group of women can begin. Those feminists who were active around Essex Road have not become involved in the new centre, most of them saying, 'Oh no, not the same problems all over again'.

Feminism and the Left

Meanwhile, the traditional left was belatedly trying to catch up with the energy of the women's liberation movement, in particular they were impressed by the 40,000 strong pro-abortion march of 1975. They weren't laughing at the 'women's libbers' any more, though of course they did say we were all middle class, or at least that's what their middle-class leaders were saying. I don't feel in a position to give a complete analysis of the left's position on feminism, but I want to give my impressions of the main left groups, ignoring the smaller groups and those that choose to dismiss feminism altogether.

The reason I want to look at the revolutionary left is not to engage in any form of sectarianism, but because as socialist feminists we accept that women's oppression is an integral part of the capitalist system. As I've said, the subordination of women through the division of labour centred on the family is central to the maintenance and reproduction of the capitalist system of existing class relations of exploitation. But women's oppression (like black oppression) is not simply just another aspect of class exploitation. All men do benefit from it, by having power over at least some women, however exploited they themselves may be. But we do realize that only a revolutionary transformation of capitalist society can overcome women's oppression, class exploitation, and all forms of social domination. We know we must unite all those fighting their oppression with the struggle against class exploitation.

By the mid-seventies, most of the Communist Party (CP) did come officially to accept the need for an autonomous women's movement. The CP argues that it wishes to make broad alliances with an autonomous women's movement. Certain CP women have placed great emphasis on the importance of studying the ideology of women's oppression, the ways in which women as well as men come to accept ideas of women's inferiority and invisibility. They have also begun to theorize the role of the capitalist state as it organizes reproduction and maintains women's subordination in the interests of the ruling class. Much of the official contribution of CP feminists has tended to be more of a theoretical and intellectual one, though many CP women do actively support NAC, and other feminist initiatives.

The intellectual contribution of CP feminists is consistent with the direction of the CP as outlined in their publication the *British Road to Socialism.* This direction encourages an ideological offensive against capitalist domination while doing little to build any form of mass working-class resistance. Indeed the CP often finds itself in the position of having to curb actual militancy, which potentially threatens its broad alliances with reformist leaders of the labour movement. For example, in Islington through their control of the Trades Council they have consistently failed to offer any practical support to the most militant industrial struggles which have occurred in the borough. And again, on the whole issue of unemployment they have failed to respond in any practical way to the five occupations which have occurred against redundancies, the largest being the occupation of Crosfields electronic factory in 1975 when 300 people were made redundant. They were also opposed to the industrial action of the Tyndale teachers in 1976 who were eventually sacked after a campaign was launched against their progressive education methods, supported by the Labour right of the council. These alliances are part of the CP's general acceptance of a peaceful parliamentary road to socialism in accordance with what is now called 'Eurocommunism'.

Thus women CP members could be given the space to develop an ideological critique whilst having little impact on their parties overall political direction. The *British Road to Socialism* does often mention the importance of the women's liberation movement. But the political contribution of the women's movement or of other autonomous movements as they affect the actual potential for a real revolutionary unification of the working class is not discussed.

Indeed, in the final analysis the *British Road to Socialism* does not depart from orthodox Marxist analysis. And this is an analysis which overlooks the significance of existing divisions within the working class, and the demands of the women's movement and of the black movement that the fight against their oppression must be an essential part of the struggle for socialism.

So the CP support for the autonomous women's movement does not seem to have served to educate its leadership when they write:

> Only socialism can overcome the basic contradiction from which every aspect of the crisis flows. Socialism replaces private ownership by public ownership. *The basic contradictions of society are removed.* [My italics. British Road to Socialism, line 465.]

It seems that CP women have been allowed to do what they wanted, while the CP leadership did what it wanted. Though even this situation of tolerance for feminism has begun to change within the CP today. As the CP and other left groups begin to scent the long-awaited revival of industrial militancy, feminists in the party will be told not to obstruct the 'turn to the class'.

The International Marxist Group (the British section of the Trotskyist Fourth International), does appear to have a more consistent theory and practice in support of the need for an autonomous women's movement.

Their weekly paper, *Socialist Challenge*, now takes the question of women's oppression seriously. But while claiming to support the women's liberation movement in its totality, there is still a strong tendency to reduce women's oppression entirely to class oppression. For example, in 1978 a centre spread in *Socialist Challenge* which argued for women's liberation made no analysis of women's oppression as distinct from class exploitation. It gave no analysis of patriarchy.

The point about this is that while the IMG are prepared to accept women's right to organize separately, they don't seem to accept what we have to say on the limitations of orthodox Marxism.[16] The way in which they want to integrate feminism and socialism is by adding on 'women's demands' to their existing programme, adding on demands for nurseries, abortion facilities, etc. But again they do not seem to see the need for feminism to transform the whole nature of working-class politics and the left.

As feminists we argue that we are not simply fighting together with men against capitalism as a more exploited section of the class. We are also fighting against male domination now, which manifests itself in all aspects of life, both within and outside of the working class. (Black people of course have a similar theory about their oppression.) So women are central to the struggle against capitalist social relations not only in the workplace but also in the home. We are demanding that men change themselves, that they change their relations to women, and to children, and take on some of the nurturing and caring work which women have always done. And this is the way in which we want to transform the nature of working-class politics, and overcome the divisions within the working class. It is presumably because of our talk about everyday life, about finding new, non-patriarchal and non-authoritarian ways of relating to and caring for each other that the women's movement has been dismissed by certain leading members of the IMG as a 'cultural movement'. The analysis is that because we are not simply making demands on the state, we are not making 'political demands'. In 1977, John Ross, who sees the women's movement as a social movement which can make political demands, stated that the issue of women's rights to abortion only became political when it began to make demands on the state.[17] Such an analysis obviously would be rejected by most feminists.

So while the IMG has accepted the organizational autonomy of the women's movement, and indeed have now set up women's caucuses within their own organization, I don't think that they accept the political autonomy of feminism as adding a new dimension to the nature of class politics. The fact that we believe that women's oppression cannot be understood simply within the Trotskyist analysis of 'the historic interests of the working class' does not necessarily mean that we as socialist feminists ignore the working class and fail to prove ourselves true revolutionary socialists. The fact that some of us may not have joined a revolutionary organization which we feel has not adequately taken up and integrated the insights of feminism does not mean that we are not a part of the struggle to build one.

The Socialist Workers Party (SWP), the largest group in the Trotskyist tradition in Britain and one which has broken from many orthodox positions of Trotskyism, does not accept the need for an autonomous women's movement at all. Their basic attitude to the women's movement is determined by the way they see themselves as the only 'real revolutionaries'. This means that for the SWP, fighting for women's liberation, like building the class struggle, is one and the same thing as building the SWP. If you accept the need for a revolutionary socialist perspective, then you join the SWP, they say. So they reject the need for either the organizational or the political autonomy of the women's movement.

'Class struggle is a form of warfare, and in warfare there has to be a single leadership,' says Chris Harman from the central committee of the SWP, echoing Lenin, in *What is to be Done?* in 1902. So the need for any organizational independence of women is rejected. Women's oppression is derived from capitalist exploitation, he argues, so they reject the need for a political independence for women organizing.[18]

When the SWP comes to write about the women's movement, all that I have ever found are jibes about it being middle class. Thus Anna Paczuska, one of the SWP's leading writers on women's politics, dismisses the 1979 socialist feminist conference like this:

> All we've got is a movement of middle class women, many in their thirties, polishing their memories for the glossy magazines, complacently surrounded by mortgages and monthly subscriptions to *Which* magazine. . . The movement is dying on its feet or rather in its Habitat armchairs. It is being choked to death by respectability, nostalgia and direct aid from the state and the Establishment. [*Socialist Worker*, 7 April 1979.]

The term 'middle class' is one of the favourite terms of abuse used by the SWP. Of course, they never bother to define the contemporary working class, or the position, for instance, of teachers. For the SWP, teachers are working class when they are in the SWP or are attending union meetings, but middle class when they attend a women's liberation conference. I think that many workers would be surprised and insulted to learn that they have never had mortgages, magazines or comfortable furniture. It is true that we do need to distinguish a person's class origin from their class perspective, but the SWP certainly makes no attempt to do so. As they are aware when it suits them, there is a real need to develop a new understanding of the working class which includes proletarianized white collar sectors such as teachers, technicians, etc. So why resort to mere hypocrisy?

In this piece and many others which have appeared in *Socialist Worker*, the weekly paper of the SWP, and elsewhere, Anna shows herself to be not just ambivalent about but quite blatantly hostile towards the women's movement. She is concerned to dismiss us and our activities altogether. In a more recent article in which she is referring to the three of us writing this book, she comments:

> They do not believe that the working class has the capacity or the creativity to win the struggle for women's liberation. They have no trust so they separate off their struggles for themselves. [*Socialist Worker*, 18 August 1979.]

Here Anna is illustrating the SWP position, which I have referred to as the orthodox Marxist position, which takes no account of divisions within the class as barriers to class unity. Against this position, we argue that a strong and independent women's movement, which seeks to understand and organize itself around the struggles of women, is a political necessity for changing the nature of the left and, more importantly, overcoming the divisions within the class and society.

Moreover statements made by Anna should not be seen as the voice of an individual – they represent the views on women of an overwhelming majority on the male-dominated Central Committee of the SWP. However, within Women's Voice, the women's magazine and organization started by SWP members, the situation is more complex. The Central Committee of the SWP want Women's Voice to be a 'periphery organization' of the SWP, organizing with working-class women, primarily in the workplace, in order to draw 'the best of them' into the SWP. However, many SWP women in Women's Voice are opposed to this position. They want a greater degree of independence for Women's Voice as a sister organization of the SWP, and they do want to give more importance to women's struggles against all aspects of their oppression. Unfortunately, however, many of them still continue to dismiss the women's movement as middle class and reformist, unorganized and unable to relate to working-class women. It was this sort of attitude which led them a few years ago to organize a separate abortion demonstration after the official NAC one.

Contrary to this view, I believe that there are many women in the socialist feminist current of the women's movement who do also want to locate their politics in the current situation and build a working-class base to the women's movement The SWP is not alone in holding this perspective, though they have perhaps done more about it. Although we may not get many working-class women along to our conferences and local meetings, many of the initiatives of the women's movement in Women's Aid, rape crisis centres, nursery campaigns, cuts campaigns like the one to defend the Elizabeth Garrett Anderson Hospital in London, and others, clearly do involve working-class women. The women's movement did mobilize in defence of the Trico women on strike for equal pay, and the Grunwick strikers who were demanding union recognition. Many feminists have been active in trades councils and tenants' associations. We don't deny that we have problems in developing a working-class orientation, but we think that it is politically wrong for Women's Voice to dismiss the importance of the women's movement and to deny what they have learned from it. Even the success of their new *Women's Voice* magazine came after it began to model itself more closely on the women's liberation magazine, *Spare Rib*, borrowing many ideas from that publication.

I also cannot accept the degree of workplace orientation of Women's Voice which leads them still to accept a priority of struggle which places many of women's central struggles against male domination at the periphery. Thus Lindsey German writes of women's movement initiatives:

> Working class women are related to in most areas where they are weakest (in battered wives' homes or rape crisis centres) rather than when women are strongest (in unions and tenants' associations)... [*Socialist Review*, November 1978.]

And 'Reclaim the Night' demonstrations, against the harassment and violence which women daily face in the streets, are referred to as 'a "soft" issue'. There is an argument for considering where women are strongest. But *in fact* women are not strong in unions today, and are not getting any stronger, even if their membership is rising numerically. We believe that the only way women in unions will get stronger is if they are supported *from the outside by a strong women's movement.* It's a dialectical process, which the SWP in spite of its Marxism, seem unable to see. Of course, 'Reclaim the Night' and NAC are helped by support from women in trade unions, and women in trade unions are helped by the support they can get from the women's movement.

While Women's Voice has shown itself at times to be effective in mobilizing support for women's struggles, I think the priority which they place on recruiting to the SWP, and the fact that they accept the identification of joining their party with holding a revolutionary perspective, means that Women's Voice could not itself become the focus for building a mass women's movement.

What we have got to get right in the women's movement, to confront the left and the labour movement, is the interplay between sex and class oppression. Not only are they both central, but they feed off each other. And they are not reducible either one to the other. Whereas the orthodox Marxist analysis puts class before sex, and Lindsey German writes: 'The fundamental division is not between the sexes, but between those who produced the wealth in society and those who rob them of it' (*Socialist Review*, September 1979) there are also 'revolutionary feminists' who put sex before class. They say: 'Women's revolution is the revolution. Sex struggle is the struggle.'[19] This is not the place to develop a critique of revolutionary feminism. Though I see a political theory which seems to write off half of humanity as a *biological* enemy as absurd. However, some of the issues revolutionary feminists have emphasized, those of rape, pornography and male violence against women are central to feminism and need to be taken up by socialist feminists and the socialist movement as a whole.

But I would argue now that it is not sufficient simply to talk of organizing around your own oppression, as libertarians and revolutionary feminists have done. For instance, although we are all oppressed as women, it is not true that we are all oppressed in the same way, even as women. Black and working-class women are oppressed in distinct ways, and we need to understand this in order to build solidarity amongst women. Without a more general perspective we won't be a part of many of the most important anti-capitalist struggles today, struggles which involve women obviously, black struggles, anti-imperialist struggles, and the growth of the new working-class offensive that is needed in this period of ferocious Tory attacks on the working class. Feminists do need a socialist perspective, but a Marxism which does not base itself on feminism, which does not recognize that the division within the working class and society as a whole necessitates a strong and autonomous women's movement, is not what we call 'socialist', it will not liberate women.

Socialism in One Borough

The main left groups did not seem to have found adequate ways of integrating Marxism and feminism in their theory or practice. But by the mid-seventies it was also becoming increasingly clear to me that there were problems and limitations in the political perspectives of many of us active simply within the women's movement. Most of us did believe that full women's liberation depended on the destruction of all hierarchical relations, of class, race, and sex. 'There will be no women's liberation without revolution. There will be no revolution without women's liberation.' The women's movement alone, however, didn't seem to equip most of us with a full interpretation of modern capitalism, and the way things were moving in the struggle against it, both nationally and internationally.

A split remained between women's politics which produced a clear understanding of personal relations and personal oppression in everyday life, and the politics of the left groups which seemed more able to produce an understanding of the world as a totality. This in turn reflects, of course, the traditional division between women's concern about people and their feelings and men's concern about practical matters and the big wide world. We could always take up the subjective side of struggles, but in some areas could not always go further than this.

This was one of the reasons why towards the end of 1974 I started shifting my energies more towards a local political paper, the *Islington Gutter Press.* This was a libertarian socialist and feminist paper which some of the women who set up the women's centre had also worked on.

It was our inability at Essex Road to get working-class women involved, as well as the fact that women who had established the centre were no longer enthusiastic about it, that led me to seek new political initiatives. But it had been the writings of, and the discussion in, the women's movement that enabled me to get a clearer theoretical perspective on the world, or at least a real understanding of women's subordinate place in it. Our activities at Essex Road did increase our confidence that we could contribute politically, and so we became more confident both emotionally and theoretically. I think this point is made more generally by the American socialist feminist Linda Gordon when she writes...

> ... once people do connect deeply felt personal problems to larger political structures, they often go on to make political sense out of the whole society rather quickly. This is not merely hypothetical; many women in the last decade moved rapidly from complaints about sexual relationships to feminism to socialism.[20]

Working on the *Gutter Press* gave us an understanding of the area we lived in. It took us several years to get to grips with the complexities of the local political scene. We began to understand some of the workings of the local state, and how local authority finance worked. We made more contact with local men and women. We learned more about housing problems in the borough, the various struggles for better services, the inactivity of the Islington Trades Council, and the activity of the small Labour left in trying to get more progressive policies adopted inside a Labour council.

We tried to make the links between the different struggles and activities we were reporting on; for better housing, and against the abuses of private landlords and property boom speculators, against the decline of local industry, for better education and for more space for youth, against racism, against sexism, against all welfare cuts and for control over services. We were not parochial in our approach to these issues, but always tried to place them 'in a global perspective' declaring ourselves interested 'in what went on, in Hackney, in Haringey or even Haiphong'.

We had remained independent of any of the left groups because we didn't want them to tell us what to do. We thought they were all authoritarian, hierarchical and male dominated. Though, of course, similar problems of professionalism and male domination cropped up – continuously – on the paper. More importantly, we also knew that apart from Big Flame they did not take seriously our politics which emphasized local work and attempts to organize on an area basis, which differed from their focus on industrial activity or particular national campaigns.[21] We believed, and rightly I think, that their emphasis on recruitment and party building, and their reliance on launching national campaigns, could interfere with our attempts at sustained local organizing in a way which was open and sensitive to the particular activities and needs of all those engaged in any form of resistance or struggle. But we did also worry about becoming isolated as a small group producing a local socialist paper but not being accountable to any wider socialist grouping.

In May 1978, the *Gutter Press* organized a local socialist conference, partly to overcome our own feelings of isolation, and our own failure to grow as a collective and get more people directly involved in the paper. We also wanted to see if there were ways in which the paper could become more efficient in its attempt to provide support for and link different areas of struggle, by becoming more accountable to a larger grouping of socialists with a similar political perspective to ours. We wrote that we wanted, 'to help stimulate enduring organizational links bridging the community and industrial struggles. . . We feel that it is possible to create greater co-ordination and support between people involved in local struggles. In the absence of a militant Trades Council, which could do just such a job, we are looking for new possibilities of co-ordination.' (*Gutter Press* leaflet, March 1978.) At the conference, which was attended by

150 people, we found that there were a large number of people, inside and outside of left groups, and inside and outside of the Labour Party, who were keen to set up a socialist centre in Islington. This socialist centre now meets weekly in a local pub, and is supported by most of the left, in particular by individuals in the Labour Party, the CP, the IMG, and Big Flame as well as by most socialist feminists and many non-aligned socialists.

The centre has organized many very well-attended and successful meetings, on Ireland, on feminism, on racism and on fascism, on struggles internationally and nationally, as well as attempts to understand the local situation in more detail and provide entertainment and pleasure. Evenings are planned to fit in with wider struggles; for example, a meeting on Ireland before or after a big Irish demonstration. It has therefore provided a useful base for meeting other local militants. It has increased the possibilities for more regular joint work when struggles arise, as well as providing political education, and entertainment which strengthens the growth of an alternative socialist and feminist culture. I think it was the consistent work done by the *Gutter Press* in establishing contacts and trust between militants that made the centre a real possibility in Islington. The paper collective has also now expanded, and become politically more diverse.

The socialist centre has therefore, in part, served to validate attempts made originally by those outside of the traditional left to find new ways of organizing. It is true, though, that at present the centre serves better as a focus for co-operation and discussion between the left than as a place for extending our base further within the working class. Some of us are hopeful that the support that we can give to people in struggle will begin to overcome this problem. Others are less worried about it. In fact, one of the most interesting, or perhaps most distressing, aspects of the centre is how clearly it often defines and separates the two groups of people, those most concerned with creating left alternatives and those most concerned with class struggle. Nevertheless, most of us still feel that the centre does create real possibilities for strengthening co-operation amongst socialists and feminists, as well as a way to reach out to working-class women and men in the area. This does not mean that we reject more traditional forms of political work centred on the workplace and the unions.

Some Conclusions

In this last section I want to return to some of the problems created by the way we organized in the women's movement and the libertarian left. As I have illustrated, we always emphasized the importance of local activity and tended to under-emphasize, and were suspicious of, national organization. In national structures we felt women, in particular, couldn't overcome the problems of male domination and leaderism and feel able to contribute their own experiences. This of course contrasts with the traditional revolutionary left who tend to have an over-emphasis on national and international politics and to dismiss attempts at local organizing as mere localism. The national organization which the women's movement has achieved is only around particular struggles, for example, NAC, Women's Aid or WARF (Women against Racism and Fascism). But this leaves us with problems, even in linking up these particular struggles. How do we arrive at any overall perspectives, decide which activities to get involved in and evaluate the results of our work?

I think the final collapse of the Essex Road Women's Centre and our failure to replace it are linked to the general problems which can occur for any loose network of small local groups. It's not easy to work out where you are going on your own as a small group, or to work out where you have succeeded and where you have failed. It's difficult for other people in other places to learn from your experiences, and for you to learn from them. We could have benefited from more regular exchange of experiences from other groups, comparing and contrasting our activities.

The problem of not really operating within an experience sharing and learning process is a difficult one. At a recent conference on women's centres in July 1979 all the old debates and conflicts came up, as though for the first time. Were women acting as unpaid social workers? Should men ever be allowed in? Should centres be funded? Why was it hard to reach working-class women, and was this important? Resolving the conflicts seemed to be as hard as ever. There was no agreement on how the centres fitted in to an overall strategy for achieving liberation. These recurring conflicts do seem to be a strong argument for some form of national organization. Though it is also true that national organizations can be slow to learn if they rely on old formulas and dogma seen as universally valid, instead of learning from new movements. For instance, issues like sexism, racism, national autonomy, and energy policies are all ones which the revolutionary left has been slow to take up. But the women's movement does need some way of assessing its past effectiveness, and using this to develop future directions in less random ways.

At Essex Road we did learn that it was hard to extend our politics outside of ourselves, and to relate to local working-class women, but we never really knew what to do about this. It is not an easy problem to solve. But if you are trying to involve working-class women, you sometimes need to take up issues which don't relate only to women, for example nurseries, housing, etc. Though you can carry a feminist perspective into these issues, you will need to go outside of your women's group to do this, extending the base of your activity. Our lack of structure perhaps made it difficult for working-class women who were outside of our friendship networks, to know how to get involved. I know of one woman who used to walk past our women's centre every day before she had fled from her violent husband, and never dared to come in. She now works at a women's refuge, but in those days, not knowing who we were, it would have been difficult for her to have looked to us for support.

This is linked to another problem. Women correctly realized the importance of including a struggle around personal relations within the struggle for socialism, and argued that without this many women would not become involved at all. 'The personal is political' was a central slogan of the women's movement. But this slogan did come to be interpreted in a very vague way, as though it meant that whatever you do, your actions have political significance. I don't think that this was the idea behind the slogan. What it did assert was that there is a connection between how you choose to live and relate to people and the struggle for social change.[22] This was all the more obvious to women in that our training into inferiority and passivity made it even more difficult for us to struggle or to feel a part of a male-dominated left. We had to create new supportive structures if we were to feel confident enough that what we said and did in our struggle against patriarchy and capitalism was important. Women said that how we relate to each other in everyday life is a part of the struggle for socialism, and in this way socialism can begin to grow within capitalism itself, but the struggle against oppression remains to be fought and won.

Over the ten years since 1968, however, there has been a complex development in the often overlapping areas of libertarianism and feminism. It does seem that many libertarians have overstressed the prefigurative lifestyle element. This has led many of them to retreat from public political activity and class politics into rustic bliss, or mysticism, or whole foods or ghetto-ized co-ops. But these forms of retreat are not options which are open to many peoples in particular; working-class people do not have the freedom to choose them. They are more trapped within the capital-labour relationship, both at home and at work, as they do what they must to support themselves and their families. But this withdrawal from consumer and urban life does have deep roots in English socialism (Carpenter, Owen, etc.) and it does maintain a visionary strand in the socialist movement that we can ill do without. It exists most clearly today in what is known as the 'communes movement'. Some parts of the women's movement have shown the same tendency, which others have characterized as 'cultural feminism', on the analogy of cultural nationalism.[23] Perhaps it is also possible to talk of a 'cultural libertarianism'. These politics do show us the possibilities of new and better ways to live, but exactly how they relate to the building of a combative feminist and socialist movement is something that remains ambiguous both historically and in the present.

The preoccupation more with lifestyles than with building the women's movement increased in Islington once the women's centre had closed. Because then it became less clear how women could help build a movement which was open to all women in their struggle for liberation. Women in their different groups, whether women's groups or mixed groups or campaigns, found it more difficult to get support from each other. We became more isolated and have difficulty in responding to specific feminist issues as they arise. In Islington there are now moves from one local study group to change this, by organizing open discussions on women's liberation locally. Obviously in many areas socialist feminist groups are working towards a similar goal. Nevertheless, I think it's true to say that at least some women have lost some of the confidence they had in the early seventies in the struggle to build the women's movement and have become even more suspicious of any overt political work.

Part of the problem is related to the general crisis of the profitability of capitalism, and the defeats of the working class. As I said at the beginning, the early seventies was still a period of economic boom. In these conditions it was clear that militancy did pay off. In many places people were able to fight for, and win, particular struggles, whether it was setting up a nursery, the funding of a youth project, improved housing conditions, or the establishment of a workers' co-operative, such as the women's co-operative at the shoe factory in Fakenham, Norfolk. People could feel more optimistic about the possibility of changing their lives collectively, and feel that it was worth the effort of trying to do so.

In the women's movement we did seem to be winning some of the things we fought for in the early seventies, even if in a deformed way. For instance the demands for women's liberation did seem to get rid of some of the more superficial forms of women's oppression. It is now becoming more and more acceptable that sexual discrimination in jobs, pubs and clubs is wrong, and its days may well be numbered. Though it is still clear that, despite equal pay, the relative position of women to men in the workforce, as the most exploited wage earners, was not changing very fast – in fact it has got worse since April 1978.[24]

But the economic recession of 1975 began to undermine the earlier forms of militancy, both in the workplace and the community. The ruling class – at first through a Labour government, and now with a Tory government – has been able to launch a general offensive against working-class organization. So we began to see unemployment rise, the thorough-going dismantling of welfare services, increasingly restrictive and racist immigration policies, and the continuous expansion of state repression, seen daily in Northern Ireland but also used against any large-scale industrial or oppositional militancy whether at Grunwick, or in the housing struggles of Huntley Street in London, or in the anti-fascist demonstrations at Southall.

In this situation industrial militancy was on the retreat, forced back into more sectoral and negotiating tactics, as each group of workers tried to have themselves declared a 'special case'. In this way they hoped to fight off the attacks on their living standards caused first of all through the 'social contract' (government-imposed limits on wage increases) and state expenditure cuts. Today, under the Tories, the workforce is being further disciplined primarily by the threat of unemployment as the state cuts its public spending even more drastically and reduces its subsidies to industry. This means that both in the workplace and the community, victories, whether local or national, have become much more difficult and there is an increasing demoralization amongst militants in all sections of struggle. So it is also becoming clearer that there cannot be local victories against the forms oppression is taking; for example, cuts in the

NHS are nationwide. This is the reasoning behind the creation of national organizations such as 'Fightback' in the area of health care, campaigning both against all hospital closures and cutbacks and against low pay as well as for better services in general.

This means that it is forms of organization which have national and international perspectives and links which seem to be even more necessary for successful struggles today. It's also true that, more urgently than ever, the current period demands that we ally with the traditional institutions of the labour movement. We need to understand the possibilities and the limitations of these institutions. The tendency in the past of libertarians and some feminists to by-pass these institutions (trades councils, union branches, etc.), which perhaps was never really justified, is quite definitely not possible today. There is always the danger that these forms of national organization and these alliances can lead to a dismissal of the dimensions of struggle which libertarians and feminists brought into the political arena. A sense of urgency can create a stronger pressure on the left to push aside the significance of the more personal areas of struggle. This danger will now be with us for a long time. And so the split between feminists and the traditional left remains, despite the attempts on both sides to build new bridges.

What I am wanting to focus on in this last section are three main problems which need a lot more thought. First, the relation between feminism and personal politics, and left groups and the general political situation. Secondly, the relation between local organizing and national organizing, and how this relates to the conflict between libertarians and feminists and the traditional left in the current situation. Thirdly, how we move on to a perspective for building socialism which can incorporate both feminists politics and the new ideas and ways of organizing which have emerged over the last ten years.

The problem for both libertarians and feminists, focusing on the importance of local work and the need to build local organizations, is how to create a larger socialist and feminist movement. A movement, built from the base up, which could mobilize enough people to fight and win, not just any one struggle – difficult as this is – but strengthen us so that the experience of each struggle is not lost but contributes to the next. Libertarians tried building a network of local groups to link up experiences and activity. There were three national conferences in 1973 and 1974. But there wasn't the political will to maintain any national organization at that time. The libertarian rejection of vanguards meant that we could not really accept the necessity for any politically coherent central organization. But, we cannot assume that links will just happen spontaneously as they are needed.

Today the women's movement also finds it difficult to take political initiatives, except in very specific areas such as fighting off attacks on women's access to abortion. Yet right now we face an enormous ideological attack on all our recent gains. Women are under attack not just in our struggle for equal pay, for more nurseries and better health care (now all threatened by Tory cuts), but attacks on even more basic things, such as the threat to women's right to maternity leave. This amounts to an attack on women's rights to waged work at all, if we have young children. Thus we increasingly hear, as was argued recently in the House of Lords, that 'unemployment could be solved at a stroke, if women went back to the home'. *As a way out of the economic crisis, the ruling class is seeking to strengthen the ideology of sexism to justify its attacks on the working class in general, and women in particular, thus revealing more clearly than ever the links between sex oppression and class exploitation.*

In this deteriorating situation, it's going to be harder for the women's movement not to feel politically marginal, unless we can find ways of making alliances with all those in struggle, both women and men, to co-ordinate actions to defend women's interests. We are not well organized in the women's movement. Although the socialist feminist current is trying to organize regional networks, and has been quite successful in some areas, it has been less successful in others. The useful national socialist feminist newsletter *Scarlet Women* has not yet managed to serve as a co-ordinating focus. We know that socialist feminists are not a minority in the women's movement – over a thousand women attended our last two conferences. But in the coming period we do need the support not just of a strong and autonomous women's movement but of the general perspectives and priorities of the socialist feminist current within it. The structures we agreed to build at our last conference mean that we must put a lot more energy into developing our regional socialist feminist organizations, and use them to co-ordinate the different campaigns we are involved in.[25] This would enable *Scarlet Women* to be more effective as a national co-ordinator.

I think we are also going to have to go beyond a criticism of the left and labour movement forms of politics, however correct we are to say that they have failed to take up the issues of feminism except in a tokenistic way. We do have to relate to both the left and the labour movement, but only by insisting that they learn from what we have to say as feminists. The left will have to understand and criticize the way in which working-class organizations through the labour movement have consistently failed to fight women's oppression. A wages offensive, for instance, is of little use to women unless it also recognizes the need for more nurseries, for a shorter working week, and actively seeks to change women's position both at home and in the work-force. We need to argue, for example, that the struggle for a shorter working week is a crucial struggle for women because it allows men to share in the childcare and house work. A recent article in *Red Rag* makes this point as follows:

> Implicit in our strivings of the last years has been an adaptation to the world of work, rather than an adaptation of that world to one that allows time for children, leisure, politics.[26]

This means that we insist that the labour movement takes into account the needs of women not just as waged workers, but also as housewives and consumers. At the same time we must strengthen our ideological offensive against the acceptance of separate spheres for women and men on which our subordination rests.

For women who want to be active in left politics outside of the women's movement, I think it is also true that male domination, elitism and passivity can exist in unstructured local groups and sectoral campaigns as well as in national organizations. People who are less confident, and less experienced at organizing, or who have less time, will find it harder to participate effectively in such groups. I have found that sometimes it can be even harder to combat 'leaderism' within the small group, as interactions are more likely to be seen in purely individual and personal terms, rather than as political manifestations. Nevertheless, we do need to find alternatives to the old structures of organizing used by the left and the labour movement, of large meetings and platform speakers which clearly silence people and do not encourage any sort of mass involvement.

There is no easy solution to the problem of creating new political structures which overcome rather than reproduce existing hierarchies of sex, class and race. For this reason most feminists could not take seriously any national organization which did not actively support the autonomy of groups to organize against their particular oppression, which did not realize that it had as much to learn from as to teach those in struggle, or one which ignored what women have said about how to organize, using truly egalitarian and supportive structures which build the confidence and participation of all involved. Alongside the need to organize in workplaces, I do think it's important to build up open and active local organizations which can increase left unity, and can be easier for people to participate in. I have in mind the sort of structures which have been developed in socialist feminist groups, community papers, socialist centres, and other community resource centres, which are different from those characteristically used by the left.

But for me today as someone wanting to be active both within and outside of the women's movement, local organizations are no longer sufficient. I also want to be a part of an organization which is trying to build upon and generalize from different situations, and thus develop overall strategies. I don't think that it is possible to build a single unified revolutionary organization in Britain in 1979, or that any one left organization has all the answers. But revolutionary groups do have a vital role in helping to build the widest possible support for all areas of struggle, and the widest possible unity on the left.

What possibilities are there for combining socialist and feminist politics in a national organization which is not subject to the degeneration, splits and paranoias which plague all the left groups? Could such an organization work out a supportive practice in relation to the autonomous groups and activities which occur all around the country? We will not all agree on the answers. My own way to find out has been to join Big Flame, a group which in its theory and practice seems to put the class struggle before its own organizational development, which recognizes the need to fully support and help to build the autonomous organizations of women and other oppressed groups, and in general strives for a vision of socialism which includes a theory of personal politics. Time will tell whether I was right.

Notes

1. It would be hard to draw up a list, but some of the most important books for us were Marx*: Economic & Philosophical Manuscripts of 1844* and *The German Ideology.* Marcuse: *Eros and Civilisation* and *One Dimensional Man*, Laing: *The Divided Self*, Reich: *The Mass Psychology of Fascism* and Vaneigem: *The Revolution of Everyday Life* Henri Lefebvre, in *The Explosion – Marxism and the French Upheaval*, attempts to give an account of what led up to the ideas and actions of May 1968.
2. See the discussion on libertarianism and personal life 'Coming Down to Earth', Paul Holt, in *Revolutionary Socialism*, no. 4,

Autumn 1979.

3. This theory was outlined by Michael Kidron in *Capitalism and Theory*, Pluto Press, 1974.
4. This relates, as many people will know, to Althusser's now famous essay on ideology, 'Ideology and Ideological State Apparatuses' in *Lenin and Philosophy*, New Left Books, 1971, in which he argues that class relations are produced through two kinds of interrelated state institutions, the 'repressive state apparatuses' (the police, etc.) and the 'ideological state apparatuses' (in particular the education system which slots a person into their class position through a process whose operation is disguised from that person). Some Marxists today point out that Althusser is only a modern and vulgar variant of earlier Marxists like Gramsci and the Frankfurt School. Back in the thirties Gramsci was writing in his *Prison Notebooks* of the importance of 'civil society', referring to those institutions like the family and the media, which are not directly controlled by the state, but nevertheless play a crucial role in maintaining existing class relations and the capitalist state.
5. An attempt to do youth work in the local community in Islington from the base of a libertarian squatters' group, is colourfully described in *Knuckle Sandwich* by David Robins and Philip Cohen, Penguin, 1978.
6. For example, Elisabeth Wilson, 'Women and the Welfare State', *Red Rag*, pamphlet no. 2, 1974.
7. This is well illustrated by Barbara Ehrenreich and Dierdre English in *For Her Own Good*, Pluto Press, 1979.
8. This concept is used by Barbara Ehrenreich in her excellent speech on socialist feminism in *Socialist Revolution*, no. 26, October-December 1975.
9. Patriarchy has been defined by Heidi Hartman as 'the systemic dominance of men over women', referring to the social structure and all the social relations through which men dominate women. ('The Unhappy Marriage of Marxism and Feminism: Towards a More Progressive Union' in *Capital and Class*, no. 8, Summer 1979.) There is a debate over the usefulness of this concept, because some people feel it does not explain the way in which women's subordination, though universal, is different in different societies. I do find the concept useful, but for a fuller discussion see R. Mcdonough and R. Harrison, 'Patriarchy and Relations of Production' in Kuhn and Wolpe, *Feminism and Materialism*, Routledge and Kegan Paul, 1978, and Z. Eisenstein, 'Developing a Theory of Capitalist Patriarchy and the Case for

Socialist Feminism' in Eisenstein, *Capitalist Patriarchy and the Case for Socialist Feminism*, Monthly Review Press, 1978, and P. Atkinson: 'The Problem with Patriarchy' in *Achilles Heel*, no. 2.

10. Mariarosa Dalla Costa, 'Women and the Subversion of the Community' in M. Dalla Costa and S. James, *The Power of Women and the Subversion of the Community*, Falling Wall Press, 1973. For a fuller discussion of this debate see Jean Gardiner, 'Women's Domestic Labour', *New Left Review*, no. 89, 1975.
11. Valerie Charlton, 'The Patter of Tiny Contradictions', *Red Rag*, no. 5, 1973.
12. See Mandy Snell 'The Equal Pay and Sex Discrimination Acts: Their Impact on the Workplace', *Feminist Review*, no. 1, 1979.
13. See Mary Kathleen Benet, *Secretary: An Enquiry into the Female Ghetto*, Sidgwick and Jackson, 1972.
14. Despite some claims to the contrary, radical and revolutionary feminists were not the only ones to talk about rape and violence against women. Though it is true that recently they have perhaps been the main impetus behind some of the large demonstrations on these issues.
15. Similar victories of this sort over a nursery, play space and other community facilities are described in Jan O'Malley, *The Politics of Community Action*, Spokesman, 1977.
16. The limitations of orthodox Marxism in its analysis of women's oppression has been discussed elsewhere, for example, in Rosalind Delmar's, 'Looking Again at Engel's "Origins of the Family, Private Property and the State"', in A. Oakley and J. Mitchell (eds) *The Rights and Wrongs of Women*, Penguin, 1976 and Heidi Hartman, ibid.
17. John Ross, 'Capitalism, politics and personal life' in *Socialist Woman*, Summer 1977.
18. This account of the SWP's present position on women's politics and what is described as 'the crisis' in Women's Voice is obtained in part from detailed discussions with SWP comrades.
19. From the 'Revolutionary Feminist statement' to the Birmingham Women's Liberation Conference, 1977.
20. From 'Sex, Family and the New Right' in *Radical America*, Winter 1977/78.
21. Judging from the impact of the first edition of *Beyond the Fragments* in the Trotskyist press, where this section on local organizing was completely ignored in almost all the reviews, the situation has not changed very much. I had hoped that it might have.

22. Barbara Ehrenreich makes this point when discussing the importance of developing political morality, 'Toward a Political Morality', *Liberation*, July-August 1977.
23. See Brooke, 'The Retreat to Cultural Feminism', *Feminist Revolution*, 1975.
24. See 'Equal Pay: Why the Acts Don't Work', Jenny Earle and Julia Phillips, *Spare Rib*, no. 86, September 1979.
25. A discussion of the points of agreement which were reached at the Socialist Feminist Conference in March 1979 can be found in *Scarlet Women*, July 1979.
26. B. Campbell and V. Charlton, 'Work to Rule' in *Red Rag*, January 1979.

MOVING BEYOND THE FRAGMENTS* (1979)

Hilary Wainwright

That going beyond the fragments is a problem for many socialists is very much a sign of our times. If we were socialists in the twenties we might be agonizing over whether we should join the Labour left through the ILP or whether we should join the Communist Party which anyway was trying to affiliate to the Labour Party, but there would be little doubt that the Labour Party, warts and all, was the way to go 'beyond the fragments'.

Since the Labour Party became a *party of government*, and, more particularly, a party of reactionary government, joining the Labour Party is no longer the automatic choice of people looking for a way of changing society. In the absence though of any socialist alternative, with roots in the local labour movements, it does still offer many socialists a way of gaining a wider political influence than, say, involvement in the women's movement can achieve. There are many socialist feminists who feel like Sally Alexander from Pimlico, London, that

> After ten years in the women's movement a lot of us felt the desire to take our feminist politics into the socialist movement. The women's moveent had brought me closer to socialism because our demands, even at their minimum, cannot be achieved without a fundamental reorganization of society. And feminism led me to a serious study of Marxism. In this way the urgent need for a socialist strategy was confirmed

* Thanks to all those friends and comrades with whom I have argued about and discussed these issues, especially those in the Tyneside Socialist Centre.

through my feminism. So for some time I hovered round, wanting to join a socialist party. The Communist Party seemed a possible option. But in their debates on the 'British Road' the Communist Party argued for a policy of working with left Labour and changing the Labour Party. I thought it was better to join the Labour Party directly. Another thing was that I wanted to be involved in local politics, with socialists from other situations and experiences. The Labour Party offers that possibility. The local Labour Party is very divided but on the left I find a surprising number of people who are very militant socialists. They just would not have given the revolutionary groups a thought but they are just as deeply committed to socialism. A third factor which led me to join was a desire to understand this mammoth institution, and the extraordinary hold which it has. Having been at Ruskin College, involved with many active socialists in the Labour Party, I was always interested in this. For any historical relationship between the working class and the socialist intelligentsia in Britain has taken place mostly within the Labour Party. It is the programme and organization of the Labour Party which have shaped the aspirations of much of the socialist left and of the working class. As far as I can see, it will continue to do so.

Any discussion of new forms of political organization must take account of these peculiar staying powers and pulling powers: the Labour Party. For in the revolutionary euphoria which followed May 1968 and the Vietnam movement, occurring against a background of the Wilson government and the decay of the Labour left, it was too easy to sound the death knell of the Labour Party without taking these peculiar staying powers into account. As a result there is a danger of there being two lefts, inside and outside the Labour Party, split partly by generation, partly by region, partly by educational and class background, rather than by politics. These two lefts are often in agreement about all the practical struggles of the day and about the general objectives of social ownership and a new popular form of political power. Yet the issue of whether someone is inside or outside the Labour Party holds back any unified political framework for common action, sustained political debate, and clarification of strategy and policy. However, there are now strong pressures at a local level and within national movements – e.g., in the anti-racist movement, among socialist feminists, etc. – for unity between Labour Party and non-Labour Party socialists. We will describe some of these later. These pressures are vital signs of the ways in which existing party political structures no longer reflect the reality of practical political alignments and struggles on the ground. The working-out of these pressures into new forms of socialist organization are held back partly by overdue respect for the old political structures and partly by the assumption that the only viable political form of organization independent of the Labour Party must even at this early stage be that of an alternative party. This latter assumption immediately precludes the possibility of a political alliance – more than unity on a single issue, single movement basis – between socialists inside and outside the Labour Party. In order to see the urgency of such alliances, to understand the problems they would be up against within the Labour Party, and to see how far the positive experiences of unity within, for example, the socialist feminist movement, have a wider application, we will look at three main problems concerning the Labour Party and socialists within it.

Labour Governments, the Labour Left and the Vision of Socialism

First is the way that Labour governments have killed the idea of socialism as a practical alternative and the way that the message of the Labour left has in effect got tarred by the same brush. The first point is generally accepted by socialists in or close to the Labour Party. John Bohanna, a shop steward at Ford, an active socialist, not in the Labour Party himself but from a strong Labour family, sums up the way this has happened, what this has done to the commitment of 'ordinary folk' to the idea of socialism:

After the war there was a vision of a real alternative, and not just among the activists. The people of this country returned a Labour government with a great majority in the hope that a new, and this time positive, socialist society would be born. I don't find anything like these feelings now. People just think it's a choice between the bad and the very bad, Labour or Tory. After the war the government did seem to carry out its manifesto promises, and what people thought would be the first concrete steps towards a just and fair society. All to the good. But by 1959 the Labour leaders, now out of office, began to argue that inequalities of class were no longer a problem. They tried to write Clause 4 – for social ownership of production – out of the party's aims. Yet to many party members this clause was the proof that it could be a party for the working class. Although these leaders were unsuccessful at the time, ever since, the leaders' policies have repeatedly conflicted with working-class needs. It's very difficult now to see what good will come of a Labour government. Of course people can see some good fellers and women in the Labour Party; real tryers like Eddie Loyden. But they see the likes of them getting battered all the time so those that aim for socialism within the Labour Party become no more than the likes of Callaghan and Wilson in the eyes of ordinary folk. And everyone's bleedin' disgusted with them.

This moving away by the Labour Party (if it was ever anything different) from what people expected has meant that there are less activists around the Labour Party than in my dad's day. It's strongly felt that there's little worth in fighting for the Labour Party. So people take the easy way out and grab what they can; ignoring the wider fight for a society in which we can all have the opportunity to live a more fulfilled life.

Perhaps things will get revitalized now we are forced to fight the Tories. I can sense something on Merseyside. Attempts are being made by the left to set up industrial branches of the Labour Party in Fords and elsewhere. It's a good way of getting political debate on the shop floor. But I don't hold out much hope of change in direction of the whole party. Still, although the arrow towards socialism has one shaft it has many heads, and socialists in the Labour Party are one of them.

What about the people who seem to get 'battered' all the time, those people busy organizing in the Constituency Party General Management Committees and at the party conference to turn the Labour Party into a real socialist party? Why cannot they reach out to would-be Labour voters and potential socialist activists to persuade them not to be misled by recent Labour governments? For these governments, it is argued, are not the real thing.

Somehow this argument has lost a lot of its appeal. The Labour left have not, since Bevan, been able to establish a credible and distinct identity from the leadership in the eyes of most working-class people. They've become compromised by their long association with the policies of the party leadership. In fact they often come off worse, for their message comes across via Labour Party debates as 'more of the same'. Left and right have always tended to appear as just different ends of a spectrum of policies on state intervention. The debates between left and right in the Labour Party have normally been about more or less nationalization, and more or less state control.

This used to be enough to establish a distinct vision of socialism. Before the war when Labour's ability to control the state machinery had not been tested, and when the state's distance from production and economic life gave credibility to the idea that the state was a neutral instrument to be used for socialist ends, their vigorous advocation of Clause 4 provided a clear strategy and programme for socialism. It made sense to think of the state as 'a sword at the heart of private property', as Bevan put it. People knew what socialism was, and in general they saw the Labour left as its true representatives, even if they were wary of supporting them. But for the past thirty years people have lived through and been brought up in an economy in which the state plays a leading role, differing little from government to government. In this situation the policies of the Labour left, for slightly more state intervention (though not even as much as Bevan used to argue for) on more social criteria, do not add up to an inspiring or even distinct alternative to the policies of the right.

A fresh and convincing vision would require a move away from the traditional framework of Labour Party debates, away from the issue of what an elected Labour government would do with the state – as if the state were as malleable as putty. It would require a move to confront the reality of private capital's extra-parliamentary power and the constraints of international trade, both of which make the state so resistant to the good intentions of many parliamentary socialists. It would require a strategy for organizing the extra-parliamentary powers of working people, on an international scale.

The 'Bennite' Labour left which emerged out of the debris of the Labour governments of the sixties made some tentative moves in this direction by establishing ad hoc links, while in opposition, with a number of shop stewards' committees and by putting greater stress on some form of workers' control. But, at a national level at least, they are inhibited from developing this further. They are trapped in the contradictions created by their belief that the way to implement their policies is to win power within the Labour Party. For this they have to concentrate their energies on winning positions within Constituency Parties, getting policy resolutions to conference, and winning the support of trade union leaders in order to get conference support for a change in the constitution and in the leadership. At a local level much of this might well be compatible with developing the extra-parliamentary power of workers' organizations. (Although it would require some improvisation on present forms of constituency organization to make close links with socialists outside the Labour Party possible.) But as a consistent national strategy it comes up against the purely electoral priorities of the party, the pressures for unity when the conflict comes to any kind of crunch, the reluctance of trade union leaders and officials to encourage or even allow industrial action on political issues – other than in defence of normal trade union organizing and bargaining rights.

In this way then, the left within the Labour Party cannot establish an independent credibility with – or even a means of communications to – the mass of working people. It is tied to a platform of politicians to whom fewer and fewer people are in fact listening with any hope or expectation.

Can They Change It?

Is this just a temporary problem, a result of the left's cramped, ineffectual tactics while the party was in government? Could there come a time when socialists in the Labour Party could remove the consensus politicians from this platform and turn the Labour Party into a socialist party able to confront the power of private capital through extra-parliamentary as well as parliamentary action? This is an important issue, for there are many thousands of active socialists, some actually members of the Labour Party, some just paying their political levy and canvassing at election time, who are instinctively reluctant to create a political alternative to the Labour Party. They feel that as the party of the working class, it could, as workers' struggles grow and political consciousness is heightened, become a socialist party. 'The left has nearly won control over the NEC; with just a few more heaves we'll have won control of the Party.' Under the present government and with the struggle for succession to the Labour Party leadership, these pressures for 'one more go' are intensifying.

Gertie Roche who has been active in the labour movement in Leeds for many years, in her union, community groups, the Communist Party and now the Labour Party, sums up this feeling with a very cautious optimism.

> I think history is made very slowly. People are slow to change their attitudes. They have an emotional involvement in

something that concerns them and then it melts away. So I do not think the Labour Party will change quickly and do not expect very much from it. But people are pushing all the time. I watched the debate at the party conference today and we managed to get MPs made accountable for their behaviour. I think that's a big step forward. There's so little accountability in the public services.

I get angry when some of the people I work with on different issues attack me for being in the Labour Party. At least when you're in the Labour Party you get listened to which is more than used to be the case with the Communist Party. I think we should stop fighting each other's allegiances and get on with the issues. There are so many things that I find I can work together on with socialists and others outside the Labour Party – on women's liberation, the cuts, supporting a centre like TUCRIC (Trade Union Information and Research Centre) in Leeds. I support the emphasis of these people on extra-parliamentary action. That's very necessary, although the small amount of support you get can sometimes be depressing.

Before we talk then about the sort of socialist organization we need, and the contribution which feminism can make to it, we need to see the blocks which its development will come up against as far as the Labour Party is concerned, and why therefore organizing for socialism will eventually be based outside the Labour Party.

There are many factors which weigh heavily against the possibility of changing the Labour Party: the power and autonomy which the British Constitution gives to the moderate parliamentary leadership, the overwhelmingly electoral priorities of the party, and so on. It may seem as these problems could be overcome if the Constituency Parties won more formal power, giving them more say in electing the party leadership and drawing up the manifesto. But there is a virtually insuperable problem for the left in making much real headway even in this constitutional direction. The problem is inherent in the origins and basic make-up of the party. It lies in the overwhelming dominance of the unions, and the power of the trade union leadership to determine how this influence is exercised. Of course different unions will move to the left on specific issues and vote for generally left motions at conference. But to change radically the direction of the Labour Party would require trade union leaders, under pressure from their members, to actively commit themselves and a Labour government to overthrowing the economy and the state in which, despite Tory threats, they have such an established role and status. Of course we hope for a time, when the majority of trade unionists will be actively involved in achieving such a transformation, dragging their leaders behind them. But such mass socialist activity could not be built up, unless there were already a socialist organization giving a lead in the factories, offices and communities.

In this way, socialists trying to change the Labour Party are caught in a vicious circle. To turn the Labour Party into a socialist party there needs already to be a socialist party. And there are insuperable constraints to possibilities of such a party operating within the Labour Party. The constraints are especially strong as far as any left grouping making an open organized alliance with rank and file trade unionists against right-wing trade union leaders. At the first signs of such a threat the trade union leadership is able to use its power within the party, directly or behind the scenes, to mobilize rules and disciplinary powers against the left. This was one of the problems facing the Bevanites in the fifties when they gave support to dockers rebelling against the pro-Gaitskell T&GWU leadership. Benn and his supporters have similarly faced the wrath of right-wing trade union leaders when they have made common cause with shop stewards through unofficial channels. The left rarely resists such threats because to take on openly the trade union leadership in this way would jeopardize all their short-run ambitions of winning control over the party. This contradiction is likely to become increasingly apparent as the smouldering resentment and frustration of trade union members with their leadership flares up out of control.

The Communist Party's national strategy of pushing the Labour Party leftwards is weakened by the same contradictions. For although it has the organizational independence to build up left oppositions within the unions, its considerable success in this is blunted by depending too much on national left leaders like, in the past, Scanlon and Jones who offer the illusion of a short cut to a left Labour government. In a few important localities, however, left Labour constituencies and left groupings in the unions are sufficiently strong and autonomous from national Labour and trade union leaderships to create an impressive and powerful alliance. South Yorkshire is the best – perhaps the only – example. Such a local alliance is one of the many heads of the arrow which John Bohanna talked about earlier. But it is not the basis for the single shaft.

Why Don't They Split Then?

However we cannot leave the matter like this: we cannot leave the Labour Party socialists to stew in their own contradiction while we hurry away to build a separate party in the hope that one day they'll see the error of their ways. That would be to ignore all the important points of agreement between socialists inside and outside the Labour Party; and the strength which can be gained from ways of organizing that provide for both joint action and sharp debate.

Historically, in Western Europe any new socialist parties with a degree of mass influence have been created out of splits within a pre-existing mass workers' party. However in Britain this scenario is slowed down and blocked by the peculiarly ambiguous and deceptive structure of the British Labour Party, with its appearance of being the united, democratic party of the workers' movement, giving full and free expression to every socialist view, concealing the reality of power in the hands of a well-protected parliamentary group, shielded as it is by the trade union leadership. Mainly because of its link with unions the Labour Party does not have the normal character of a political party. It is a hybrid of a radical party made up of individuals committed to a radical programme, a powerful trade union lobby, and a parliamentary leadership of professional consensus politicians. For while the left is continually being defeated by the practice of every Labour government (the professional consensus politicians), defeat and failure never seem conclusive, for, after all, 'we won at conference', 'we are in control of the constituencies' (the radical party) – it's just a matter of putting on more pressure next time, of making the parliamentary leadership accountable. But the powerful trade union lobby working behind the scenes, with varying degrees of unity, makes success perpetually elusive. People are always leaving in disgruntled little groups, when they've had enough, and when one issue, entry into the Common Market, incomes policy, the cuts, etc., is 'the last straw'. And many are no longer joining, because trying to change it, after fifty years of failure, seems a dead end, and there are better things to do. But these same people carry on paying the political levy, voting Labour and canvassing for Labour. Most of them could not really imagine setting up an alternative political party unless a major split took place in the Labour Party, even though they may be involved in all sorts of campaigns and projects which have little significant support from the Labour Party.

Some socialists wander in and out of the Labour Party, not out of any enthusiasm and hope for national change but through the absence of any other adequate political framework and the existence of many congenial and left-wing constituency parties.

Val Clarke, for example, who used to be in the IS (SWP) is now very active in the local Labour Party near Huddersfield, Yorkshire, not because of any confident belief that the Labour Party can become a genuinely socialist party but because

> When we came here and got involved in campaigns on industrial issues, housing, and education problems, virtually all the main socialist activists were in the local Labour Party. That's where socialist policies on all these issues were being

thrashed out. Being outside the Labour Party meant we got all the discussion and information second hand. We could not influence things. And it would have been impossible to set up any alternative left focus. In a sense there was no need to, any militant who was any good was in the local Labour Party. This may not be typical, I recognize that, but Labour Parties like this must be taken account of when we talk about alternatives.

This blurred, indecisive quality of socialist politics in Britain is partly a product of local variations and partly of the ambiguous structure of the party. But it is also reinforced by the fact that when it comes to who should represent them in Parliament socialists and other radical activists have little political choice. This monopoly that is reinforced by the present electoral system gives Labour MPs and councillors an important hold on socialist militants whose campaigns and struggles can often be strengthened by having allies within the political system.

If then Labour Party socialists are unable to turn their local socialist politics into an effective national strategy and socialist party, and yet if the inevitable postponement of the final outcome of debate within the Labour Party and the wider trade union movement makes conditions for an alternative party extremely unfavourable, how and from where will the sort of socialist organization we referred to earlier be created?

Filling the Vacuum

Ever since the growth of CND, and then the movements which grew up in the late sixties and early seventies among students, trade unionists, women, blacks, gays, and, more recently, youth, there has been a growing force of people, inside and outside the Labour Party, who are impatient with the fruitless reliance on a Labour government, who are organizing directly for control over political and industrial decisions, and who are contesting the state in almost every sphere. But, partly as a result of the ambiguous features of the Labour Party, partly because of the pro-Stalinist record and present-day lack of internal democracy of the Communist Party, and partly because of the sectarianism of the revolutionary left, these activists do not have a political voice which expresses their grass-roots strength. That is, we are without a sustained way of organizing beyond our specific oppressions and experiences. We lack the means to develop a general theory and programme for socialist change from these varied experiences. And we do not have adequate ways of convincing people of the wider political changes which need to be fought for if their specific demands and needs are to be met. Our fragmented movements and campaigns are that much weaker without this political focus and back-up. This will become more and more painfully obvious as a strong, determined Tory government makes isolated victories more difficult. Many of the socialists involved in such movements and campaigns are instinctively aware of these weaknesses. As a result, there is a growing tendency to develop and make explicit the wider political implications of whatever movement or project socialists are involved in. Some people thought that the pressure of the political vacuum on the left would draw such activists towards the banner of a new socialist party. Instead, it has tended to induce people to make the wider links, elaborate the more general policies and theories, create the cultural alternatives, through a whole variety of industrial, community, and cultural organizations. In effect left-wing trades councils, socialist resource centres, socialist women's groups, theatre groups, left bookshops, militant shop stewards' committees often carry out, in sum, the functions of a socialist party but without the co-ordination and long-term perspectives of a party. It is as if the different parts of a piece of cloth – a political organization – were being woven creatively and with ad hoc contact between the weavers, but without anyone having a master plan. Though occasionally we need, from different points of view, to stand back and see where we've got to, where the cloth is weak and where the pattern is becoming blurred.

This sounds all very well, and perhaps a bit over optimistic. Where are the signs of these developments? it is not a uniform picture and no one person could draw it. We can only outline certain indications from our own experiences.

In some areas, for example, trades councils have come to act increasingly like socialist alliances, taking up militant socialist positions, directly critical of the Labour and trade union leadership, and through their subcommittees organizing together local women's groups, unemployed youth, active tenants' groups, socialist research workers, with the relevant local trade unionists. In Coventry, for instance, the Trades Council has played a leading role over housing in fighting the council and private building companies, in giving practical support for the demands of the women's movement, in organizing anti-imperialist campaigns, in organizing anti-racist campaigns, and, more recently, in rethinking socialist policies towards state intervention in industry, in the light of Labour's rationalizations and closures. The Trades Council in Newcastle has played a similarly political role, in addition, taking a strong stand against British imperialism in Northern Ireland. On Tameside in the North West the Trades Council set up what began as a cuts committee but which for a period became the focus for all sorts of different issues – abortion, anti-racism, unemployment, and so on. The Hull Trades Council is launching a weekly newspaper which is likely to become one focal point for socialist activity in the area. There are many other examples from trades councils throughout the country. The point here is not that trades councils have taken an occasional militant stand. There's nothing new in that. What has developed in the last ten years or so is a pattern of trades councils which act pretty consistently as socialist organizations, as consistently, that is, as the limits of being a trade union body will allow. We shall return to these limits later.

Another indication of the strongly felt need to reach beyond our own problem and shape a more general political perspective is the development of widely supported socialist tendencies within the women's movement and the gay movement which play an active role in trade union struggles, e.g., organizing contingents on the Grunwick mass picket, organizing against racism and fascism, and playing a leading role in fighting the cuts. Along with this, these groups have considerably deepened and extended Marxist theory and socialist policies.

There are similar, though less developed signs coming from a number of tenants' organizations, in which there is a strongly felt need to make more effective links with industrial workers, and women's groups. For example, there is the work of the Socialist Housing Activists Workshop which brought together activists in local and regional tenants' movements with socialist research workers to produce the 'Red Paper on Housing', a set of proposals for socialist policies on housing that is being discussed in places where there is a reasonably strong tenants' group, like Tyneside, Cardiff, Liverpool and Coventry. The activities and policies of the National Tenants' Organizations also reflect a strong socialist influence, the effect of an alliance of socialists from different localities and different political tendencies.

Similar developments can be seen in organizations connecting industrial issues and the interests of working-class communities. Since the late sixties there have been numerous local industrially-based organizations, formed over one issue but developing to take on many others, and acting almost like a political alliance for many of the activists concerned. For example, in South-East London an organization was formed from different shop stewards' committees and union branches during the fight against the closure of A.E.I. Woolwich. Its purpose was to campaign against closures and redundancies in the area more generally. But very soon it was taking on incomes policy, racism, and all the other issues that socialists campaigned over at that time. As Jim Coughlin, its chairman, said

> It really became a political focus at the time; local right-wing MPs like Mayhew and Marsh could see that. They did their best to stop us being represented at important meetings. But for a period SELAC [South East London Action Committee Against Closures] provided a very militant forum and propaganda organization.

In Speke, on Merseyside, a few years later, the Speke Area Trade Union Committee (SATUC) brought together industrial and community-based militants to fight on the single issue of no redundancies on the Speke estate, but the committee got involved in other matters as well.

Maureen Williams, a member of SATUC describes its origins, political potential and the problems it faced:

> It was set up in early 1975 as a direct outcome of the fight to prevent the closure of a local factory. From there we got involved in a wide range of disputes in Speke where jobs were at stake and we were asked to help. As it developed SATUC took up wider issues. We had speakers on Chile and Portugal and sent delegates to conferences on these issues. After a year or so members of the committee actually got involved in fighting a rent rise and joined a community picket of the town hall. This was very different to when I had first raised the issue and been met with disinterest or considered diversionary. Within eighteen months members were prepared to fight – even if only as individuals and not as representatives of their organizations. SATUC also got involved in organizing conferences on health and safety at work and unemployment.
>
> Late in 1977 our activity began to diminish. As a committee we were totally dependent on whether or not a fight was going on on the industrial estate. If workers did not fight redundancy we couldn't. In a sense we fell between two stools. On the one hand we were too much a trade-union-based and orientated body, with delegates and finance from branches and shop stewards' committees, to carry on as a militant alliance when active support from the branches began to dwindle. On the other hand we were too unorthodox to get support from trade union officialdom. Many trade union officials were outright hostile to us.
>
> SATUC did have potential as a political alliance. Various socialist organizations were in it, left Labour, IS, Big Flame,

as well as unaligned 'lefties', but to develop in this way we would have had to clarify our relationships to the Labour Party, the trade unions and the shop floor. [The Garston Labour Party (and many local union branches) are left wing and we needed to work with them rather than appear as a complete alternative.] We also would have needed to reassess ourselves as 'political' rather than 'militant to protect jobs'. Neither of these items was ever seriously on our agenda.

Another radical movement in which many people are developing and extending a socialist perspective and organizing more closely with working-class organizations is the movement of radical technologists and environmentalists. This 'movement' covers a multitude of sins as well as many creative and highly political advances. While some have remained interested only in individualistic improvements in the quality of middle-class life, others like the British Society for Social Responsibility in Science, the Socialist Environmental and Resources Association have become increasingly concerned to link their critique of capitalist technology with the working-class organizations which alone have the power to fight for alternatives. The initiative of the shop stewards in Lucas Aerospace in drawing up and fighting for products which used and modified modern technology to meet social needs and to enhance rather than destroy the skill of the worker was an important catalyst in this.

This initiative by the Lucas Aerospace Combine Committee is itself an illustration of new ways in which activists are building on their own resources and organizations to meet the new political needs that no single socialist organization fulfils. The combine committee brings together trade unionists from all sorts of political traditions but it was, and still is, faced with the problems of structural, technological unemployment to which no one political organization has an answer. The idea of fighting around specific proposals for socially useful production, for skill-enhancing instead of skill-reducing work came from a belief in the political power of independent combine committees. That is, the power of shop-floor and technical workers to take on management over the highly political issues of investment, the purpose of production, and the nature of the labour process. Of course no combine committee can take on these issues alone. The Lucas Aerospace stewards make this clear in the introduction to their plan where they deny the possibility of 'islands of socialism in a sea of capitalist exploitation'. But the principles behind workers' plans for production according to need have been taken up, modified and developed by other shop stewards' committees; for example, in power engineering, in some sections of the armaments industry, to a small extent in shipbuilding, the rubber industry, and elsewhere. And the tentative beginnings of organized links between these shop stewards' groups is taking place.

Another rather different process of politicization has been going on among Marxist academics, many – but by no means all – of whom are increasingly sensing the need for their work to be engaged with socialist, political, community, and industrial organizations. There is a sense of unease about the sort of theory produced without the discipline, the stimulus and the constraints of interaction with political movements. Discussions at the Conference of Socialist Economists have come increasingly to concern issues of strategy and working-class politics; many of its members on a local level are working with trade unionists, tenants' and women's groups. The *History Workshop Journal* explicitly sees its work as closely related to the wider socialist movement; it gives special support to, for example, locally-based publishing projects, like Strong Words in the North East, Centerprise in East London and others in Brighton and elsewhere. These local publishing projects have begun to recover and inspire critical working-class writing as part of the tradition of workers' self-education through which working-class people develop their consciousness and creativity. State research is another example of the growth of research and writing with a political urgency and purpose. State Research is a collective of journalists and researchers which investigates policing, intelligence and the military. Through a bi-monthly publication it spreads its findings to the activists who come up against these parts of the state, and to the wider media, sympathetic MPs, etc. *New Left Review* in its debates on nationalism, revolutionary strategy in the West, socialist opposition in the East and on the substantive implications of materialism has served to highlight fundamental problems facing the development of a coherent socialist practice.

The women's liberation movement has been an important catalyst in many of these moves towards a richer unity of theory and practice. Its insistence on theoretical work which is accessible and relevant to the growth and strengthening of the movement has produced a self-consciousness about the political purpose and practical process of theoretical work which was rare. A recent editorial in *Feminist Review*, a theoretical journal produced by a collective within the women's movement reflects this:

> In our first issue we said that our intention in publishing *Feminist Review* was to contribute to the political development of the women's liberation movement by providing a space where ideas could be discussed and information exchanged. To do this we stressed the importance of the accessibility of the material we publish; but accessibility isn't just a question of language and presentation, although these are very important issues. Equally important is the process of discussion between readers, contributors and the editorial collective.

Feminists have taken these sort of principles into many of the projects just mentioned above, with good effect.

An important consequence of this ad hoc politicization is that many so-called 'sectoral', 'single issue' or 'merely local' campaigns, movements, and organizations have been created on the basis of consciously socialist values. This does not mean that such organizations are, or necessarily will ever be, fully socialist in their policies or ways of organizing. What it does mean, however, is that behind specific labels 'the women's movement', 'alternative press/bookshops', 'tenants' action groups', local and national 'shop stewards' combine committees', 'trade union and community resource and research centres', there is often – not always – a wealth of ideas, experiences, and ways of organizing which are of direct political relevance to the creation of a socialist organization.

Socialist Alliances

But before we discuss bow these advances can best be built on, we need to be aware of the limits of this 'organic' way in which the political vacuum has been filled. The problems vary, but they all become apparent at times like the last five years when there is no massive tide of class struggle sweeping everything along with it. At such times the trades councils and shop stewards' bodies which have tended to become more of a left alliance than a trade union organization are in danger of becoming isolated from their mass membership, and consequently unable, when things come to a crunch, to show any real industrial strength. Trades councils do not suffer so obviously as a result, because they have long-established roots which can survive failures and isolation. Though they do come up against attempts by the TUC to restrict the scope of their activity, and sometimes the national TUC can enlist the support of the Regional TUC to keep the trades councils in check. The unofficial industrial bodies we have mentioned like on Merseyside or in South-East London are more dependent on being able to deliver some practical goods to the membership. If the organization begins to move too fast, more at the tempo of a political organization, it loses its base. And unless the leading members are conscious of its potential as a political alliance, it loses its rationale and disintegrates, as happened on Merseyside and in South-East London. In addition, because such bodies are essentially trade union bodies, they cannot usually allow for the political debate and education necessary to develop a united political strategy and programme. This in turn leads to political misunderstandings, the predominance of personal hostilities, splits, and falling away of political initiatives.

Within campaigning movements like the women's movement, the tenants' movement, radical technologists, and so on, the problems facing socialists are different. They mainly concern the difficulties of socialists making the necessary links beyond their own movement with other trade unionists and other community-based groups when they are not in any party or, when, as is usual, the links need to go beyond the small circles of existing socialist parties. The same problem arises in elaborating policies which need to take account of wider working-class interests beyond the movement initially concerned. For example, socialists in the tenants' movement on Tyneside are trying to develop pressure to extend the direct labour force. For this they need to make contact with building workers and trades councils and sympathetic sections of the Labour Party. The activists involved can see very clearly how very much easier and more effective the whole campaign would be if the socialists involved in all the different organizations affected were in the habit of meeting with each other, discussing policies, reaching some common understanding of the problem and its wider context. As Kenny Bell, one of the activists involved, put it:

> For tenants as consumers the issue of who does the repairs and the building and what control tenants have over it is really important. In this way they have a clear interest in expanding the direct labour force. But there's been so much rundown of the direct labour force in Newcastle, jobs are so insecure, wages and conditions so bad, that many building workers are glad of a job in the private sector. So creating the links, putting over the argument about the potential of direct labour isn't easy. We need to be working closely with socialists in the building trade. But it's difficult to make that contact out of the blue. It is much easier if there is some tradition of wider contact between socialists in the different unions and campaigns. The Tyneside Socialist Centre's network has been

useful and also the various resource and information centres. The socialist centre has also been helpful as a way of clarifying ideas about strategy. But we need to build a lot more on that.

Similarly with socialist feminists in the National Abortion Campaign wanting to make contact with hospital workers and other trade unionists. Small numbers of socialists across the sectors are in organized contact with each other, through being in the CP, the SWP or the IMG, but this nothing like covers even the majority of the activists who would/could be politically united and be very much stronger for it.

Experience of these sorts of problems has, in several localities led to socialists from different campaigns, movements, unions, and from different political tendencies, creating local socialist alliances, forums, or centres. In Hounslow, for example, the need to provide a focal point for socialist activists in the area arose from the experience of the thirteen-month occupation of Hounslow Hospital. The occupation had demonstrated to many of those involved the possibilities of a new way of organizing; Karl Brecker, Chairman of the shop stewards' committee at the West Middlesex Hospital, describes this:

> To sustain such a long occupation we had the problem of raising people's political awareness, and therefore of taking political discussion beyond minimal agreement on action, without allowing sectarian differences to destroy the cohesion of the occupation. It took a long time to work this through; but gradually people learnt to debate with, and yet respect, each other's views. It wasn't a matter of yielding your opinions into a mish-mash. And gradually people learnt how to speak and discuss in a non-sectarian way. They had to. There were a lot of hospital workers at the meetings, not in any political organization, who would not tolerate the sort of rejection of people's views because they are members of another organization, which often goes on in sectarian circles.
>
> The other thing that was important was the ways that

all the time we had to break down hierarchies and make people feel involved. The whole occupation would have disintegrated unless the normal divisions such as those between ancillary workers and nursing staff were broken down. We had to make sure people did not feel put down, that their personal problems were recognized, and that they were given support. The influence of the women's movement was important here. The occupation became a base; a centre for other campaigns and struggles in the area. It became a sort of school for activists, learning how to do leaflets, and so on. It was used by the firemen in their strike, by the NUJ, also by some Labour Party socialists who stood in the local elections on a no cuts, no unemployment platform.

Many of us felt that with all this that we had created something different, a stronger way of organizing, and we did not want to lose it once the occupation was over. We thought we should build on this experience modestly. That's why a group of us setup the Hounslow Socialist Forum in the third week of January this year. We hold meetings every fortnight, on topics which put local issues into a broader context. Forty or fifty local activists turn up from all the main socialist organizations as well as a lot of independent socialists. People use it as a place to get support for campaigns and local disputes. We meet at the Labour Hall. We have not thought about premises, or anything more ambitious yet. We need to move slowly, as people get used to working together and we define the areas of agreement and debate.

On Tyneside in 1975 a socialist centre was set up initially for educational, cultural, debating and general propaganda purposes. But since the centre was bringing socialists together – albeit in a haphazard way – it began to take on a more practical role: organizing anti-fascist leafleting, helping to provide support for strikes, initiating local campaigns and debates around political issues such as the deportation of Agee and Hosenball, the oppositions in Eastern Europe, workers' plans for socially useful production, British investment in Southern Africa and support for the Zimbabwean liberation movements. Then for a year or so it became overwhelmed by the practical problems of maintaining and improving the only socialist bookshop and book service in the area. But it is now re-emerging from this, stronger perhaps as a result of the very practical, material responsibilities that this entailed, and able to strengthen united action against the Tories and to extend debate about policies and strategy. Its constitution provides for the representation of affiliated political tendencies (e.g., the SWP, and the CP), trade union organizations and other movements on the Centre's co-ordinating committee. It has regular general meetings of individual supporters and representatives of organizations. Working groups take more specific responsibility for the Centre's projects, like the bookshop, the bulletin and meetings.

In Islington a similar sort of alliance and forum was created out of a conference called by the *Islington Gutter Press* in early 1978. The conference was attended by activists in local campaigns against racism, on women's groups, in unions (mainly the public sector) in the Labour Party, the CP, IMG, SWP and Big Flame. This conference elected a Socialist Centre committee which now organizes regular Sunday evening debates, educational meetings, and socialist cultural events. At their last conference they decided to look for premises, and also to play a more active role in supporting strikes and campaigns. Lynne's piece in this book describes this in more detail.

In Hackney too, meetings of socialist and radical activists to learn from one another and discuss common problems and different views have begun. The existence of a local alternative paper, bookshop and café as well as a trades council building with a pub and meeting rooms help in communicating this development.

There are many factors which could make for these local socialist alliances. In some areas like Tyneside and Merseyside, Clydeside, parts of Yorkshire, the steel towns, and indeed, increasingly, just about everywhere beyond Westminster, the stimulus could be the real threat of decline and collapse.

In most such areas some kind of official campaigns against the threat usually grind into motion. But after ten years or more of decline in some regions, many socialists have learnt from the campaigns of the past. They have witnessed the demoralization which comes from relying on these leaders, from the futility of their lobbies, their token demonstrations, and their reluctance to agitate and argue among the membership and the community for something more. Such socialist activists are increasingly aware of the need to come together to take more militant initiatives and to elaborate policies of more a socialist content than the 'grab what we can get for this region' sort which often dominate official campaigns. Alec McFadden, a former member of the Communist Party, now in no political organization, Treasurer of Newcastle Trades Council and an organizer of the Trades Council Unemployed Centre summed this up from his own experience:

> We can't just unite vaguely against the Tories like we did under Heath and leave it at that, like the TUC is talking about now. Though that was necessary, it wasn't enough. It meant we weren't ready to deal with the policies of the Labour government, we had not got alternative policies and we had not got the strength to act independently when MPs, officials and the like wouldn't fight.
>
> We need to get real socialists together in the area, to build up a fight, yes, but also to prepare for the future. It can't be a matter of uniting for unity's sake. If it's just that, we'll be back to the same sort of Labour government as before. We've got to prepare alternative policies. I learnt that from the closure of Tress [part of Fairey, owned and closed by the NEB of which McFadden was AEUW convenor] and from the failure of the campaign to keep Vickers Scotswood open. The socialists involved should have got together more and worked things out, to give a lead.

The way such alliances might come about will vary tremendously according to local conditions. Sometimes under the pressure of the onslaught from the Tories and the hopelessness of official campaigns, the local branch of the strongest left-wing organization or left Constituency Labour Party might set an alliance in motion. It might break with the normal customs, and making its discussions the forum for socialists, in other smaller organizations or unaligned.

In other areas the experience of successfully working together over some nationally-initiated campaign might lead people to seek ways of establishing that unity on a more permanent, wider political basis. Or there might already be some form of unity, a local socialist newspaper, a shared resource centre, a bookshop, socialist club or centre, which can be built on to create a more active political alliance. Whatever the process, the signs are that conditions for such alliances – ad hoc and loose though they may be – are especially favourable at a local level. There are many reasons for this, one is closely related to what was said earlier about the nature of debates within, and splits from, the Labour Party. Because of the endless postponement of decisive conflicts in the Labour Party; because of the poverty of political debate within most constituency and ward Labour Parties; because of the absence of a mass circulation socialist paper, the left in Britain has not been through a common process of debate on strategy and programme – even of the kind which precedes major splits from socialist and communist parties on the Continent. As a result there is a lack of agreement or even discussion of strategy and programme between any sufficiently strong groupings at a national level to determine nationally the framework of unity at a local level. At a local and regional level however there are plenty of opportunities, first, for unity around the major practical problems of the day; also around socialist projects like bookshops, socialist trade union information and research centres, resource centres, alternative newspapers. So many of these projects are quite beyond the resources of any one political organization. (For example, the SWP could not sustain any socialist bookshop outside London and Glasgow, although they tried.) Their success, though, is vital to the creation of a popular socialist party. There is a peculiarly restrictive notion of unity which holds back revolutionaries from creating these sort of alliances. It is argued that if unity goes much beyond specific issues or within particular unions then it will either suck away our energies in endless argie-bargies with other left groups, or it will be so wishy-washy as to be useless and passive. Yet we have found in the women's movement and among socialist feminists that it is possible to have a single unifying framework within which we unite to act where we agree, e.g., abortion, equal pay, nurseries, fascism, and other issues, and within which we have useful debates over things on which we go our own ways. This can work if you are not defensive about debate and argument and do not see it as ruling out unity on other issues, etc. The unity will have to be vague and loose to begin with. But in developing the basis for political unity one vital function such alliances could perform would be to provide exactly the forum for political debate and education which is so lacking nationally. Without the (re)building of this groundwork of political debate and socialist culture, related to problems and differences encountered in practical struggle, national political co-ordination is bound to flounder.

The pace at which these local socialist alliances coalesce and develop, the dialectic between them, and, emergence of a national socialist organization, cannot be laid down in advance. A revolutionary upheaval in Italy or Spain, for example could rapidly extend people's horizons for united socialist advance far beyond the local or regional level.

The Revolutionary Groups

Isn't this all a bit ramshackle? Wouldn't it be much simpler, clearer and ultimately more effective to encourage everyone to join one of the revolutionary groups/parties and hope that through proving itself in action, this organization will eventually encompass the activists, some of whose diverse projects we have just sketched? The problem with such a solution is not 'Leninism' as a theory of the class nature of the state. Nor is it what follows from this in terms of a need to destroy the coercive state machinery and establish a new form of democratic political power. Neither is the organizational condition for such a transformation, a mass revolutionary organization based in the movements of the working class and other oppressed groups in question. The problem is rather with the way in which most of the existing revolutionary groups seek to establish such a mass revolutionary organization. One of the main problems lies in the leap they make from a belief in the need for mass socialist organization to the conclusion that they are the infant stage (SWP), or the nucleus (IMG) of such an organization. They therefore take on the essential structure and features of the central leadership which they hope one day to be. Like the Elizabethan children who were dressed up like full-grown adults, the result at worst is absurd, puffed up and very constricting! Perhaps the problem can be more seriously elaborated by applying Marx's basic principles on the relation between revolutionaries (Communist) and the rest of the workers' movements.

As he puts in in *The Communist Manifesto*:

> They [communists] do not set up any sectarian principles of their own, by which to shape and mould the proletarian movement ... The Communists are, on the one hand, practically, the most advanced and resolute section of the working-class parties of every country, that section which pushes forward all others; on the other hand, theoretically, they have over the great mass of the proletariat the advantage of clearly understanding the lines of march, the conditions, and the ultimate general results of the proletarian movement.

The major revolutionary groups in Britain tend to make the mistake of assuming that it is they alone (and their close contacts) who are, in Marx's phraseology, the Communists. In fact they are merely a small section – though with a specific and important contribution to make – of those who are, at the grass-roots, giving a political lead to workers and other oppressed groups. The mass of 'Communists', are the socialist activists whose diverse projects and struggles I have just sketched. Some are in other workers' parties, some are in none, but, as already argued, they are none the less socialist for that. In this way then the 'vanguardist groups', though alert, in abstract, to the dangers of substituting for the class, tend all the time to substitute themselves for the diverse emerging vanguard of that class.

This criticism applies most directly to the Socialist Workers Party. The International Marxist Group, a much smaller organization, but none the less, an influential one, does not make such a claim. It conceives of itself as merely the nucleus of a future party which will be formed through a lengthy process of united fronts, splits and fusions with other organizations. This leads them to put more emphasis on projects aimed at unifying the left (e.g., the initial launching of *Socialist Challenge* around a basic programme on which many socialists not in the IMG could agree, similarly with the idea of a united electoral alternative to the Labour Party, organized through 'Socialist Unity').

However, their attitude to the way in which a correct programme is developed weakens their ability to make these projects anything much more than ways of slightly widening their own 'periphery' of contacts and supporters. Their model is premised, correctly, on the belief that the creation of a socialist society is, above all, a conscious political process, not an outburst of irrationality or the unintended effect of thousands of uncoordinated decisions. There is therefore, they argue, a need for a scientific approach to politics. So far so good. Their model, however, of such a scientific approach is based on far too monistic a view of scientific development. For they do not merely fight for their own beliefs as we all do; they also argue that their own internal processes of democratic discussion and decision-making are the processes through which a scientific socialist politics is elaborated. Of course, they assume in this that their members learn from their involvement in wider struggles and campaigns. But the process of synthesis goes on within the IMG. Such a notion flies in the face of the way that all other scientific ideas develop, that is, through a process of more or less structured contestation and of diverse but co-ordinated experimentation. Of course the development of a science of practical politics differs from other sciences in that its practice does not involve artificial experiment but human struggles. But in a way this makes the substitution of the processes of theoretical/political debate and practice of one political tendency for the possibilities of co-ordinated debate and action of the wider socialist involvement, even more disastrous. It seems to flow from the assumption that there is one timeless organizational interpretation of the concept of democratic centralism. Ironically, it is Ernest Mandel, a leading theoretician of the Fourth international (of which the IMG is the British section), who points to the real political significance of this concept when he says:

> The essence of democratic centralism is not really organizational, but political, or better, socio-political. The immediate experience of workers [we should add 'and other oppressed people' – H. W.] is always partial and one-sided. Real workers, as opposed to idealized ones, are active in one factory, in one branch of industry, in one city. The lessons they draw from their immediate experiences are therefore always partial. The spontaneous activity of the working class, while it may be quite varied, is always fragmented and therefore always tends to lead to fragmented consciousness. The essential function of democratic centralism is to overcome that fragmentation by centralizing the experience of the working class as a whole, thawing the proper lessons from it, and organizing a strategy that can unify the proletarian front in its battle for state power. [*Revolutionary Marxism Today*, New Left Books, London, 1979, p. 222.]

No single organizational form is implied by such a process. Neither is there any justification for making the logical leap from a belief in the IMG's ideas to the conclusion that it is only through the processes of democratic discussion in the IMG or the Fourth International that an adequate programme can develop. The forms of organization which provide the most favourable conditions for a scientific socialist politics will vary. For example the forms required in a period when the majority of socialist activists have come from a variety of different political traditions and experiences rather than mainly from, say, a split in a previous mass party (as was the case with the Bolsheviks who came from a split within the Russian Social Democratic Labour Party) are likely to be very different from those required when there is the sort of political homogeneity which is usually produced by such a common political experience and debate.

The extent of the pluralism of political tendencies and sources of socialist inspiration and vision then will vary, as with all forms of scientific development. When a dominant theory of socialist changes collapses in the face of economic and social problems that it can no longer explain or resolve, and when no alternative has matured in previous contestation with the dominant view, then there is likely to be tremendous variety in the attempts to fill the vacuum. Especially when the objective problems are urgent and there is a periodic groundswell of mass activity in response to them. This, in effect, is the situation we have described earlier, with the decline of left reformism. Out of this diversity can then come new solutions, greater agreement, and greater strength. But only if we create a new way of organizing through which to carry out sharp, principled debate between the diverse traditions and movements, and at the same time to achieve unity in action on the major issues of today.

We are not arguing that revolutionary groups should dissolve themselves, as some have done in Italy, into an illusory idea of an undifferentiated mass movement. In any mass socialist organization which is eventually created out of the fragments, there will always be different political tendencies with some degree of national organization of their own. Among other things, these tendencies are in a sense carriers of the revolutionary traditions of the past; they have kept those traditions alive in periods where there was no wider layer of socialist militants. Learning from, debating with and developing the traditions which these revolutionary groups apply to contemporary problems will be vital to the process by which a socialist organization is woven together.

At present the components of such a mass organization are far from reaching the political cohesion and the clear understanding of the lines of march to which Marx refers, and for which he has provided the markers. The revolutionary groups could be important catalysts in overcoming these weaknesses; they have at least mulled over the lessons for the present, of the marches of the past. But their ideas are inevitably limited. They have been able to develop only the bare bones of a strategy and programme for socialist revolution in the modern capitalist world. As small organizations emerging only in the last ten years from discussion groups, their politics are not especially 'advanced' on most of the issues which have come to the fore in these ten years in new and complex ways: sexual politics, the contemporary institutions of ideology and bourgeois culture; the massive extension of state intervention in production; the extent and form of the recession; the new forms of technology and its impact on workers' living and working conditions, and so on.

This is partly because of the major gulf between the last period when revolutionaries in Britain could achieve any significant hearing – the 1940s – and the period 1968 onwards when thousands of militants began to search again for socialist alternatives. When this happened, the revolutionary organizations were not in any position, either in terms of organizational strength or in terms of the richness and breadth of their analyses, to provide an overall political leadership. The result has been many centres of socialist initiative and analysis, of leadership, of political growth.

The unwillingness of the groups to fully recognize this and adopt a more humble political stance towards these many foci of socialist activity has reduced their capacity to influence and catalyse these initiatives towards a more co-ordinated political movement. It has also reduced their capacity to work together.

Once these groups had, as they saw it, made the leap from being propaganda/discussion groups to being fully-fledged democratic centralist parties, or embryos of such, the contradiction between their grandiose conceptions of themselves and the reality of political life on the ground, in the localities and in the various movements and struggles often became too much for many members or possible members to accept. I remember sensing this very sharply when I was a member of the IMG while being very involved in the women's movement. At first we in the IMG used to prepare our 'interventions' as if we really could, and had a duty to, give an overall political lead to the movement. This soon seemed too absurd to carry on, not because we were a politically isolated vanguard trying to convince a mass of 'backward elements', but because all sorts of other socialist feminists had developed better ideas and initiatives along similar lines. Gradually our rather ridiculous pretensions were abandoned by many of us active within the movement. We continued to benefit from the sustenance of the political tradition and analysis which the IMG represented and from the contact it provided with socialists involved in other activities. But for us this became a basis for working on one or two issues without any wider pretensions. In this way we probably made a much more valuable contribution, and we worked much better with other socialists and feminists. But we were not acting as the revolutionary leadership of the women's movement, neither were we aspiring to it. We just became one of, or part of one of, the many sources of leadership and initiative. Neither were we acting according to strictly democratic centralist norms. Sometimes it would be a help to convince the IMG to take a national initiative, e.g., support for the Working Women's Charter. Sometimes we would just work out and test out in the movement our own ideas and then feed them back into the IMG. We did not feel bound by the discipline of the IMG; on any one issue we felt as if we might just as well work with another political tendency if their ideas seemed better. We felt accountable to IMG only in the sense of the comradeship of being accountable to people with whom you share ideas and with whom you carry out collective projects. In other words, so long as the IMG recognized its limits as one socialist grouping among many, and always likely to be so, then being a member of it was a source of strength. But whenever it puffed itself and the Fourth international into something more, into an embryonic party with all the pretensions that go with it, then it became a problem.

This over-estimation of their own importance became a problem not only for the real contribution which members of the revolutionary groups could make to wider movements and struggles, but also because of the opportunities which are missed by refusing to work together on more than single-issue campaigns. Because each of the groups assume that they are the infant party then their relations with each are, on the whole, thoroughly two-faced and imbued with mistrust. The majority of members are probably genuinely committed to the real strength which united work gives to a campaign. A section of the leadership, on the other hand, are more concerned with recruiting 'the best elements' of the opposing groups. This in turn creates mistrust and rivalry at a local level, and so it goes on, considerably weakening the real political strength which exists on the revolutionary left. For example, take the two main papers of the revolutionary left, *Socialist Worker* and *Socialist Challenge.* Both in their own ways can be very good, Socialist Worker as a popular socialist paper arguing the basic case for socialism, for workers' control, for women's liberation (recently), and putting over a consistently strong attack on racism. It suffers from a tendency to report only on struggles and campaigns in which its own members are involved and from very weak analysis at times (which is not a necessary cost of being accessible and readable).

It would benefit from a much wider source of reporting and commenting. *Socialist Challenge*, on the other hand, contains some extremely good analysis and occasionally some good popular journalism, especially on racism and international struggles. It falls between two stools though. On the one hand, it is under pressure to provide IMG militants with an equivalent to *Socialist Worker* to sell on picket lines, outside factory gates, in shopping centres on a Saturday, etc. Yet on the other, it aspires to a form of debate and analysis for socialist activists in different organizations. If the two groups controlling the papers were to drop their party pretensions and recognize that they are both tendencies in essentially the same political movement, resources could be combined – and with others, like Big Flame and unaligned revolutionaries – to produce both an effective popular socialist paper and a paper of debate and analysis for the left. Such papers, not tied to any particular group, would also benefit from a much better relation with the independent socialist and broadly radical newspapers which are produced in numerous localities.

The Relevance of the Women's Movement

All this concern with the Labour Party, with local socialist alliances, with national socialist papers must at first sight seem a long way from feminism. But women have a strong vested interest in the success of the socialist movement. And after organizing ourselves for some years we feel we've got things to say about all the wider organizing and agitating which needs to be done if we are to create a truly democratic and egalitarian society.

The movement that feminists and socialist feminists have succeeded in organizing may not have achieved many effective legislative and industrial changes. But it has increased the strength and confidence of thousands of women, both those working in the home and those earning a wage, both in white collar unions and in manual unions. It has drawn into political activity many of the millions of people who have always considered politics wasn't for them, it was for the politicians.

In other words, the women's movement, in all its diverse ways, through all its different political tendencies, has helped to give women the power to organize ourselves to fight for control over the decisions by which our lives are shaped. And that surely is what socialist organization should most centrally be about, for all oppressed and exploited people.

Some might say that the objectives of the women's movement are very specific and limited, that, for example, it takes on the state in only marginal ways and over issues on which some concessions can and will be granted. Whereas, by contrast, a socialist organization has a far more fundamental, difficult task. The corollary of this is that the organizational forms of the women's movement may be appropriate for its specific tasks but organizing for socialism requires something very different. Not much can therefore be learnt from feminism, in a crude sense this contrast has some truth in it. A socialist organization will have to take on many issues and problems which do not now confront the women's movement. We are not holding out the organization of the women's movement as a complete model on which the left should base itself. But the women's movement has made an absolutely vital achievement – or at least the beginnings of it – which no socialist should ignore. It has effectively challenged, on a wide scale, the self-subordination, the acceptance of a secondary role, which underpins most forms of oppression and exploitation. This may not be confronting the state – though the women's movement does plenty of that – but unless such a self-subordination is rejected in the minds of men, of the unemployed, of blacks, gays, and all other groups to which socialists aim to give a lead, there will never be much chance of confronting the existing state with a democratic socialist alternative.

The ways in which the women's movement is achieving this then have a wider relevance. From the point of view of learning from the women's movement it is the values which underlie our organizations which are important. The particular organizational forms have relevance only to the specific purpose they were created to fulfil. The values underlying our ways of organizing have been ones which put emphasis on local control and autonomy; on small groups within wider co-ordinating structures; on local centres and social and cultural activities; on relating theory to practice; on discouraging forms of procedure and of leadership which make others feel inadequate or uninvolved; on recognizing that different views on strategy and tactics come from some real experience and are worth listening to and discussing. Sheila and Lynne explain these ways of organizing in detail and point out the contrasts with more traditional ways.

These values have created a groundwork on which national and regional structures, co-ordination, theoretical debate, and self-disciplined national action around an agreed programme of demands have been built. They have led to the creation of a movement with many focuses of initiative and leadership and a movement which combined unity with the existence of many different political tendencies. Such unity is not a matter of complacent tolerance. After periods of conflict and mistrust, the movement builds on the distinct contributions of different political views. For example, the movement gained a lot of its ability to influence the trade unions, to get trades councils to set up women's subcommittees, to involve union branches in actively campaigning for the demands of the movement from women in or close to the IMG and the CP. Recently Women's Voice has been a strong influence in many areas in adopting a more aggressive, outward-going approach in many of our campaigns.

These ways of building a movement are not specific to women. They have been a necessary part of the women's movement because the subjective experience of political organizing, whether it is 'off-putting' or involving, whether it builds up your sense of your own power to change things or makes you feel powerless, is so vital to whether or not women become active. Distant national structures over which you feel little control, formal procedure which does not seem to achieve anything, rigid notions of the correct line which suppress hesitant disagreement and questions, theoretical debates which do not shed light on practice, solidarity based on abstractions with little commitment to each other – none of these could have moved women to cast off their passivity and self-subordination. And this probably applies to a lot of working-class men as well.

There are many lessons to be drawn from the women's movement which would help us as socialists to create structures, arrange meetings, debate with each other, plan tactics, take decisions in ways which draw new people into socialist activity, and which keep them involved far more effectively than in the past. Another shift which the lessons of the women's movement would produce would be a greater respect for initiatives which people are already taking in a socialist direction. I have tried to show in this piece how important this recognition is at the present stage of creating a more co-ordinated socialist movement out of the fragments. It has been the experience of the women's movement which has made us sensitive to these areas of growth. Finally, the women's movement, at its best, has taught us how to unite as a movement on the major practical issues of the day while debating and respecting each others political differences and frequently agreeing to differ and go our own ways without jeopardizing the single movement. If the left could achieve that, at least at a local level, we'd be a long way towards showing people that there could be more than a choice between the 'bad and the very bad'; there could be real alternatives which they will have a hand in shaping.

Sheila Rowbotham is a professor in the School of Social Science at the University of Manchester. Her latest book is on Edward Carpenter.

Lynne Segal is Professor of Psychology and Gender Studies at Birkbeck College, University of London. Her latest book is *Making Trouble: Life and Politics*. She is just completing *Out of Time: the Pleasures and Perils of Ageing.*

Hilary Wainwright is an editor of *Red Pepper* magazine. She has appeared on BBC Question Time and is a research director of the New Politics Project of the Transnational Institute, Amsterdam.